Speaking Intelligently

Speaking Intelligently

Communication for Problem Solving

Otis M. Walter

Professor of Rhetorical Theory
University of Pittsburgh

Macmillan Publishing Co., Inc.
New York

Collier Macmillan Publishers
London

Copyright © 1976, Otis M. Walter
Printed in the United States of America

Macmillan Publishing Co., Inc.
866 Third Avenue, New York, New York 10022

Collier Macmillan Canada, Ltd.

Library of Congress Cataloging in Publication Data
Walter, Otis M
  Speaking intelligently.

  Includes bibliographies and index.
  1. Oral communication. I. Title.
PN4121.W323   808.5   74–11753
ISBN 0–02–424341–8

Printing: 1 2 3 4 5 6 7 8   Year: 6 7 8 9 0

The Speaker

"Why has he brought us here?" they said.
"I cannot walk for fear I sink," one said.
"The children cry, and we all long for home," they said.
"Contentment is only on the faces of our dead.
"Before the trees had lost their leaves,
    We should have turned toward home."

"Why has he brought us here?" they said.
"The land we knew was sweet.
"It gave us more than we could store in those great bins,
"And as time passed, we rested some and loved."

"Follow me," he said. And so we did, and left with him,
But before the leaves fell from the trees,
    We should have turned toward home.

At last they say,
"Ask him why he brought us here;
"Ask him where we go, how far;
"Ask him: 'Will we return? And when?'
"Ask him: 'Is it likely we'll be found at all?' "

At last, I asked.
"We must know; why did you bring us here?" I said.
"Before the trees had lost their leaves,
We should have turned toward home."

No answer came. I shouted; then I shook him. Then I said:
"We should have known; the great speaker and our leader, was
Forever dead."

O. M. W.

to Everett Lee Hunt
and Henry Nelson Wieman

In addition to having influenced and inspired me, these two always spoke intelligently

Preface

The only book for beginners that is steeped in rhetorical theory and in the problems of contemporary communication is *Speaking Intelligently: Communication for Problem Solving*. More precisely, this book—from start to finish—has *problem solving* as its main concern. Much of this book is original and consists of materials I have developed myself and have taught to small sections of twenty students and to large sections of over a hundred students. The book, therefore, is designed to be versatile and to be adapted to the needs of various kinds of instructors.

I have used the materials in this book myself. Parts of the text, the questions for understanding, discussion, and research at the end of each chapter, and the assignments in the appendix I have used, revised, and used and revised again and again until I have developed teaching materials that seem to have worked well. In a sense, I have spent thirty years developing this book, trying to make it flexible enough to be useful in many ways and yet unlike any other book in speech-communication ever written. I believe that I have succeeded. So much for the uniqueness of this book.

Education should lead one to work at his upper limits, and under our best teachers, it does. To reach these limits is difficult and often painful; yet with intelligence and practice, that which was once beyond one becomes gradually possible and eventually, the easy thing to do. Once, only Newton and Leibnitz could solve problems using calculus; now high school students can. When the upper limits become the normal way, one's mind can rest a moment and glimpse another horizon yet beyond. By such a process, mankind rises.

To this process, unfortunately, speech courses seldom contribute. Courses in speech-communication are often the least imaginative and the least demanding among college offerings. Yet few activities are more important or more difficult than intelligent speaking, whether from the platform, in the television studio, the small group, the classroom, the pulpit, the courtroom, or at the dinner table. Speech-communication, far from being among the easiest of courses in college, perhaps should be the most demanding. This book is written so that minds will push to their upper limits and find new limits that are now beyond us.

In a real sense, however, there are no rules for intelligent speaking, for intelligent speaking derives from a superior intelligence that tends to fracture the rules, or better, rises above them with a sense of what is appropriate, strong, necessary, or fulfilling. Just as Beethoven rose above the classical rules of music or Descartes invented a way of solving algebraic problems by geometry, genius rises above rules. But genius does not ignore the rules. It usually knows them and knows when to fracture them. This book is not about "Genius in Communication," but rather attempts to answer the question, "How can we recognize, achieve, and teach intelligent communication?"

I regret that there is only one book in speech-communication entirely devoted to problem solving, for much work remains to be done in this field. As one who has spent thirty years of college teaching working on problem solving, I know that if a thousand colleagues did research in problem solving for a thousand years, we might have removed no more than a few grains of sand from the beach of ignorance. *Far more about problem solving remains unknown than is known today.* In sincere humility I hope that others will be motivated to work on problem solving in the future, and I look forward to hearing that such work has begun. If the reader is interested in writing about the matter to me at the address at the end of this preface, I will be happy to hear from him, although I cannot always answer.

I must thank many to whom I am indebted, and probably those mentioned here are outnumbered by those of whom I am not aware but who also helped. The good students I have known inspired this book, and it was written with them in mind. I owe much to students and colleagues at the University of Illinois, the University of Houston, the University of Alabama, and the University of Pittsburgh, and to my former professors, especially the late Lew Sarett, the late John J. B. Morgan, the late Robert Seashore, the late Ernest Wrage, the late Clarence Simon, and the late Irving Lee. The following might be surprised to learn I am indebted to them: Professor Lester Wolfson, now President of Indiana University at South Bend; General Harold Harding, H. Y. Benedict Professor *Emeritus* of Speech and Rhetoric at the University of Texas, El Paso; Professor Marie Hochmuth Nichols of the University of Illinois; and Robert T. Oliver, Research Professor *Emeritus* of The Pennsylvania State University. I especially thank Professor Don M. Burke of Purdue University for reading the manuscript and offering insightful suggestions.

At the University of Pittsburg, Marilee Kodis and Mark Krangle have given me helpful suggestions, and Professor Jack Matthews, chairman of the Department of Speech Communication and Theater Arts, and Professor Robert P. Newman, professor-in-charge, arranged a class schedule that enabled me to finish this book. Professor William S. Tracey painstakingly read the entire manuscript and offered valuable suggestions for improving it.

I thank Lloyd C. Chilton, executive editor, College and Professional Division of Macmillan Publishing Co., Inc., for his unbelievable patience in permitting me to dawdle when I had to.

The help of all of these, and those acknowledged in the book itself, does not entail any endorsement of the book by them. But I thank them for their kindness and help. If the book disappoints them, it is not their fault; the fault is mine.

Otis M. Walter
Department of Speech Communication
University of Pittsburgh
Pittsburgh, Pa. 15260

P.S. I must acknowledge (although she will never know and if she did, wouldn't care) the help of my eighteen-year-old cat, the gentle and saintly *Wu-wei,* for not letting mice eat up either my notes or this manuscript.

Contents

1 *The Reach of Rhetoric* 1

2 *Problems* 24

3 *Presenting Problems* 47

4 *Causation* 75

5 *Solutions* 98

6 *Values* 131

7 *Motivation by Ethos: Individual Determinism* 151

8 *Motivation by Group Behavior: Group Determinism* 174

9 *Problem Solving and the Varieties of Rhetorical Criticism* 198

Appendix 213

Speech Assignments 215
PROBLEMS 215
CAUSATION 219
SOLUTIONS 221
DEFINITIONS 225
VALUES 228

EULOGY   232

COMPARATIVE GROUPS   234

NORMATIVE GROUP   236

An Outline on Outlining   239

SAMPLE OUTLINE   243

Delivery   244

Index   249

Speaking
Intelligently

1

The Reach
of Rhetoric

. . . A man's reach should exceed his grasp, or what's a heaven for?
                                            —ROBERT BROWNING

On one of the islands in the South Pacific, at least in times before
the inroad of Western culture, whenever a visitor arrived, the islanders
expected him to make a speech; but his speech was always written for
him by one of the islanders, and it was delivered for him by another.
Such ideas about communication strike us as strange, but different cultures have different notions about communication. All people have ideas
of how to communicate, when to communicate, how much to communicate, and when not to.

Rhetoric: Implicit and Explicit

*Each tribe, each culture, and each subculture within our own has
ideas about communication implicit in its habits, its mores, its rules,
and its customs.* For example, implicit in our culture is the idea that,
at a party, conversation must not be allowed to falter; should it do so,
we are likely to show signs of embarrassment. Such an idea would strike
some tribes of American Indians as absurd, for among these Indians,

1

individuals were expected to remain silent unless they had wise or uniquely pertinent contributions to make. All people have *implicit* ideas about communication, which is to say that *all people have implicit ideas about rhetoric.*[1]

Although every group has ideas about communication, few have explicitly stated these ideas. Of all the cultures of the world, only one— Western culture—has left many records of its rhetorics. The best of these are brilliant and insightful works written by the brightest minds the world has produced. The value of these rhetorics is largely overlooked today because most students, as well as many rhetoricians or specialists in communications misinterpret them. These works are classics, and classics—especially in rhetoric—require a special approach to reveal the differences among rhetorics.[2]

On the Classics

Mark Twain once said that the classics were books that everyone wants to have read, but nobody wants to read. The classics, indeed, suggest to the popular mind the idea of dullness and heaviness. Many are accessible only through translations that distort the beauty and sense of the original. In addition, classics have sometimes been badly taught and poorly read. Even worse, knowledge of the classics used to be thought of as the mark by which to distinguish members of an establishment from supposedly lesser persons, and this "snob appeal" has reduced the popularity of the classics. But, as Jacques Barzun insists, if one lends one's

[1] See, for example, Margaret Mead, "Some Cultural Approaches to Communication Problems," in *The Communication of Ideas*, ed. by Lyman Bryson (New York: Harper & Row, Publishers, Inc., 1948), pp. 9–26. Few studies have been made of implicit ideas about rhetoric that characterize different cultures, or different subgroups in our own culture. Among the most recent is Robert T. Oliver, *Communication and Culture in Ancient India and China* (Syracuse, N.Y.: Syracuse University Press, 1971), and Gerry Philipsen, "Speaking 'Like a Man' in Teamsterville: Cultural Patterns of Role Enactment in an Urban Neighborhood," *Quarterly Journal of Speech*, 61 (February 1975), 13–22.

[2] A few rhetoricians have recognized the great differences among the better explicit rhetorics, and the enormous variety of implicit rhetorics. See, for example, P. Albert Duhamel, "The Function of Rhetoric as Effective Expression," *Journal of the History of Ideas, 10* (1949), 344–56 (also published in Maurice Natanson and Henry W. Johnstone, Jr., *Philosophy, Rhetoric and Argumentation* (University Park, Pa.: The Pennsylvania State University Press, 1965), pp. 80–92); Otis M. Walter, "On Views of Rhetoric, Whether Conservative or Progressive," *Quarterly Journal of Speech, 49* (December 1963), 368–82 (also published in *Contemporary Theories of Rhetoric: Selected Readings*, ed. by Richard Johannesen [New York: Harper & Row, Publishers, Inc., 1971], pp. 18–38); and Otis M. Walter, "Creativity and the Rules of Rhetoric," *Journal of Creative Behavior, 1* (Fall 1967), 383–90, (reprinted in *A Reader of Speech-Communication*, ed. by James W. Gibson [New York: McGraw-Hill Book Company, 1971], pp. 139–45).

mind to a classic, "It will be returned to him, not as good as b
than new." [3]

The important part of a classic—for our purposes, at least—*is the
question that the classic attempts to answer.* The question serves as a
kind of handle by which we can pick up the hot griddle of the classic.
The question gives the classic its fire, suggests the reason it was written,
and serves to help us interpret it. Thus, *Macbeth* may be said to raise
the question, "What is the result of 'vaulting ambition' on different
kinds of people?" Machiavelli's *The Prince* attempts to answer the question, "How do rulers hold their power in spite of the natural opposition
of the ruled?" Most literature asks, although in an amazing variety of
ways, one basic question: "What is the human condition?"

LOCATING THE QUESTION IN A CLASSIC

The question or questions posed by a classic must be *imaginatively
discovered* by the reader, and not all readers will agree on the precise
nature of the question. Each age may interpret a given classic differently.
Great works such as *Hamlet,* the "Mona Lisa," or *Oedipus Rex* have
been given dozens of interpretations through the ages. These interpretations give rise to a limited number of questions, and those questions
provide the handle by which to grasp the work.

The most characteristic aspect of the classic is that it asks the
"right" questions—questions that are stimulating and timeless, questions
that bring into being a host of new subquestions, questions that demand
new methods of investigation and new ways of looking at old knowledge,
ways that are fresh, ways that may work intellectual, social, economic, or
political revolutions.

But if a classic asks the "right" questions, it often, especially in
nonfiction, gives a "wrong" (or an inadequate) answer. Nevertheless,
our schools have generally required memorization of the often inadequate answer and have failed to focus on the original questions. We
must return to the classics and see them as works that asked original,
fundamental, searching, profound, and stimulating questions. If we do,
these books will cease to be the dead hand they sometimes have been
thought to be, and will serve as Emerson said books should: to inspire.

Some Classics in Rhetoric

Classical rhetoric has not been the energizing force it might have
been because twentieth-century scholars tend to see all rhetorics as posing only one question: "What are the means of persuasion?" That this

[3] *The Art of Teaching* (New York: Vintage Books, 1955), p. 72.

is the great question for rhetoric is the "conventional wisdom" of our century.[4] Let us take an unconventional, but more accurate, view of some of these rhetorics.

PROTAGORAS

Protagoras, a fifth-century Greek, seemed to ask, *"How can a person push his intellect—and, presumably, that of his audience—as far as it can go?"* [5] His answer is inadequate, for he believed that when intellect had probed the limits of any question, it would find two answers, equally true and irrefutable, but irreconcilably contradictory. (Thus, perhaps, he meant that in studying the tides one would find that both high tide and low tide, though opposite, exist. Or, in studying the human being, one would find man and woman. More likely, he meant more sophisticated matters; we cannot tell because most of his works were burned after he gave a speech insisting that no possibility exists of having knowledge about the gods.) Even so, "How can we push intellect to its furthest limits?" is still a good question, and like the questions of many classical rhetorics, is still largely unanswered. This book asks the same question, and attempts a more adequate answer.

PLATO

Plato, founder of the first university, the Academy, which lasted for 916 years, was much concerned with rhetoric. In Plato's day, speaking was the means by which a man persuaded a jury to award him more land, people to give him more freedom and more power, or persuaded the legislature (of which all free Athenians were members) to pass favorable laws. By persuasion, citizens achieved social standing, wealth, and influence. Plato condemned the conventional rhetoric of the day as "making the worse appear the better reason," and suggested the outlines of a new rhetoric. His outline seems to be answering the question, *"How may the speaker find the ethical ideas on which life must rest and, by finding them, transform himself and his society into the best it can become?"* His answer is not so inadequate as that of Protagoras, and his question is still important today.

---

[4] "Conventional wisdom," a useful term popularized by John Kenneth Galbraith in *The Affluent Society* (Boston: Houghton Mifflin Company, 1958), Chap. II, signifies those notions that everyone believes are true, but that happen to be false.

[5] Most interpretations of Protagoras have been influenced by Plato's condemnation of him. For an interpretation that is not, see Mario Untersteiner, *The Sophists*, trans. by Kathleen Freeman (New York: Philosophical Library, Inc., 1954), Chaps. I, II, and III.

ISOCRATES

Isocrates, the most successful teacher of rhetoric in the ancient world, placed rhetoric at the center of his curriculum. He was opposed, as was Plato, to those speakers who sought only their own advantage. He asked, and partially answered, the question, *"How may we educate future speakers so that they will become great citizens?"*

ARISTOTLE

Aristotle wrote the best-known and most frequently read of the ancient rhetorics. It is not true, as it is commonly thought, that he asked only this major question: *"What are the available means of persuasion in any given case?"* Aristotle asked a variety of questions, perhaps the most important of which is, *"What besides rhetoric should the speaker understand?"* He answered it by urging speakers to study what we now call political science, psychology, logic, and ethics as well as rhetoric. Today, he would probably also urge an understanding of sociology, economics, anthropology, literature, and history.

Thus, we see that Protagoras, Plato, Isocrates, and Aristotle all asked different questions about rhetoric. This brief survey is sufficient to show us that classical rhetorics asked certain stimulating questions that require answers today.

Asking Unconventional Questions

When one forms the habit of reading a classic by constantly asking, "With what question is this classic concerned?," he soon acquires a new tool for thinking. Werner Heisenberg, winner of the Nobel prize for the discovery of quantum mechanics, has stressed the importance of this tool:

We must stress the fact that the whole strength of our Western civilization is derived, and always has been, from the relationship between the way in which we pose questions and our practical actions. . . .

Whoever delves into the philosophy of the Greeks will encounter at every step this ability to pose questions of principle; in this way he can learn to command *the strongest tool of Western thought.*[6]

The questions implied in the classics can also become an important tool, not only in helping us *develop a sense of what a good question is* but, more important, in helping us *improve old questions and ask new ones.*

[6] "A Scientist's Case for the Classics," trans. by Arnold J. Pomerans, *Harper's* (May 1959), 25–26.

Let us examine three of the questions that have not been adequately treated in works on communication and rhetoric. One of these was first asked in the last days of the Roman Empire; the other two did not arise until recently. These questions concern the liberal arts, democratic speaking, and civilization.

Liberal Arts and Communication

The term *liberal arts* has had several meanings. In the eighteenth century it meant "activities suitable to wealthy persons to enrich their leisure times." Since most of us lack such wealth, the definition is irrelevant to us. In the nineteenth century *liberal arts* meant "knowledge that distinguishes aristocrats from lesser persons." The definition is so snobbish as to be repulsive. In the twentieth century *liberal arts* became confused with "general education." Our century saw curricula that required students to take a little bit of everything; some science, a bit of history, a smattering of a language, at least one social science, some course in English composition, perhaps a superficial course in speech, perhaps some philosophy, but not much of depth in more than perhaps one subject. Yet a more useful meaning of *liberal arts* may yet evolve: The most useful meaning of *liberal arts* springs from the meaning of the Latin word from which *liberal* was derived: *Liberare* or "to free." A liberal education is an education for free people, an education concerned with freedom. With a liberal education, one learns how to obtain freedom, how to preserve it, how to use it responsibly, and how to extend it. Intelligent speaking, in this sense, is part of a liberal education.

In our own country, when concern for freedom was greatest, our speaking reached its greatest heights: from Patrick Henry to Abraham Lincoln, Martin Luther King, Jr., and Malcolm X. We must indeed concern ourselves with education for freedom if our nation is to fulfill the unique experiment that was begun two hundred years ago. To fail to understand the liberal arts as "those arts needed by free people" may be to fail in the purpose for which this country was founded. Little in education today is taught to provide the tools free men need, and our needs grow more desperate yearly. Let us return to the ancient meaning of *liberal arts,* not only in higher education but in education at all levels.

Democratic Communication

Nearly all rhetorics, and certainly all classical rhetorics, were written in a dictatorship. Moreover, they were written at a time and by people who did not understand democracy. Yet *the most salient characteristic of good democratic speaking is that it is directed at the solu-*

tion of problems of the citizens of that society. No existing rhetoric describes the process of problem solving; it is time we tried to do so.

Communication and Civilization

Among the questions that must be raised in rhetorical theory are the following: "What kinds of communication cause a civilization to develop and grow?" "What kinds of communication cause a civilization to stagnate and decline?" Because the welfare of all of us is tied to whether or not our civilization is in a state of development or a state of decline, we should explore the relation between a civilization and the communication of that civilization.

In the Golden Age of Greece, all free men had the chance to gaze upon the Parthenon, to attend the plays of Sophocles and Euripides, and to hear philosophers debate in the marketplace. But when their Golden Age ended, the Greeks wrote no more great plays, created no more great art, and borrowed their religion, science, and philosophy from more energetic cultures.

When a culture declines, the people suffer. When the splendor of Rome at last wasted away, not only did men fail to write great books but generations were made to endure plagues, to believe in witchcraft, and to suffer in poverty and filth. When our civilization is provident, we have more freedom from economic worry. When a culture is rich in ideas and art, we have the best chance to enjoy and create more ideas and art. But when a culture is poor and the individual must battle for sheer survival, he will lose many of those human advantages and virtues. This large pattern called civilization, then, is one from which none of us can wholly escape.

This larger pattern of culture is not mere custom and habit. Whether one eats with chopsticks or with a knife and fork makes little difference, but whether one lives in a rich culture or in an increasingly unproductive one makes a great difference. What matters is not that we shake hands and Eskimos rub noses, but that we possess enough wealth, wisdom, freedom, and confidence to develop our potential.

What people say over the dinner table, at meetings, and from the pulpit or platform or television screen influences what human beings do. What they write and read in the newspaper, the scholarly journal, and the magazine influences the course of our culture. Presumably some things can help our culture, whereas others will cause it to stagnate or decline.[7] Let us add, then, these questions about the role of communica-

---

[7] For a more complete treatment of this point, see Otis M. Walter, "On the Teaching of Speech as a Force in Western Culture," *The Speech Teacher, 11* (January 1962), 1–9.

tion in civilization to our repertoire of "rhetorical questions," for no questions may be more important than those that increase our chances for a fulfilling life by improving the quality of our civilization.

Questions for Survival

We have, so far, looked at the following questions:

1. Protagoras: How may the speaker carry his intelligence and that of his listeners as far as intelligence can go?
2. Plato: How may certain values, if completely understood by speakers and audiences, transform men and states into the best they can become?
3. Isocrates: How may speech be taught so as to create effective speakers who are also great citizens?
4. Aristotle: What matters, other than rhetoric, must the speaker know?
5. Liberal arts: How can communication be taught so that rhetoric can increase one's understanding of maintaining and extending one's freedom?
6. Democratic speaking: How can speaking be taught so as to be uniquely suited to a society striving to become democratic?
7. Civilization: How may communication secure the growth processes of a civilization and prevent its decline and disintegration? [8]

Problem Solving

Although the questions that form the basis of this book appear to be widely divergent questions, they can all be unified to produce a single approach to rhetoric and communication. If these seven ideas about rhetoric and communication might be unified under one concept, we will then have something more than "notions" about rhetoric and communication; we will have a theory of rhetoric and communication. And, in fact, it is possible to unite these questions under one important idea —*problem solving*.

INTELLIGENCE AND PROBLEM SOLVING

When Binet constructed the first intelligence test, he refused to define the term.[9] Yet, the meaning of intelligence is important. Intelligence

[8] A logical positivist might insist that one cannot define some of these terms; I would point out, however, that even a logical positivist lives as if he has done so.
[9] See Richard Herrnstein, "I.Q.," *Atlantic* (September 1971), 46. At least Binet *thought* he did not define intelligence when he constructed the test. Actually, he did have an idea of intelligence: average intelligence was that which made it possible

is not mere memory—the *idiot savant* can perform startling feats of memory but may lack the intelligence to take even normal care of himself. Nor is intelligence confined to the ability to learn, for one can absorb information without being able to understand or apply it. *Intelligence is, rather, the ability to solve problems.* These problems may be those of engineering or agriculture, of aesthetics or art, of politics or economy. The problems may be as commonplace as the question of what to do with leftovers from a big meal, or as profound as the problems contemplated by a Hindu mystic. Wherever problem solving occurs, intelligence is at work. But what is intelligence?

We can gain more insight into the nature of intelligence by pointing out that the IQ test cannot possibly measure intelligence. First of all, one of the qualities that characterizes an intelligent person is the ability to divine—to guess—which problems he is capable of solving. If one selects the "wrong" problem for himself, he may be doomed to failure. But somehow—and we know almost nothing about how—the intelligent person manages to select problems that he is equipped to solve. *Not one item on any IQ test measures one's ability to select such problems.* Often, the solution of a problem requires the location and eradication of its causes. Not one item on the IQ test measures one's ability to locate these causes. Therefore, the IQ test does not measure intelligence. It may measure a kind of puzzle solving, but not problem solving.

Puzzles and Problems. Problem solving obviously requires that one be able to identify or devise solutions to problems. IQ tests seem designed to measure the ability to solve *puzzles* rather than to solve *problems*. A problem is as different from a puzzle as is the creation of a great painting from the effort to copy it. The genius of Michelangelo created the Sistine Chapel's famous fresco; almost any hack may copy it. Taking a superior photograph of the ceiling may be a hard puzzle, but painting the ceiling in the first place was so great a problem that Michaelangelo needed all his genius to do it at all. Let us review the difference between puzzles and problems.

A puzzle has one, or relatively few, solutions. In chemistry, you are given an unknown chemical to identify by qualitative analysis. The unknown has a precise amount of certain chemicals. Finding what they are and how much of each exists is the solution to a puzzle, although it

---

for an individual to do what most people of his age group were able to do; superior intelligence was the ability to do what older people could do; low intelligence, of course, was the inability to do what people in one's own age group could do. Herrnstein's article holds that intelligence is nearly entirely the work of heredity; such a notion is, as we show, untenable.

may be a difficult puzzle. A "problem" in algebra is really a puzzle because there is only one answer possible. Not so with problems. In a problem, there may be no known or agreed-upon answer. For any particular problem there may be many solutions, or no solution, and experts may disagree on all such matters. Moreover, the solution may raise new problems. Problems are also generally more important than puzzles, even though little of our education is concerned with either problems or puzzles.

But one thing is clear: the IQ test does not measure intelligence of this kind, although it may measure whether or not we can do things that upper-middle-class white members of our age group can do. Children raised in a black ghetto, for example, will often rank low on IQ tests. Yet, they can survive living in the ghetto, although their upper-middle-class white age peers might not. Intelligence involves the ability to solve problems, and this book is devoted to helping speakers learn how to choose, analyze, and solve problems and then to communicate to others that these choices, analyses, and solutions are worthy of acceptance. Thus, problem solving incorporates the necessity of considering Protagoras' attempt to study the nature of intelligence.

VALUES AND PROBLEM SOLVING

The concept of problem solving also subsumes Plato's concern with the transformation of man and of society. To transform man, Plato realized, the very basis of man's choices must be changed. Behind any kind of problem solving are values—attitudes that lead one person to identify a given situation as a problem and another person to ignore it. If human brotherhood is a powerful value for us, we may feel that the suffering of ghetto inhabitants is a problem; but if we value efficiency more, we may conclude that the alleviation of that suffering is too costly. Values likewise influence our identification of the causes of a particular problem, and our selection of acceptable solutions. Because Plato's major concern was with values, he can offer a contribution to any theory of rhetoric or communication that is based on problem solving.

CITIZENSHIP AND PROBLEM SOLVING

The concept of *citizenship* has become distasteful to us because of a meaning imparted to it by many members of the establishment: "to become a harmless person." Nevertheless, the word is still a useful one because we can give it a more substantial meaning. What is a good citizen? Surely he is not merely one who habitually prattles of patriotism and goes through the prescribed patriotic rituals. *The good citizen is he who best understands the problems of his people and is best equipped to help solve these problems.* Superpatriots seldom meet this standard.

The superpatriot may even help to destroy his country by refusing to acknowledge the problems that plague it. The great citizen is one who recognizes the problems of his society and thereby helps to ensure its survival. Thus, citizenship—or patriotism—requires problem solving.

MATERIALS OUTSIDE RHETORIC AND PROBLEM SOLVING

To solve the great problems that confront our civilization today, we must know more than doctrines and techniques of persuasion. The best rhetoric texts strongly urge the student to use the library, and to become acquainted with a wide variety of subjects. In so doing, these texts are following the example of Aristotle. But to solve problems, we must draw on subject matters with which these problems are concerned; for economic problems, we must of course study economics; for political problems, we will find help in the study of politics. Yet to understand problem solving itself, we must grasp some concepts that were originated by philosophers, some that have been developed by psychologists, some that were developed by logicians, as well as some that were devised by experts in communication and by rhetoricians.

CIVILIZATION AND PROBLEM SOLVING [10]

Perhaps the best of the unconventional questions on which this book is based is one that rhetorics have never discussed carefully: "What is the relation between communication and civilization?" Let us show that here, too, problem solving is a key to understanding civilization and its rise or fall. Here, too, those who communicate can influence the course of even the mighty conglomerate that passes national boundaries and continental barriers: Western civilization.

How can communication be a force that sustains and strengthens Western Culture? How can it help save our civilization from the destruction that has been the destiny of all previous civilizations? The question is of the utmost significance, particularly in our times. It can be given no perfect, certain, nor final answer, especially in the confines of a single chapter. But our times demand the best answer possible lest we be a good-willed but unwitting force for evil. If our answer is only a shrewd guess or at best a probable hypothesis, such answers are still better and more likely to help our culture than completely unlit darkness. All that can be offered here is a supportable hypothesis that one hopes will encourage debate and further research to the end that even-

---

[10] Taken from Otis M. Walter, "On the Teaching of Speech as a Force in Western Culture." *The Speech Teacher 11* (January 1963), pp. 1–9, and reprinted, with modifications, by permission.

tually we may know how communication and speaking operate to create, sustain, weaken, and destroy civilizations.

That communication is at least a link in the chains of causes that create and destroy civilization is easily seen. Most of the world's business is transformed into symbols that must flow through the filter of communication. If that filter were suddenly forever blocked so that no man could again communicate with another, civilization could not exist. Left alone with only our private perceptions and personal thoughts, we would all be terrifyingly isolated, with the best in human life beyond our helpless reach. And without communication, the signs of civilization would disappear, some of them, overnight: no philosophy, no literature, and no science could exist. No courts could enforce justice, no schools could educate, no buildings could be erected, no legislature could pass laws, and no newspapers could tell us of the fate of our fellow man. *The communication of ideas over space and through time is the great drive-shaft that propels all civilized activities.*

But to understand how communication drives a culture, we must probe deeper. *If we know how civilizations arose and what effected their decline, we might be able to infer the part that communication plays in these processes.* We would then have an hypothesis about the way communication can be a force in Western culture. We will, therefore, try to analyze the process of the rise and fall of civilization. This analysis will suggest hypotheses about the function that communication must fulfill in growth or may fail to fulfill in decay. We shall then be in a position to offer a guess as to how speech, communication, and rhetoric might be a beneficial force in Western culture.

The Rise of Athens. Let us examine the circumstances leading to the rise of Greek culture. Much is known about the birth of civilization in Greece, and, more important, the Greeks produced the greatest number of geniuses *per capita* of any other civilization before or since. Greek culture was not born because the Greeks had an easy life.[11] By the seventh century, B.C., the thin, rocky soil of Greece could not raise enough grain to feed either the men or the cattle of Greece. The natural increase in population together with the increase that came with the Dorian invasion produced the possibility of perpetual famine. But the Greeks noted that certain agricultural items, especially olives and grapes,

---

[11] Arnold F. Toynbee, *A Study of History,* abr. by D. C. Somervell (New York: Oxford University Press, 1947), p. 90. Toynbee has done the most thorough job attempting to show that civilization arises from a challenge. The writer is indebted to him for much inspiration as well as information. Unfortunately, Toynbee is not content to write a philosophy of history, but his late volumes have become muddled with concepts of eschatology, so that he has not continued to think clearly about the problems on which he made so fine a start.

grew so well on Attic soil that a surplus could be raised. If Attic farmers gave up raising grain and planted only olive trees and grapevines, an enormous surplus of grapes and olives could be produced. This surplus could then be traded to Asia Minor for grain. Athenian civilization and Athenian wealth began their rise with this solution to the problem of starvation. Thus a *problem,* to which a *solution* was found, laid the basis for Athenian civilization. Athenian civilization, furthermore, continued to develop by the same pattern—that is, by finding solutions to problems. *The striking manner in which other solutions to other problems forced the rise of Greece suggests that a civilization rises when it is faced with problems to which the people of the civilization discover or devise solutions.*[12] This idea is further supported by other activities that encouraged growth. The Athenians, for example, faced many problems in the development of trade. The principal traders of the world at the time were the Phoenicians, but to ship the olive oil and return the grain in Phoenician ships would be to give the profits from the venture to a foreign land. The Athenians responded to the problem by developing a ship-building industry, which not only provided jobs but gave Athens the largest merchant marine in the world. The shipping industry faced a problem because other nations and pirates would attack the ships and wipe out the profits from the trade. Athens solved the problem by building a navy that gave her control of the seas. This navy, developed as a solution to the problem of safeguarding Greek ships, destroyed the Phoenician-built fleet of the Persian Empire at Salamis and thus saved perhaps both Greece and the West from Oriental domination.

Moreover, to ship olive oil and wine required a special container, with the result that a lucrative pottery industry grew up in Athens. In addition, to trade with highest profit often required that olive oil be sold in one port and grain bought in another, but to sell goods in one place and buy in another requires a medium of exchange. This problem hastened the development of the rich silver mines of Larium and forced Athens to coin money. After the Persians had burned Athens and its Acropolis, both of which were built of wood, another problem arose.

---

[12] Unfortunately, the hypothesis, although it can be extensively illustrated, cannot be conclusively proved. The beginnings of civilizations are shrouded in a lost past. Moreover, the thesis demands that we approach the problem phenomenologically— that is, to know how *the people in the culture themselves* perceived the problem and what *they* felt the meaning of the problem was to them. Such data cannot be obtained except very indirectly—especially since there are few records of the early stages of a culture. The best we can say for the hypothesis is that it is an informed guess. But the guess itself is an attractive one that seems capable of explaining many of the phenomena of civilization and capable of helping us make predictions about our own civilization.

Greek soil no longer produced enough lumber. The Athenians were forced to look for another material. The solution was to build with marble, with the result that buildings of such permanent and inspiring beauty were constructed so that the Greeks would still deserve fame if their architecture were their only claim to it.

The problems the Greeks faced forced on them solutions that were powerful forces in the development of Greek civilization. Without the problem of starvation, there might have been no Greek trade, with the result that Athens would not have made stimulating contacts with other peoples and civilizations. Without the need to own their ships, the shipbuilding industry would not have been forced on Athens, with the possible result that Athens might have fallen to the Persians before the Golden Age began. Without the problems posed by trade, the Greeks would not have been forced to develop their urns or coinage. Without the thin soil that could not raise enough lumber, the Parthenon might have been built of boards.[13] *In each case, a solution to a problem forced the rise of Athens.* Thus, the stimulation of a problem was necessary to jolt people into problem solving. Solutions both enrich a civilization and provide opportunity for further material and cultural enrichment.

Bergson makes an illuminating comment on why a problem must be the starting point of a civilization.

But to get on this road [to civilization] . . . requires perhaps the menace of extermination, such as that created by the discovery of a new weapon or by an enemy tribe. Those societies that have remained more or less "primitive" are probably those for whom life has been too easy. They were not called upon to make the initial effort. Subsequently, it was too late; the society could not advance . . . because it was contaminated by the products of its own laziness. These products are precisely the practices of magic, at least inasmuch as they are excessive and all encroaching. For magic . . . temporarily calms the uneasiness of an intelligence . . . which is vaguely aware of its ignorance. . . .[14]

Thus a problem is the starting point of a civilization because the operation of intelligence on an extended and systematic scale does not begin unless a *jolt,* such as the threat of destruction, is experienced first. The

---

[13] Of course, an ugly building can be built of marble. To create the Parthenon, far more than calcified stone was necessary; human genius was necessary to create the Parthenon, and human genius is necessary to the building or civilization. But the point is that for human genius to arise, to be channelized usefully on a grand scale, and to be accepted requires a special social field—a field that is created by a problem to which people demand (and, consequently, reward) the act of genius that solves the problem. Thus for genius to function, a social setting that stimulates genius, disciplines and channels genius, and rewards genius is created. Thus, genius is inseparable from the causes of the rise of civilization, but for it to become operative, the social setting of problem solving seems to be required.

[14] Henri Bergson, *Two Sources of Morality and Religion,* trans. by R. A. Audra and C. Bereton (Garden City: Doubleday & Company, Inc., 1954), pp. 171–72.

jolt energizes a people to develop those solutions that we recognize as the activities of a civilized society. Bergson noted that the process of civilization can be stopped by the antithesis of problem solving, which is magic.

THE GROWTH OF A CIVILIZATION

Problem solving not only helps to explain the *origin* of a civilization but also helps to explain the *growth* of the high culture of the Golden Age. The struggle to find solutions to certain problems, for example, is found in the origins of Greek philosophy. The first philosopher on record is Thales, who investigated the nature of matter. Although he concluded that the fundamental component of matter was water, Thales' idea was truly a sophisticated one. The sophistication of his idea becomes clear when one sees the assumptions and reasoning behind his conclusion. Thales, first of all, took the nature of the universe *as a problem*. Moreover, he assumed that the problem must be solved by finding a *natural answer* to it, a solution very different from the superstitious explanations of the Egyptians and Persians. Thales' conclusion especially suggests that he hit upon a new means of solving the problem of the nature of matter. Thales' conclusion indicates that he systematically used empiricism; his answer was, doubtless, made by observing that water falls from the sky, water exists in the rivers and the ocean, water comes from the ground, and that both animals and plants contain watery fluids.

More complex, but more crucial, was Thales' notion that water was the foundation of earth, of fire, and of air. The evaporation of water into the air made it appear that it was turned into air—and, therefore, a constituent of the air. Water in the form of steam rose toward the sun—making it appear that it was the basis of fire. A cold dish held over a fire accumulated water on it, a sign interpreted to mean that water came from fire. Water was absorbed by the ground and could be squeezed out of it. To say that the thinking is wrong is to forget that we look in the light of the knowledge of physics built since the time of Galileo. But in the light of man's knowledge during the hundred thousand years before, it is one of the most brilliant guesses ever made, and we still cannot answer the question. Thus the first philosopher took the nature of the world as a problem, searched for a natural solution to the problem, and hit upon empiricism as a way of looking for the answer. Thus a special kind of problem solving gave birth to Greek philosophy.[15]

Other philosophers, perhaps stimulated by Thales' attempt, offered

---

[15] See Susanne K. Langer, *Philosophy in a New Key* (New York: Mentor Books, 1942), Chap. I. Langer shows in other ways how new questions—new problems—can generate new schools and new interpretations of philosophy.

different explanations of matter using the same method. Since many philosophers took the same problem, used the same method, and found *different* answers, the result was, to some, bewilderment but to others, stimulation. *The Greeks had begun to think.* Soon the Greeks were taking as problems the nature of mathematics, of drama, of political activity, of the good life, and especially, of man. The problems of justice and metaphysics inspired Plato to write the *Dialogues.* Moral and religious problems inspired Aeschylus, Sophocles, and Euripides to write the only other plays that can be compared to Shakespeare's.[16] Tools for problem solving such as logic, mathematics, and argument were refined and developed. The Golden Age had arrived. No society anywhere has so delighted itself with the problems of the nature of things as did the small but brilliant band in Athens. The Greeks thus took as problems nearly all matters, and found new ways of working with the problems and new solutions to them. *So it was that the attitudes of problem solving not only laid the basis for the development of strength and wealth in Athens but served to generate science and philosophy, and even had its effect on art and architecture.*[17]

VARIETY IN CIVILIZATIONS

Problem solving is not only the generating force behind civilization; it likewise determines the direction that a civilization takes. The kind of civilization a people develop is determined by the kinds of problems they choose to solve. Although the Greeks chose to solve the problem of starvation, some Orientals looked upon starvation as something to be accepted in the normal course of human existence. Instead of developing methods to combat the problem, the Oriental developed attitudes and philosophies that made the problem of extreme poverty

---

[16] Again note how problem-solving attitudes provided a social field in which genius could flourish. See footnote 13.

[17] Many philosophers, including Toynbee, have assumed that a civilization is a kind of gestalt or whole that rises as a unit and declines as a unit. Careful observation has shown that such is not the case. There seems to be no uniformity in the times at which art, science, religion, mathematics, and the like are developed in the various civilizations. Some of these may come early in one culture, late in another, or not undergo any significant development in still another. (See Pitirim Sorokin, *Social Philosophies in an Age of Crisis* [Boston: Beacon Press, 1950], Chaps. XI, XII.) *This kind of situation is precisely what one would expect if problem solving offered the key to an understanding of civilization.* A culture would advance only in those areas and at those times when there was a strong interest in certain problems, or when there were new methods discovered for dealing with the problems. Stagnation would occur when there were no new available ways of solving the problem or interest in the problem was low. Decline would follow the situation in which past knowledge was being "lost" or in which the problem was worsening. Thus a civilization may grow in some respects, stagnate in others, and, simultaneously, decline elsewhere.

bearable—philosophies that would be useful to any Westerner in helping him accept whatever tragic matters are inevitable. So the Oriental
chose to "solve" the problem of starvation by developing a philosophy
that would enable him to accept privation; many of the qualities of
Oriental cultures spring from this difference in the choice of problems.

The civilization of Rome, although much like Greece, developed
in a different way from that of Greece because a different set of problems was chosen. The practical Roman was not, like the Greek thinkers,
interested in the nature of things; he preferred to accept the formulations of the Greeks without much question and with little refinement.
Consequently, Rome never developed much in science, philosophy, or
the arts that rose above the level of mere imitation. Moreover, the imita-
tions were generally inferior just as Cicero was inferior as an orator to
Demosthenes, or Plautus was inferior to Aristophanes in the art of
comedy. No Roman philosopher could match Plato or Aristotle; Phidias,
the sculptor of the Parthenon, had his imitators but no equals, and
there was no Roman counterpart of Archimedes. Consequently, no new
forms of art nor theories of it, no new ideas about the nature of man,
nor any new formulation about the universe were produced in Rome,
for the pupils did not exceed their teacher.

But there was one area in which the Greeks were manifestly weak
—the problems of managing an Empire. Here the Romans proved themselves as ingenious as had any Greek. This ingenuity was to shape the
Roman way as much as the problems chosen by the Greeks shaped them.
To the problem of government and law, the Roman brought his vigor
and his skill. Rome's codes of law, her policies of local administration of
government, local collection of taxes, and local creation and enforcement of law, continued in the face of forces under which other civilizations had foundered. Whereas the Greeks found their glory in
individuality, *Rome built her grandeur upon order and system,* and in
her greatness preserved the civilization of the Greeks and spread it
throughout the world.

The Decline of Civilization

But why did Greco-Roman civilization die? *The concept of problem solving as a fundamental key to civilization here gains double
strength—for not only does success in problem solving generate a civilization, but failures in problem solving mark its decline.*

As Greek civilization was absorbed by the Roman Empire and
thus was permitted to live on, failures in problem solving rendered the
civilization relatively stagnant and, finally, destroyed it. Let us look at
some of these.

A failure of the Greeks to solve a special problem is worthy of mention. The Greeks emphasized individuality. Each Greek felt he was responsible for each major public decision. In Athens each citizen was a member of the Assembly and each could sit on the huge juries that often numbered in the hundreds. Men were even elected to generalships, so jealously did the Athenian guard his right to express his judgment. Individuality was prized—so much so that it seems to have *blocked* the thinking of the Greeks about a problem that this very individuality brought about. The individuality of the Greeks led them to feel that the small city-state was the ideal form of government. Plato observed that the ideal *polis* was no larger than 5,005. Such governments, indeed, permitted a maximum of individuality. City-states, however, are apt to be jealous of each other, and to use their vitality and strength to fight wars among themselves. The Greeks fought three such wars in one generation. And so dear was the individualism of the Greeks that their thinking on the problem of "city-state rights" seems to have been blocked; no major Greek philosopher conceived of the possibility of forming some kind of federal union based on government by consent to preserve individuality and yet kept peace. At last the Greeks, perhaps too weary of ceaseless wars, succumbed, after only one battle, first to Philip of Macedon and later to Rome. The problem was that of preserving the diversity and individuality permitted by the *polis* while still establishing the unity of all the Greeks. For want of a solution to this problem, the Greeks wasted their energy in wars among themselves and failed to unify at the decisive moment when Greek liberty was threatened by invading armies.

When thought is stifled or thinkers are persecuted, problem solving is apt to falter. The ancient world had, on the whole, little regard for personal freedom. Waves of persecution were directed against those who searched out problems. Socrates pointed up the moral problems of Greece so vividly that the Greeks, irritated at his questioning, condemned him to die. Even the mild and conservative Aristotle left the citizens of Athens "in order not to give them a chance to commit a second crime against philosophy." Protagoras, Socrate's contemporary, although over seventy, was banished from Athens because of his agnosticism and was lost in a storm at sea while the mob burned his writings. Rome never quite welcomed the Greek thinkers with an open heart. The Epicureans were expelled from Rome in 173 B.C., and all philosophers (and rhetoricians) were expelled in 161 B.C. The Gracchi brothers urged the Roman Senate to enact laws that would improve the standard of living of the destitute. These two brothers might have helped solve the problem of poverty, but they were murdered. For his attempts to re-establish the Republic, Cicero, previously declared the father of his country, was banished from Rome and for his part in backing the least obnoxious faction of the dictatorship in the civil war, was beheaded. Finally, in A.D. 529 Justinian closed the nine hundred-year-old schools of Greece. They did not open again. Moreover, the interest in order and system stultified certain kinds of creativity. To keep order and unity, the emperors hired poets and playwrights. Needless to say, there was no critic of the emperor or of the institutions of Rome, nor was there even an attempt to understand the problems of Rome. Instead, the emperors saw to it that unity was achieved by superpatriotism and by a revival of the Roman state religion. *For problem solving to take place, people must be free of persecution, free to admit that there are things wrong, and free to consider and advocate various ways to right those wrongs.* The people were not free, and, hence, the problems of Rome were not solved.

Then, as one might expect, one or more of the unsolved problems reached such proportions that the civilization became seriously weak within. There is not space here to treat the final end of the Roman Empire, but some of the problems it faced can be sketched. The poverty of the masses was appalling. One third of the inhabitants of the city were without any sources of livelihood whatever. The Romans kept these people from revolting by giving them a dole of free grain and by giving them a kind of entertainment for which the Romans have become infamous. But the program of "bread and circuses" did not diminish the poverty. Another third of Rome's people were just barely able to survive. Thus, two thirds of Rome's inhabitants were too weak to make a real contribution. Hardly one in fifty was comfortably situated. The stench, filth, and disease on the streets of ancient Rome could not be imagined by a modern American. The morale of the masses of Romans sagged because they had no economic stake in the community. Rome had to work harder to court the favor of the masses by giving more bread and circuses and finally, by exempting these citizens from military service; afterward, the legions of Rome were filled and even commanded by foreign mercenaries.

Since criticism of the system that begot these difficulties could not be given, the problems were not diagnosed and solved. Since the principal writers and teachers of Rome were in the pay of the emperor, they were required to glorify Rome to earn their keep. Criticism, of course, would have been a higher form of loyalty than unceasing praise because it might have permitted Rome to survive. But Rome refused to permit freedom of criticism, blinded herself to her problems, persecuted those who might have helped her, and invoked false substitutes for problem solving. The city was already weak when Alaric entered.

COMMUNICATION AND CIVILIZATION

Communication is the instrument that begets decisions about problem solving. When communication is stupid, problem solving will not occur; when communication is weak and dull, problem solving will not occur. But in rhetoric and communication the tools of problem solving are (although not exclusively) our subject matter. We must learn the ways to bring audiences to see that an apparently remote problem is closer than they realize; we must learn the logical requirements of a plan of action, and how an idea can be made attractive. We must learn the merits of this problem or that solution and how to gain acceptance for a program. Indeed, the spoken word, the organized idea, the well-supported point, the intelligent and discerning attack upon the fallacy—these are at once the categories of problem solving and the categories of speaking.

We can use these strategic materials to speed the growth of Western culture. But we must do more. We must help others see the significance of problem solving in society, understand the rewards of problem solving, and know the dangers of failure. We must debate and discuss problems so that the most important will be selected, and we must struggle to find or devise solutions for them.

I am not sure that we in communication are doing enough to help problem solving. I suspect that we have some ideas that hinder problem solving. Too often, speech is taught as if its aim were *merely* to develop one's confidence, or to gain personal influence over others, or to win a tin cup for Alma Mater or merely to encourage talk. Too often, the course is merely one in delivery with a few hints on organization. Too often, *we have bowed to the hostility of a community toward the controversial and permitted our students to speak the least on the problems about which they should have talked the most.* We have done too little to treat the traditional myopia of society toward its problems. We should remember that if speakers become tranquilizers instead of gadflies, Western culture will have lost a source of strength for which there is *no substitute.* Sometimes we lacked the knowledge to stimulate an interest in a problem or to stimulate our listeners to think deeply about its solution. In one or more of these ways, all of us have fallen short. But if communication is to be a force in Western culture, we must avoid cheap and superficial approaches. We must speak well and think hard—and to speak and think about more than the harmless, the popular, and the trite. *Above all, we must encourage intelligent thought and clear, vivid, logical expression about the problems that beset us.*

The great need of any society is to produce situations in which problems can be discovered and solved with the least resistance. This need is just as great for Western culture as for any other. Our part of the bargain ought to be to help channel the power of a rich and energetic people behind the obliteration of our present problems. The successes of our culture must not engender a false sense of security that would blind us to our unsolved problems while they grow so great that they can weaken us. The time of unprecedented prosperity in which we live is a time when our strengths make it most easy to solve our problems; but that same prosperity makes it possible that we will neglect our problems because they are not now so pressing—and save them until the time when we are weaker and less able to solve them, as we have done with the food shortage, and the energy shortage.

Communication must, *vis-à-vis* problems, help the muddled become clear, the fallacious more accurate; we must wake up the apathetic and the sleeping; we must stimulate the recalcitrant; we must fire the soul of the energetic to the end that we earn survival by the solution of our problems.

Such communication will always require intelligence and goodwill. There are times, too, when it will require great courage and even sacrifice. But there are rewards for the risk. Our civilization can be destroyed, for the first time, by bombs, and only a few are needed; or biological warfare, perhaps even more horrible, could destroy crops or kill billions of people. Moreover, we are threatened by polluted air, water, and land. We seem momentarily sick from lack of energy, and weak from shortages of everything from food to safe drinking water and fertilizer. We have experienced a partial—but not necessarily fatal —decline. But this decline need not be permanent. *For if, through our communication, we can help others see that unsolved problems are a source of weakness and that a problem solved is a source of strength, we will have been a force for strength in Western culture.* The reward will be sufficient, for we will not only have helped the survival of Western culture but we will have helped make Western culture the only one that *deserved* survival.

Summary

This book re-examines many of the important questions with which classical rhetoric is concerned. These questions appear to be divergent and unconnected, but *they can be unified into a single system, a single rhetoric, under the concept of problem solving.*

1. *Intelligence.* We can answer Protagoras' question, "How may we push our intellect as far as it can go?" if we can understand how to develop the greatest possible skill in solving problems.

2. *Values.* Because the problems one identifies and the solutions

one selects (and, often, the causes of these problems one prefers to select) depend partly on one's values, we must consider the subject that intrigued Plato. Moreover, we should not merely look for solutions to isolated problems but for values that may lead to a transformation of human beings and of society.

3. *Knowledge.* Because to solve problems one must draw on many subjects, Aristotle's point of view is essential. Speakers must draw on concepts of anthropology, geology, economics, history, philosophy, literature, and psychology, as well as on concepts of rhetoric and communication.

4. *Citizenship.* The great citizen is not the superpatriot, but he who understands the problems of his society and who can work toward solving them. Isocrates seems to have tried to write a rhetoric of citizenship that was partly a rhetoric of problem solving.

5. *The liberal arts.* The most useful meaning of *liberal arts* is "the education free men need to understand, to maintain, and to extend freedom." We need education that helps us understand how problems limit our freedom and how some solutions may protect our freedom. Especially, we need to sharpen our sense of values so that these values may influence our choices without limiting our freedom. Nothing limits freedom more than the great unsolved problems that have defeated every civilization before us—war, poverty, caste, tyranny, and disease. To be free, we must dedicate ourselves to the solution of problems that stunt and stifle the members of our society.[18]

6. *Democratic communication.* The characteristic of a democratic society is that problems, and possible solutions, can be discussed. Citizens in a democratic state are free to select, to argue, to ignore, or to consider whatever problems or solutions they will. Yet no classical rhetoric is addressed to democratic problem solving, and time for one is long overdue.

7. *Civilization.* Civilizations thrive as solutions to problems are discovered; civilizations stagnate or decline as attempts at problem solving fail. Hence, concern with problem solving reflects concern with civilization.

The concept of problem solving serves as a unifying principle for seemingly divergent approaches to rhetoric. *Each of the seven points of view furnishes an original and necessary but incomplete contribution to a theory of problem solving.* The aim of this book is to evolve a rhetoric

---

[18] Perhaps the best American advocate of liberalizing and humanizing rhetoric is Everett Lee Hunt, from whose works I first was inspired to see and respect the humane tradition in rhetoric. The best works in communication have always been in this tradition.

of problem solving by combining the traditional with the new. I have selected those aspects of traditional rhetoric that have meaning for us today; I have added some contemporary aspects that can give us hope or that can terrorize us. All of these aspects can be unified under one idea. The idea of problem solving includes much of the best of the past and the best of the present. Perhaps more important, the rhetoric of problem solving can give some hope for the future.

Questions for Understanding, Discussion, and Research

1. What aspects or concepts of rhetoric and communication theory might justly be called conventional wisdom? Explain.
2. If you are a member of a minority group, try to discover aspects of the implicit rhetoric of the group that contrast with the implicit rhetoric of other groups.
3. How does the implicit rhetoric of your generation differ from that of your parents' generation?
4. Can you usefully approach plays, paintings, films, poems, architectural works, conversations, and other forms of communication by reducing them to questions as described on pp. 3–6? Are there limitations to this technique? Explain.
5. Read some conventional commentaries on rhetoric, especially those that deal with Protagoras, Plato, experimentalism, classical rhetoric, communication theory, and so on. A list of some banal commentaries may be obtained from your instructor. What are the limitations or flaws in these commentaries?
6. Why are so few rhetorics written for democratic societies, even in democratic societies?
7. If the analysis of civilization, on pp. 11–21 is correct, are we presently in a stage of growth or of decline? Why? What uncertainties do you have about your own answer?
8. What is the current thinking among psychologists about the testing of intelligence? Do you agree or disagree? Explain.
9. What courses does your college offer that are (as defined on p. 6) genuine liberal arts courses?
10. What ways other than problem solving might be used to unify rhetoric and communication theory? What are some of the merits and limitations of each?

2

Problems

Identification of Problems

If we understand why problems remain unsolved, we may be able to develop lines of communication to solve them. Let us look at one problem that can symbolize many kinds of problems.

A MODEL PROBLEM

In 1889, a dam broke near Johnstown, Pennsylvania, and a wall of water six stories high roared down toward the town. Nearly every building, including the steel mills, in the thriving community was destroyed. No one knows how many drowned; nearly all those left alive were homeless. Strangely, nearly everyone in Johnstown had known that the flood was coming. A few minutes before the flood hit, they had heard a warning roar as the water tore down the canyon, and traveling at thirty-five miles an hour, pushed before it mud, houses, barns, trees, livestock, and people.

In the spring of that year, Johnstown recorded the heaviest rains in its history. The artificial lake created by the dam—a dam improperly maintained and leaking dangerously—had filled and overflowed. The inhabitants of Johnstown had known for years that the dam was defective, but the lake created by the dam was the site of the South Fork Fishing and Hunting Club, an organization of about sixty-five wealthy families. Among its members were some of the richest men in the world:

Andrew Carnegie, Henry Clay Frick, and Andrew Mellon. The members had voted, just before the dam broke, to "patch" it with straw. You can still see the sides of the dam if you go to Johnstown; you can see that it has been made a national monument; and you can see that the sides are too steep to support so high a wall of water.

At about 3:15 P.M. on May 31, 1889, the water in the lake burst through three fourths of the dam, and surged down the canyon toward Johnstown.[1] The rest is history. For a decade after the Johnstown flood, corpses and skeletons kept turning up in the valley below Johnstown. After the dam broke, the members of the South Fork Fishing and Hunting Club who were at the former lake climbed on their horses and headed in the opposite direction from Johnstown.

If everyone knew the flood might come, why did no one act to prevent it? Why did no one solve the problem posed by the dam? What made the townsfolk continue to live and work in a place where their lives were in danger? By hindsight we know the lake could have been carefully drained and the dam rebuilt with proper sluices and spillways. Our "solution," although it could have been applied in 1889, is nearly a hundred years too late. Yet the Johnstown flood serves as a model of the ways in which human beings fail to solve their problems.

What makes men continue in patterns that seem certain to lead to catastrophe? Some of the problems we face make that of the Johnstown dam look simple indeed. Yet, only if we *recognize* these problems and *try to solve them,* will our fate be better than the thousands of citizens of Johnstown. If our solutions come a hundred years too late, we, too, may face obliteration. Let us try to understand the problems we face, so that we can communicate the nature of these problems to our fellow man. If we cannot so communicate, we will not survive.

THE NEED FOR SENSITIVITY

To solve a problem, one must be sensitive to it. The owners of the Johnstown dam—the members of the South Fork Fishing and Hunting Club—were insensitive to the weakness of the dam and hence never solved the problem it presented. The citizens of Johnstown manifested a sort of insensitivity as well; because they did not own the dam, they could not themselves repair it, but they brushed off fear of doom by jokes and took no action.

Survival requires sensitivity. Dinosaurs, for example, became extinct long before *homo sapiens* evolved, beaten in the race for survival by smaller but more adaptable species.

Gerald Heard describes the sequence of events:

[1] The most scholarly description of the events are in David McCullough, *The Johnstown Flood* (New York: Simon and Schuster, Inc., 1968).

[T]he giant reptiles were themselves hopelessly decadent before the rise of the mammals. . . . They had begun as small, mobile and lively creatures. They grew so vast that these land-ironclads could scarcely move. . . . [T]heir brains remained practically nonexistent. . . . Their heads were no more than periscopes, breathing tubes, and pincers.

Meanwhile, as they slowly swelled and hardened up to their doom . . . there was already being fashioned that creature which was to leap the boundary and limits then set for life and start a new stage of energy and consciousness. And nothing could illustrate more vividly the principle that life evolves by sensitiveness and awareness; by smallness, not by size. The fore-runners of the mammals . . . are minute rat-like creatures. In a world dominated by monsters the future is given to a creature which has to spend its time taking notice of others and giving way to others. It is undefended, given fur instead of scales. It is . . . given those sensitive feeling forelimbs and, no doubt, those antennae—the long hairs of the face and head—to give it irritating stimulation all the time. Ears and eyes are highly developed. It becomes warmblooded so it may be constantly conscious throughout the cold when the reptile falls into anesthetic coma. . . .[2]

The most sensitive (or at least potentially the most sensitive) of all animals is man. But man often reacts insensitively to his own plight, and to the plight of those less fortunate than he. Perhaps seventy billion people have lived on earth since man first evolved. Until recently man lived less than thirty years, and that short life was spent dwelling in hovels, dressed in rags, and enslaved by the rich and powerful. History takes little note of such men; they could not read nor write, so they left no record of their pains and sorrows. Thomas Hobbes characterized the life of the Anonymous Man: ". . . worst of all, continual fear and danger of violent death; and the life of man [is] solitary, poor, nasty, brutish and short." Saint Bernard wrote, "It is a misery to be born, a pain to live, a trouble to die." Human life, as Samuel Johnson said, is "a state in which much is to be endured and little to be enjoyed." Why is the most amazing product of nature, man, generally in a state of torment and today in danger of obliterating himself?

Classical Problems

Past civilizations were "killed" by one or more problems. The problems, like disease, weakened, stultified, and finally dispatched the civilization. If we could discover what problems killed each of these civilizations, and then inquire if these same problems are invading our own culture, we might be able to stop them from destroying the last

[2] Gerald Heard, *The Source of Civilization* (London: Jonathan Cape, Ltd., 1935), pp. 71–72.

remaining civilization on earth. We might, that is, if our communication is sharp enough, powerful enough, and intelligent enough. Let us see what problems have destroyed all previous civilizations.

War completely destroyed the civilization of Carthage, and it has destroyed, or weakened, nearly every other civilization. The greatest resource of a civilization is its human beings, but these human beings died in the eight thousand wars mankind has fought in its seven thousand years of recorded history.

Poverty weakens human beings, thus reducing their potential wisdom, energy, love, and creativity they might have if they did not have to spend most of their time merely trying to survive.

Caste, or built-in prejudice against birth, sex, or color, wastes human resources and forces the weak to serve the powerful, and the penniless to serve the rich.

Tyranny can convert human beings into servile creatures to serve the tiny minority that control establishments.

Disease can obliterate whole peoples and can weaken, permanently, those who otherwise might have contributed to the civilization, making them instead a pitiful drain on the energies of that civilization.

The pattern of insensitivity to the problems of war, poverty, caste, tyranny, and disease destroyed every civilization before our own. These destructive forces are the *Classical problems* to which all civilizations, sooner or later, developed a fatal insensitivity. We can describe this built-in insensitivity by two points:

1. *Those who suffer from the effects of these destructive classical problems have little power to remove or to reduce the problems.* A few people, perhaps one in a thousand, can climb out of the pit of suffering, but most cannot help themselves. Of the more than 200 million people who are threatened by starvation today, we cannot justly say, "They could and should have helped themselves."

2. *Those who have power do not suffer from these forces, and hence do not comprehend the urgency of man's problems.* No white man can truly understand the problems of the black because he does not share them. Nor have the powerful and the rich grasped the intensity with which help is needed by the poor, the helpless, and the sick. The sufferings of mankind are not really perceived by those who do not suffer. Most men of power are not sensitive, yet only those with power can effect solutions to these problems.

If we could teach those who suffer to communicate, or if our communicators could develop sensitivity, or if those with power were forced to recognize the rights of the powerless, then we might free our civilization from the problems that crush it. Let us, therefore, develop some sensitivity to these problems, and let us study the ways in which communication can make others sensitive to the plight of the oppressed. Let us survey each of the classical problems and then ask whether it is afflicting people today.

WAR

War seems to have been a major cause of the downfall of Athenian civilization. The Greek city-states each had their own armies and used them frequently. In just one war Athens lost one third of her manpower. Energy and wealth even in the fifth century B.C. were drained by wars that even the "winner" lost.

In the twentieth century, the bloodiest in human history, the danger of war is greater than ever before. A growing number of nations possess the atom bomb. Enough nuclear explosive has been created to deliver the equivalent of twenty tons of TNT for every man, woman, and child on earth. Some of the poisons from these nuclear explosives have a half-life of forty-three thousand years, posing a threat to countless generations to come. No people before ever lived in danger of being vaporized. Never before could great nations destroy each other twenty times—as if one time were not enough "overkill." War is a greater danger now than ever before.

POVERTY

Poverty was so widespread in ancient Rome that only one third of the inhabitants lived above a bare subsistence level. Whenever large masses of people are poor, everyone suffers. The poor cannot pay taxes or purchase goods and services to help keep the wheels of industry going. Rome, with most of its wealth in the hands of a few, could not withstand the ravages poverty visited on her. Plagues and invasions decimated the Roman population so that by A.D. 600, the city was almost uninhabited.

Of course, we can produce and distribute goods and services far more efficiently than Rome. Still, two thirds of the people on earth go to bed hungry every night. The average annual income *per capita* is $150, and roughly 1.5 billion people make less than $150 a year. In our own country, 20 million people live below the official poverty level; of these, 10 million go to bed hungry every night.

We fail to realize how poverty weakens all of us. The Baltimore slums, for example, produce only 6 per cent of the city's revenue, but consume 45 per cent of its budget. Sacramento's slums contribute only 12 per cent of the city's tax revenues, but consume 50 per cent of the city's health budget and 41 per cent of its police budget.

Of course, gains against poverty have been made; but the Aswan Dam on the Nile River may serve as a paradigm of the problem. The dam added millions of acres to Egypt's arable soil, but by the time it was completed, the population of Egypt had so increased that no more food *per capita* is available now than there was before the dam was built. In South America, food output dropped 2 per cent in 1969 while the population increased 2 per cent. In Africa, in 1970, food production increased by 2 per cent, but population increased by 2.5 per cent. The net result is that today more people suffer from poverty than ever before in human history.

CASTE

India is the classic case of a caste system that holds down people, keeping them weak, assigning them to jobs and status on the basis of their birth. Millions of Indians, permanently poor because of their birth, suffer and labor to support a few rich people.

Caste systems award goods and power on the basis of an irrelevant criterion—birth, color, sex, or social status.

Such a system exists in the United States. Black people, for example, live about seven years less than white people. The average black worker receives $1,400 less in annual income than the average white wage earner. The unemployment rate among blacks is generally twice that among whites. At present, 37 per cent of black youths who are out of school are unemployed. Statistics often reveal a worse situation among Chicanos and American Indians. These minority groups do not find congressmen or state legislators who understand their problems nor have they access to mayors or school boards. Hence, these people are weakened. They can pay less in taxes than their proportion of the population, thus increasing the tax burden on everyone else. They have less purchasing power, hence business and industry suffer. Caste systems weaken all members of a society, as well as the groups against which they discriminate.

TYRANNY

Tyranny is a system that prevents discussion of the problems of a people. Every ancient empire ended in tyranny. Tyranny is the most certain device for destroying a civilization because it prevents discussion of problems and the search for solutions through public discussion and debate. Even articulate sufferers will not receive a hearing, and tyrants usually manage to arrange that most sufferers will be inarticulate. The twentieth century has been the most tyrannous in history. Before mid-century, monsters such as Hitler and Stalin had already subjected more people to terror than did Genghis Kahn or the worst Pharaohs of Egypt. In our own country, we suffer because of the blindnesses of big government, big labor, big business, and even big educational institutions.

However, our hope lies in breaking the chain that keeps those who suffer from reducing their own suffering and those who hold power from doing nothing. If we protect the civil rights of those who protest, we help insure the discussion of our problems.

DISEASE

Plagues destroyed one third of the population of Greece just as the Peloponnesian Wars were weakening Athens. Europe's population was nearly destroyed several times by plagues that laid waste whole cities and towns. Until recently, the average life span of man was thirty years, and in most parts of the world it is still not much longer. Perhaps disease is now checked in some parts of the world, but in precisely these "advanced" areas pollution of the air, the water, and the soil is most severe. Disease may soon again become a leading threat to man.

In 1942, when French undersea explorer Jacques Costeau explored the Sargasso Sea, he could see underwater for about 300 feet. Today, he reports the visibility has shrunk to barely 100 feet. When he first started diving in the Mediterranean 25 years ago, it was filled with life. Today? You can hardly see a fish 3 inches long. Pollution has caught up with the seas and the oceans' ability to cleanse themselves. Costeau estimates that the vitality of the seas . . . has declined some 30 per cent to 50 per cent in the past 20 years. . . .

Swiss marine explorer Jacques Piccard warned that if nothing is done, all the oceans will be dead before the end of the century. . . . . In fact, says Piccard, "Phytoplankton, the primitive plant life that generates most of the earth's oxygen, is surface matter. It absorbs dirt and acts as a sort of pollution filter. Thus all you need to knock out is the surface of phytoplankton, and the entire marine life cycle is fatally disrupted." That disruption is accelerating logarithmically. [Meaning, roughly, that pollution is increasing by multiplication instead of by addition.] At one Baltic measuring station, Environmentalist Barry Commoner points out, the oxygen content of water samples was 2.5 cc. per liter in 1900. The figure gently declined to 2 cc. by 1940, but in only 30 years since then it has plummeted to 0.1 cc.[3]

Some oceanic experts have predicted the death of the oceans in less than thirty years, and, of course, with the death of the oceans, which furnish most of our oxygen, will come the death of all plants, animals, and human beings. If this prediction becomes a reality, everyone will be affected: black, white, red, yellow, civilian and soldier, physician and patient, youth and oldster, employed and unemployed, student and professor. To be insensitive to a problem such as this is to go the way of the dinosaur, the way of ancient Egypt, the way of extinction. But our civilization has a chance to deserve survival.

[3] Anonymous, "Dying Oceans, Poisoned Seas," *Time* (November 8, 1971) , 74, 76.

The Search for Solutions

KNOWLEDGE

We have already acknowledged that no civilization before ours solved the classical problems. Can we? The classical problems are not the only ones we face. All problems act as a disease because they render people weaker, less wise, and more limited than they might otherwise have been. When we solve these problems, we restore health, and we contribute to human fulfillment. We are the first civilization to have ideas about how to obliterate war, poverty, caste, tyranny, and disease. For the first time in history, we know how to reduce the possibility of war by tying nations together politically and economically. The latter is especially important. We know how to produce enough to feed, house, and clothe all the people of the world—something no other civilization knew. We know how to distribute wealth so as to alleviate and even eliminate poverty. We have ideas about how to end caste systems, and to prevent tyranny, including the tyranny of the majority. We know how to prevent many diseases that once were epidemic, and we know how to stop the pollution of air and water. This generation, at last, has the knowledge necessary for survival.

Useful knowledge can sometimes be applied with gratifying speed. Consider the speed with which the railroad changed the world's system of transportation:

The use of steam and industrial processes spread like wildfire over the Western world, transforming in an explosive manner industry, means of transportation, and ways of life. England had ninety-seven miles of railway track in 1830, 1,497 miles in 1840, and 4,800 miles were laid in the year 1845! In a single decade, the stagecoaches had disappeared from England and along with them a whole variety of trades.[4]

We not only know more about solving problems than other cultures did but we also know how to disseminate what we know. *These two facts alone should help us see that we might be able to solve problems where others failed.*

PROTEST

The recognition of problems as conditions not to be tolerated is becoming more acceptable. When we were in primary school we were taught, by more than one teacher, that one should not criticize a thing

---

[4] René Dubos, "The Despairing Optimist," *The American Scholar, 41* (Winter 1971–72) , 18. Copyright © by the United Chapters of Phi Beta Kappa. By permission of the publishers.

(i.e., point out that it is a problem and should be remedied) unless we could offer something better (i.e., a solution). Such propaganda—unwitting as it was—prevented us from recognizing many problems. Indeed, today we may take heart because to seek out problems, whether or not we have solutions, is becoming acceptable. Let us become sensitive to problems—those that make us suffer and those that make others suffer—for this very sensitivity is the prerequisite to solving those problems.

If more people become alarmed by a problem, then more minds will be stimulated to devise a solution. We can, under our system of government, identify problems, and identification is the first step to solution. Protest often lights the road to growth:

> . . . [T]he influence of Lao-tzu, Buddha, and Jesus began with the *rejection of their times* rather than with the presentation of a systematic body of thought. Rejection of an objectionable state of affairs as much as allegiance to a new faith has indeed commonly been the trumpet call of social revolutions—whether they have been initiated by religious reformers such as Martin Luther, by social reformers, . . . or by nameless soapbox orators.[5]

"All good ideas begin with a minority of one." At one time the ideas we now consider most influential were held by only one person. Once, only Copernicus believed that the earth revolved around the sun. Once, only Darwin believed that natural selection could explain the evolution of species. Once, only Louis Pasteur believed that bacteria were the cause of most disease. Once, only Socrates believed that "the unexamined life is not worth living." If that minority of one had kept silent, the rest of us might never have learned what they had to teach.

UNEXPECTED SOURCES OF SOLUTIONS

Solutions to problems may come from the most unlikely sources and be adopted at unbelievable speed.

> Islam was born unpredictably in the mind of . . . Mohammed, who was a middle-aged merchant of Mecca early in the seventh century. The group of Arabs to which he belonged was then a small tribe, extremely poor, largely illiterate, and almost entirely isolated from the rest of the world. Yet Mohammed and his immediate followers converted these destitute Arabs into a powerful fighting force that created in little more than a century an immense empire, prosperous, artistically refined, and intellectually sophisticated. . . .
>
> In just as mysterious a manner the idea of the First Crusade was apparently born in the mind of Peter the Hermit. . . . But . . . Peter the

---

[5] Ibid., pp. 18, 20. Italics mine. One might add that Socrates and Plato protested against the systems under which they lived, as did Martin Luther King, Jr. and Malcolm X.

Hermit was influential in starting the long series of Crusades during which the uncouth European barons learned from the Arabs the refinements of civilization. . . .

Mohammed and Peter the Hermit thus set in motion immense social forces, the impact of which extended for centuries over the whole world. And so it is for all the great movements of human history.[6]

An apparent weakness sometimes becomes the source of the greatest strength:

During the reign of Augustus, the Roman Empire was the largest, wealthiest, and most powerful political structure in the world. At that time also, the Synagogue ruled supreme in religious and social matters over the Jewish people in Palestine. . . . Yet Jesus was born during this period of apparent stability, . . . and his teachings soon began to disturb the established order of things. Who could have imagined at the height of the *Pax Romana* that the Empire would collapse under the blows of the Barbarians and that the Barbarians themselves would so rapidly submit to the Cross? . . .

In our times, we have seen how passive resistance, guerilla warfare, and sabotage—the weapons of the poor and the weak—succeeded in rapidly bringing down the mighty colonial empires of the Western nations. Social revolutions and colonial wars have demonstrated time and time again . . . that technological and political power can be overcome by the determination of men. The crusade against the degradation of life and nature is facing great handicaps, but it can succeed if enough bold spirits really believe that the time has come to convert our industrial society into a humane civilization.[7]

DEVISING NEW SOLUTIONS

When we do not know of solutions to a problem, we may know how to discover them. We need, however, the kind of spirit displayed by Hannibal when he was told that there was no way through the Alps. He replied, "I will find a way or make one." [8] We are not unrealistic to recognize that in this civilization, where no way exists, we can find a way or make one. Failure is possible, but unthinkable. We, too, must find a way, or make one.

Problem Structures

What is a problem? Thinking that a problem is a problem doesn't always make it one. Perhaps a series of criteria would help one judge whether or not something is a problem:

[6] Ibid., p. 20.
[7] Ibid., p. 23.
[8] Gerald Johnson, "Hannibal for President," *The American Scholar, 41* (Winter 1971–72), 39.

(1) A significant problem may be one that has caused the decline of a previous civilization. The problems of war, poverty, caste, tyranny, and disease are the classic problems of humanity, and wherever one finds civilizations in decline, one or more of these problems was a significant part of the cause. (2) A significant problem is one that has caused or causes human suffering. (3) A significant problem is one that limits human achievement. (4) A significant problem is one that, when solved, releases new energy. (5) A significant problem is one that prevents growth and development. (6) A significant problem is one that forces on us an important change. (7) A significant problem is one that violates a human value: injustice, selfishness, treachery, lying, which violate the values of justice, generosity, loyalty, and honesty, respectively. (8) A significant problem is one that reduces strength, whether it be the strength and energy of an individual, of a family, of a community, of a nation, or of a civilization.

But perhaps we need help, not in increasing our knowledge of kinds of problems that exist but in sifting out the important from the less important. Perhaps instead of setting up criteria, we might offer a definition of a problem. But definitions cannot be proved or disproved, and neither do they necessarily help secure the kind of understanding we seek. Sociology books often define problems, and often usefully. But we are more interested in those elements in the *structure* of any situation that make it a problem. Let us examine some problem structures.

THE "JOHNSTOWN DAM" STRUCTURE

In one kind of problem structure, almost everyone in danger of the problem understands it rather well, but no one moves to prevent it from arising or moves to have a solution adopted. And then, one day, figuratively speaking, the dam breaks. This kind of structure underlies some of the most serious problems we face today. The problem of war is well known, yet little is done about it. War is a "Johnstown Dam" structure, and so is pollution, overpopulation, worldwide poverty, and tyranny. In each case, *men acknowledge both the existence and the seriousness of the problem, but do too little to solve it.*

THE "CHRISTMAS CARD" STRUCTURE

We wish our friends peace, love, and wisdom at Christmas or Chanukah, and many of us use these holiday greetings to keep in touch with old friends. These wishes and our desire to continue communication are admirable. But some things about Christmas cards are not in keeping with these aims. The Christmas card usually expresses a stereotyped greeting, often in bad poetry, and without taking note of the individuality of either the person who sends it or the one who receives it. Whole forests are cut down to make the paper on which the cards are printed. Then after the holidays, the cards add to the mounting volume of junk of which we must dispose. So, instead of peace, love, and wisdom, we have deforestation and incalculable piles of additional garbage. We may have solved a small problem, but we have created others.

The "Christmas card" structure is one in which the means of dealing with a problem not only fails to reduce the original problem, but actually creates others. The Vietnam War, designed to strengthen freedom in Southeast Asia, resulted in the devastation of the area. The war did no more to bring about freedom than Christmas cards do to bring about peace, love, and wisdom.

Marxism uses the "Christmas card" structure when it insists that a dictatorship of the proletariat will lead to freedom for all. Dictatorships do not teach people how to use freedom, and they are inept at solving any problems except those chosen by the dictator. Therefore, *the "Christmas card" structure is one in which the aim may be good, but the means to achieve that aim succeed only in creating other evils.*

THE "AMAZON VALLEY" STRUCTURE

A problem often can be solved through methods developed earlier. We can solve a problem in arithmetic by using the same method we have used to solve similar mathematical problems. We can solve problems in one city by using methods that were successful in another. Sometimes, however, the methods that work in one place don't work in another. The Amazon Valley, for example, is the largest fertile, unfarmed valley in the world. If that valley could be farmed, we might be able to feed all the people of the world. With this hope, some Americans went to the Amazon Valley a few years ago to show the Brazilians how to turn the jungles into farms and to operate them just as we do those in the rich (but somewhat smaller) Mississippi Valley. The Americans tore out the trees, plowed the land, and sowed hybrid seed, and produced a fair crop. But after the first harvests the soil in the demonstration plot mysteriously became a gumbo that a plow could not furrow. Because the fields could not be plowed, seed could not be sown. Today, the land is worthless. We have discovered that the fertility of a tropical rain forest is completely different from the fertility of a temperate region.

The problem structure illustrated in this situation is one in which we fail to realize that a solution effective in one place or time or situation may not be effective in another. In a similar situation, we drilled wells for the people in the Middle East so that they could have water, yet they continued to use the old town fountain instead of the new inside plumbing: the town fountain was the women's meeting place; moreover, followers of Islam believe that one must not drink water that is not perpetually flowing—as in a fountain. That which contributes to making life easy in New York City didn't in some Middle East towns. Conditions were different, and our good wishes, our money, our time, and our energy were largely wasted.

THE "MAGNIFICENT FAÇADE" STRUCTURE

Imperial Rome was glorious and splendid. The Emperor Augustus, as he himself said, found it a city of bricks and left it a city of marble. Even more interesting, everyone in Augustinian Rome *knew* that the age was a Golden Age—their knowledge was no mystery because Augustus paid orators, playwrights, professors, and poets to declare the new Golden Age to the people. So everyone knew about the new Golden Age, but not everyone knew about the rotting foundation beneath the façade. The dangers of a growing poverty were never seriously discussed by the Senate. After the Gracchi brothers were murdered, few cared to bring up the problem of poverty. Rome was wealthy, but most of the wealth was in the hands of very few people. The whole of North Africa, then a far more fertile country than it is now, and nearly the size of the United States, was owned by ten Roman families. The families that controlled Roman wealth also owned vast tracts of land that they had stolen, bought, or squeezed from the small farmers of Republican Rome—lands the wealthy farmed by the most inefficient and least productive means: grazing. After all, why should they go to the effort of improving agriculture, when they had all the money they needed? Unfortunately, most Romans did not have all the food they needed, and this method of grazing increased the price of food so that fewer could afford proper nourishment. But Rome did have magnificent temples, a breathtaking Forum, great public baths, and, of course, the Colosseum. They were a façade for the corruption and filth of the Empire. In a few centuries, as the buildings fell into ruins, people began to think that the buildings were erected by giants or by gods, because during the Dark Ages everyone was sure that no man could possibly have built such wonders.

The "magnificent façade" structure attempts to distract people from serious problems by emphasizing only achievements. Of course, the ancient Romans were not the only people to have been deluded by the "magnificent façade" structure. Today, we pride ourselves on our new push-button telephones, our electric-powered window openers, our automatic drape pullers, and our cordless electric drink mixers. But behind the façade of automatic can openers and electric carving knives lurks the terrifying possibility of watching the final nuclear cataclysm on automatically tuned color television.

At this point, find your own favorite illustrations of each of the problem models identified so far. Your examples might differ from mine; what matters is that we learn to identify problem structures that weaken us and that might destroy us.

Here are some examples. One who was not an insider of the Penn Central Railroad would never suspect from its advertising that the railroad was nearly bankrupt by 1970. It was America's largest railroad, and even if its stock wasn't going up, it was still paying dividends. Who would have guessed that it was going to go broke? And who would have thought that the American automobile—that magnificent device that changed the habits of a nation—was, as Ralph Nader demonstrated, unsafe at any speed?

Try to find some examples of your own. Maybe you'd like to pepper college professors or universities, or textbooks or speech classes. Whatever your target, find some examples of problem structures.

THE "GREAT PYRAMID" STRUCTURE

According to Herodotus, the Greek historian, the Pharaoh Kufu (better known as Cheops) spent nearly a generation and the lives of a hundred thousand slaves to build his crypt. The Pyramid covers thirteen acres, and is composed of three hundred thousand blocks ranging in weight from two and one-half to seventy tons. Archeologists still have not ascertained the engineering methods that hoisted these blocks. The Great Pyramid still stands, whereas the other six of the Seven Wonders of the ancient world have disappeared.

The social significance of the Great Pyramid is not so glorious. At the time is was built, the Egyptians had mastered the techniques of agriculture, reaped the benefits of the fertile Nile Valley, and accumulated a surplus of wealth. The wealth was spent not for the benefit of the people but for a building that was of no use to them or to Kufu himself. All the pyramids were rifled and the entombed corpses were stolen—along with the gold buried with them—within a hundred years of their burial. The wealth of Egypt was wasted on a monumental nothing.

The "Great Pyramid" structure illustrates that we may spend wealth, labor, and human resources on a "phony" problem. Supposedly, the Pyramid was built to preserve the body of the Pharaoh and, by so doing, to give him immortality, but there is no evidence that preservation of the body assures immortality. Yet one generation was sacrificed and the accumulated wealth of Egypt wasted. The time, ingenuity, and wealth invested in the Great Pyramid could have gone far toward solving at least some of Egypt's classical problems; instead, the Great Pyramid created poverty, provided one of the most horrifying examples of a caste system, and stands as a monument to one of the greatest tyrants in history.

The "Great Pyramid" structure illustrates that a culture may invest its energies in the wrong problems and, as a result, increase those problems that can destroy.

Recent evidence indicates that the Great Pyramid, perhaps, was never intended as a tomb, but was a kind of astronomical and geographical testament, built to keep alive some surprisingly advanced knowledge the Egyptians had acquired. The base of the Great Pyramid is almost exactly 1/480 of a degree of the circumference of the earth at the equator; moreover, from the placement of the Great Pyramid, men could immediately tell the exact direction of true North. From this knowledge, we infer that the Egyptians knew the earth was round, that they knew about how large it was, and that they could tell the direction of true North. Moreover, the Pyramid was built so that the exact date of the equinoxes could be determined, because only during the equinoxes would the light of Alpha Draconis shine down one of the corridors built into the Pyramid. This knowledge is of enormous importance to an agricultural community: a crop planted too soon will fail; one planted too late will not mature. The Great Pyramid could also be used as a surveyor's point so that after the annual Nile flood, property lines could again be re-established and each farmer know exactly where his land was.[9]

If the Great Pyramid was built to preserve this mathematical knowledge, it illustrates the "Christmas card" structure. No monolith will suffice to keep alive knowledge. It is better to make the knowledge available to the people, instead of keeping it a monopoly of the priestly caste, as did the Egyptians. If the Great Pyramid is a kind of mysterious "book," people had forgotten how to read it even by the fifth century B.C., when Herodotus visited it. The result did not justify the effort, for despite the expenditure of human and material resources, the new knowledge was soon lost.

Another theory is that Kufu built the Pyramid as a kind of public works project to reduce unemployment in times of poverty. Perhaps his intention was noble, but again, even this intention illustrates the "Christmas card" structure. The same time and effort could have pro-

[9] For the sources of this and additional information, see Peter Tompkins, *Secrets of the Great Pyramid* (New York: Harper & Row, Publishers, Inc., 1971). Almost as good is Tompkins' much shorter version, "Secrets of the Great Pyramid," *Horizon, 13* (Winter 1971) 37–49.

duced works that would have been wealth-creating. Dams could have been built, canals could have been dug, or research projects sponsored that might have resulted in better agriculture, more abundant harvests, and a permanent rise in the standard of living. As it was, the Great Pyramid remained as dead as Kufu's corpse, and the only wealth it produced was from the tourists who have come to view it.

To see the faults of others is easy, but we should learn to spot the "Great Pyramids" in our own culture and our own country. What have we done that might place us in the same category as Kufu? Some would point to our space exploration program. The program, begun when 10 million Americans went to bed hungry, has cost $30 billion—enough to build and endow thirty universities of the size and quality of Harvard. Some benefits to humanity have resulted from the space program, just as they did from the building of the Great Pyramid, but the spin-off, some feel, was not enough to justify the program. Others would point to the modern world's propensity for building (and using) armaments, for in our time the largest item in nearly every government budget is "defense." Some of the richest governments allot over half their budgets to preparations for war. Surely, the people of the Soviet Union would be better off if that money were channeled into wealth-producing activities, as would be the people of China and, some might add, those of the United States. Nations and whole civilizations perish because they do not attack the problems that have destroyed people in the past and can destroy them now; instead they attack problems that really don't matter. What do you think are the best examples of the "Great Pyramid" structure?

THE "TORQUEMADA" STRUCTURE

Tomás de Torquemada led the Spanish Inquisition, whose aim it was to stamp out heresy. By using evidence obtained by torture and from the enemies of the accused, Torquemada and the Inquisition for decades submitted about a thousand persons a year to secular authorities for the *auto-da-fé* (literally, *act of faith;* actually, the execution by fire of the convicted) and annually imprisoned or severely punished perhaps a hundred times as many. The Inquisition forgot that one might "confess" to anything to stop the stabbing pain from thumb-screws, the torture from the slow breaking of one's own bones, or from the application of red-hot metal to various parts of one's own body; forgotten also was the notion that one's enemies may not be the most objective of reporters. To be certain about how many were tortured by the Inquisition is difficult partly because the Holy Office did not care to publicize the figures, but certainly the Inquisition influenced the thought of the day:

Where it succeeded, as in Spain and Italy after the Renaissance, it also succeeded in smothering the national genius that had produced the golden ages. . . . The future belonged to the countries where it failed. The apparent lesson of the Inquisition is that insistence on uniformity of belief is fatal to intellectual, moral, and spiritual health.[10]

But no statistics can convey the terror in which the Spanish mind lived in those days and nights. Men and women, even in the secrecy of their families, had to watch every word they uttered, lest some stray criticism should lead them to an Inquisition jail. It was a mental oppression unparalleled in history.

Did the Inquisition succeed? Yes, in attaining its declared purpose—to rid Spain of open heresy. The idea that persecution of beliefs is always ineffective is a delusion. It crushed the Albignesians and Huguenots in France, the Catholics in Elizabethan England, the Christians in Japan. It stamped out in the sixteenth century the small groups that favored Protestantism in Spain.[11]

Ideas can be suppressed. The Inquisition "exterminated the Albigenses so effectively that scholars are still uncertain about the articles of their heresy." [12] We tend to remember how the Christians survived the Roman's lion-feeding program, but forget that such survival is hardly typical. Haven't *you* had ideas that some teacher or relative or friend has managed to suppress, so that you don't bring the ideas up, at least in their presence? If so, you have experienced the "Torquemada" structure.

In the "Torquemada" structure, problems may not be solved because mere discussion of them may be silenced by fear of reprisals. Until Senator Eugene McCarthy publicly condemned the Vietnam War in 1968, discussion of the war as a problem seemed so dangerous and futile that many who recognized the hideousness of the war remained quiet; another two years elapsed before the majority of Americans turned against it. Even now, some Americans believe that to fail to support any war a president undertakes is treason, forgetting that only the Congress can declare war. Fortunately, the Constitution of the United States guarantees free speech to all, but social and economic pressures ("If you continue to talk like that, you'll lose your job") keep many problems from being discussed. *Free speech is of no use unless it is protected at precisely those moments when speaking about a problem is most condemned.*

Can you find other examples of the "Torquemada" structure in American life? Examples are more numerous than you will realize at first, but try to name some of your own. For example, name situations

---

[10] Herbert J. Muller, *The Uses of the Past* (New York: Mentor Books, 1952), p. 280.
[11] Will Durant, *The Reformation* (New York: Simon and Schuster, Inc., 1957), p. 216.
[12] Muller, p. 280.

in which it would be dangerous or unpleasant to defend each of the following: the National Association for the Advancement of Colored People, the National Rifle Association, the National Manufacturers' Association, American Indians, black people, white people, Chicanos, Japanese-Americans, members of the John Birch Society, the American Medical Association, the Republican Party, the Democratic Party, Socialists, Communists, Gay Liberation, prison inmates, fraternity members, Women's Liberation, college students, poor people, rich people. Your analysis should reveal that you would be condemned somewhere in our society for arguing *for* any of these, and elsewhere you would be condemned for arguing *against* any of them. And the extent to which you would not permit any of these groups to speak freely is the extent to which you, too, perpetuate the "Torquemada" structure. Oliver Wendell Holmes, Jr., once said that the best test of truth is the ability of an idea to survive in the competition of the marketplace. If an idea is a poor one, it can be refuted. Freedom is not good merely because it is just pleasant; freedom also provides a means to discover truth. Therefore, divorce the bonds that may liken you to Tomás de Torquemada, and urge those to whom you speak to do likewise.

THE USE OF PROBLEM STRUCTURES

Other structures exist, but the foregoing ones are the most significant in our time. We can now see that the "structure" of a problem is that condition that keeps a problem from being solved, the perpetuating principle inherent in a problem. We have named them only to make them easier to remember. Let us review them.

1. Acknowledging both the existence and seriousness of a problem, but doing nothing to solve it and acting as if it did not exist: The "Johnstown Dam" structure.

2. Attempting to achieve a worthy aim but by means that not only fail in that achievement but create other evils: The "Christmas card" structure.

3. Using a solution known to be successful elsewhere but without the necessary conditions that made that solution successful: The "Amazon Valley" structure.

4. Offering pleasant or exciting distractions so that a problem will be tolerated by some and unnoticed by others: The "magnificent façade" structure.

5. Investing energy in the wrong problems and, as a result, increasing the power of destructive problems, and further dissipating energies: The "Great Pyramid" structure.

6. Failure to permit and encourage the discussion of a problem because of fear of reprisals: The "Torquemada" structure.

These structures give us a sense of a basic way to channel our problem solving. In a "Johnstown Dam" structure, we must work to fix responsibility; in the "Christmas card" structure, we must create better means to achieve our ends; in the "Amazon Valley" structure, we must become familiar with the unique problem and ready to devise new solutions for it; in the "magnificent façade" structure, we need awareness of the more basic problems and to devise solutions for these problems; in the "Great Pyramid" structure, we must find better priorities, a better sense of the problems we face; in the "Torquemada" structure, we need communicators who will select methods, sometimes devise new methods, to reach people, speakers who will be able to command enough respect to be heard, and who can stimulate the natural desire for freedom among all.

Thus, these structures give us a sense of the gross anatomy of a problem, a suggestion or hint as to where we should apply our energy, and what the most successful strategy might be.

Finding Material for Problem Speeches

EXPERIENCE

Personal experience with a problem acts on a speaker by giving him more authority, or a clear ring of sincerity by increasing his commitment to the problem, by adding to his interest in the problem, and by increasing his sympathy for those who suffer under the problem. Therefore, if you are to speak on the problem of ghettos, go to a ghetto and drive or walk through it, or talk to those of your friends who have lived in a ghetto, and listen to their ancedotes, and observations. Find and talk with those who work daily with ghetto inhabitants—social workers, city planners, members of the redevelopment authority. Do that which no library can do for you—get in touch directly with the problem. If you are speaking on problems of the aged, talk to your grandparents, or visit a nursing home, or offer your unskilled help to a county home for the aged, or a "golden age" club. *Direct experience with a problem will give you a deeper understanding and a keener outlook.* Miss such direct experience, and your speech will risk being sterile, "academic," and possibly somewhat irrelevant.

If you have had experience with the problem on which you speak —if you are speaking about war and have fought in one, if you are speaking about a farm problem and have raised stock or grain, if you are speaking about the poor and have been one of them, if you are talking about women's rights and have been the victim of male chauvinism—be certain to bring the best of your experience into the speech. The experience may provide the high point of the speech and will communicate to the audience that your speech is not merely a fulfillment of a class assignment, that your concern is genuine, that you understand the problem and feel its impact, and that you have earned a right to speak about it.

Moreover, experience with a problem may change you. Abraham Lincoln turned against slavery when, as a young man, he went down the Mississippi on a barge. Thomas Paine became the "Penman of the American Revolution" because, in part, he had observed tyranny at work. When you see how a problem terrorizes others, and when you feel that terror yourself, you gain an understanding that is different from that gained through reading about the problem.

GENERAL READING

Experience with a problem does not, of course, guarantee wisdom. Those who suffer from a classical problem are not necessarily wise about its causes or extent or solution. We need to know what the best minds have thought and said on the subject; we need the most accurate statistics that have been gathered; we need the authority of the careful student of the problem to lend authority to our own thoughts and ideas. We need the poet who has electrified readers, or the writer who has dramatized the problem. We need even the experience of the musician and artist whose works may themselves be a form of social protest. We need to put into our speeches more than we ourselves have experienced. Access to the experience of others is possible through libraries, and we need to know some of the sources in the library that will guide us to the best works on the subject.

REFERENCE WORKS

Because many indexes are arranged by date of publication (see *Reader's Guide,* for example) , they give little clue as to what are the *best* works; indeed, the most current works may be far from the best. To prepare a speech on a problem, therefore, one should first consult a general work, such as an encyclopedia. *The International Encyclopedia of the Social Sciences,* for example, has generally intelligent articles on social, political, and economic problems. The *Encyclopaedia Britannica* will often have competent, if somewhat dull, articles on problems. Each article is followed by a bibliography that may be helpful. For more recent data, however, one must consult one of the many general indexes.

The most interesting index is the *Pollution Abstracts,* which contains pictures, editorials, and summaries of books, articles, and pamphlets. Other indexes, however, will help you locate materials and are arranged by subject, as well as by author and title. Perhaps the most useful index for current books and articles on problems is the *Public Affairs Information Service*. The most standard (and overused) index is the *Reader's Guide to Periodical Literature;* similar indexes on particular areas are the *Education Index* and the *Agriculture Index*. If you have a large library that has a good pamphlet collection, consult the *Vertical File Index,* but remember, libraries do not keep pamphlets very long and unless you want current pamphlets, your library is apt to have discarded them. *The Social Science and Humanities Index* (formerly the *International Index*) is another good general index that, like the others, is indexed by subject so that you can locate materials on particular problems. UNESCO publishes the International *Bibliography of Social Sciences,* which is a series in economics, sociology, and political science. For an index of United States Government publications, consult the *Monthly Catalogue of the United States*. And if you want to see more material you might consult the *Guide to Reference Books*. Of the making of indexes, there seems no end.

INDEXED NEWSPAPERS

If you wish to locate the news story about a Supreme Court decision, particular opinion polls, or events in the Congress or abroad, a newspaper index will be of help. To locate the text of an important speech, or the events surrounding a given period of time, one might consult *The New York Times Index,* or you might prefer the *Christian Science Monitor Index*. *The Wall Street Journal Index* is by no means only for stockbrokers; it is an index to excellent articles on economic, agricultural, business, and industrial problems. *Facts on File* is more condensed than any of the other three indexes, and may be useful too.

FINDING POETRY AND LITERARY SUPPORTING MATERIALS

Often a problem can be vividly stated in a poem or a series of quotations from superior writers. In Granger's *Poetry Index,* poems are indexed by subject as well as by title and by first line. For recent poetry, consult Granger's *Supplement*. See also Lewis Leary's *Articles on American Literature,* which covers only to 1954, but is still excellent. *The Essay and General Literature Index* is an annual publication of merit. William Rose Binet prepared *The Reader's Encyclopedia* with a fair subject index, and a good title and author index. If you want to read the summary of a book to see if the book would be worth reading, you might consult the *Book Review Digest*. And, although some would not approve, if you want some quotations that suit your problem you might look up the subject in *Bartlett's Familiar Quotations, Stevenson's Home Book of Quotations,* or Bergen Evans' *Dictionary of Quotations*.

REFERENCE WORKS ON THE CLASSICAL PROBLEMS

There are many reference works on specific problems. *The Peace Research Abstracts Journal* gives summaries of books, films, pamphlets, and articles and includes material on economic peace, labor disputes, and social and political peace. *Consumer Reports* and *Consumer's Bulletin* both have annual indexes and buying guides with many articles on such subjects as consumer economics, food purity, and medical care. The *Statistical Abstract of the United States* is a general work with statistics on productivity, crime, education, and similar subjects. *Crime in the United States* is the annual uniform crime report by the Federal Bureau of Investigation.

On civil rights, a number of good references will help the student: *Report,* an annual report by the American Civil Liberties Union, has sections on educational problems, minority-group and other problems related to freedom. Some reference works are devoted to a particular minority: *The International Library of Negro Life and History* and the *Negro in American History* are multivolume works. The *Negro Handbook* and the *American Negro Reference Book* are single volumes, but contain an abundance of facts, commentary, and information. *The Handbook of North American Indians, The Handbook of South American Indians,* and the *American Indian Index* are also useful. Only about twenty libraries in the United States subscribe to the *Human Relations Area Index,* but it is valuable for research on minority problems.

It would appear that we have ample material on our social, political, economic, and agricultural problems, but we do not. *Toward a Social Report* published in 1969 by the U. S. Department of Health, Education and Welfare demonstrates the inadequacy of our statistics on health, environment, income, crime, learning, science, and art, and is also an excellent source of statistics on some of our internal problems.

One of the most useful of all indexes is your own library's Card Catalogue, provided it has a good subject index. And, one of the best ways to find a good topic is to consult the indexes and the table of contents of books on social problems. And, finally, there are the almanacs: The *World Almanac* is the best known, but many newspapers issue an almanac under their own title. These annual publications are available in paperback and are inexpensive. Also useful are the dictionaries that have been compiled on almost every subject, from the Bible to sociology, economics, philosophy, psychology, and even rhetoric. The problem is not the location but the selection of the appropriate reference work.

Questions for Understanding, Discussion, and Research

1. What other characteristics, in addition to those on p. 25, are necessary for survival? (See, for example, Charles Darwin's *Origin of Species* and a rejoinder to it, *Mutual Aid* by Prince Peter Kroptokin.) What limits any list of qualities for survival?
2. Aside from the classification of problems that have caused the decline of civilization as described on p. 27, how else might problems usefully be classified? Why is your classification useful?
3. Which current problems seem to you to be most dangerous, and, therefore, the most worth talking about? Why?
4. Can human beings control their own destiny? What arguments could be used against your position?
5. What are some of the limitations of trusting to "unexpected sources of solutions" (p. 32)?
6. Which problem structures seem most important in our times? Why?
7. What is the difference between the concept of the *structure* of problems as described in Chapter 2 and the *causes* of problems (Chapter 4)?
8. Devise a problem structure not in the book: name it; explain it; state its principle; illustrate it with both historical and contemporary examples.
9. Prepare an annotated bibliography on problem solving from sources in psychology, sociology, and philosophy.
10. Delete from the bibliography any articles that deal with puzzle solving rather than problem solving. Does research on puzzle solving have relevance for problem solving? Why?

Speech Assignment: see pp. 215–219.

3

Presenting
Problems

Strategy and Tactics

Rhetoricians, like generals, devise their plans guided by two concepts: strategy and tactics. Strategy is the "grand plan" for victory. Tactics are the smaller, specific techniques for implementing the "grand plan." Alexander the Great captured an Asian city using strategy that cost neither side a single life: he rerouted the river that flowed through the middle of the city; since the city was deprived of its water supply, it promptly surrendered.

Alexander's strategy was the rerouting of the river; his tactics involved putting his soldiers to work digging the new channel. In the Civil War, Sherman's march to the sea was part of the "grand plan" to cut the Confederacy in two; Sherman's tactics involved practicing a "scorched earth" policy by destroying the Confederacy's food supplies and buildings en route. In World War II, the Allies decided to destroy Germany's ball-bearing factories, because ball bearings were an essential component of airplanes, tanks, submarines, heavy guns, ships, and wheeled vehicles of every kind. Their tactics consisted of sending fleets of bombers over German production centers at certain times of the day. The Allied strategy was not successful: Germany's production of ball bearings continued to increase. Strategy, however brilliant, sometimes fails. Yet a good rhetorician, as well as a good general, will always have strategy in mind.

Politicians develop strategies too. When Thomas E. Dewey ran against President Harry Truman in 1948, all the polls showed Dewey to be far ahead. Dewey decided to adopt the strategy of keeping peace among his supporters. His tactic was to discuss nothing controversial, to discuss nothing that might alienate one of his supporters—in short, to discuss nothing. Of course, the strategy was faulty: Harry Truman won the election by discussing the issues with vigor and sometimes with vehemence. Select the wrong strategy, and you, too, may be a loser.

Strategy for Communication

Strategy, in rhetoric, consists of the idea you want the audience to accept and the general statements in support of that idea. Tactics consist of the means by which these main ideas are made vivid and valid.

Strategy must be selected with great care. Obviously the central idea and main points of the speech determine the thrust and direction of the speech. If you choose the wrong direction, your speech will not succeed. If you simply put into the speech all you know about the subject, as beginners often do, you will have no strategy. Large armies don't necessarily win battles; small armies, with good strategy and tactics, can win over enormous odds. In 480 B.C. Xerxes invaded Greece with an army of some 5 million men. The Athenians, with an army of perhaps forty thousand men, devised a brilliant strategy: they destroyed the navy that supplied the invaders. With no food, the invaders had to retreat— and Greece was saved. Even overwhelming power does not insure success. Minorities, especially, need strategy to defeat majorities.

To devise good strategy, a general must have thorough knowledge of the nature and size of the enemy forces, of the strengths and weaknesses of his own forces, and of the terrain. In rhetoric, a speaker must have the most thorough knowledge possible of the subject in order to be able to choose the strategy. A common reason for failure among beginning speakers is lack of knowledge. The typical beginning speaker has so little knowledge that he can just about fill the time allotted for the speech; were he to have one minute longer, he would have nothing to say. But the successful speaker has so great a knowledge that he may select those options appropriate to a particular audience, subject, or time. The more knowledge the speaker has of the subject, the more varied are his choices of strategy.

A fair command of a subject is not beyond the reach of even the beginning speaker because modern libraries have resources that enable anyone to accumulate knowledge quickly (see pp. 43–45). After such knowledge has been gathered, there remains the problem of devising an appropriate and effective strategy (see also Appendix, p. 217).

POINTS SHOULD BE FEW IN NUMBER

Main points are, by their nature, general statements, and general statements are dull or lack clarity, or require strong support to be believable. "Consumers need the protection of a better Pure Food and Drug Act" is a general statement; it is not as interesting or convincing as the material that supports it: examples of dangerous additives in our foods, ineffective patent medicines sold on the basis of unwarranted claims, food-handling procedures that allow frozen foods to thaw and then be refrozen before they are sold, and so on. Most of the speech should consist of supporting evidence—statistics, examples, and quotations from acknowledged authorities. Main points must be few in number. If a speaker who is allotted six minutes has ten main points, he will have only thirty-six seconds in which to make each general statement vivid and valid—an impossible task for even the most remarkable speaker. General statements should be kept at an essential minimum. Only those statements that are crucial to the speech should be included. In this way, the speaker gains maximum time in which to support each point, to render it compelling, and to demonstrate its validity, so that the audience will understand, accept, and remember. The ability to reduce a subject to the fewest possible directly supportable general statements is a reflection of the speaker's intellect. Student speakers are often listened to only with politeness because their inept strategy bores their audience and exposes their lack of understanding. Distilling a subject to its essence not only opens the possibility of incorporating the maximum amount of dramatic support but suggests, rightly, something about the intellectual competence of the speaker.

POINTS SHOULD BE BRIEFLY STATED

To focus the attention of the audience, the speaker should state his main points as succinctly as possible. If a given statement could be shortened without significant change in meaning, the statement is wordy or verbose. For example, the statement "It is necessary for us to make the government's program of taxation more equitable" can be shortened to "Taxation should be more equitable." Of course, the statement should, perhaps, define *equitable* by substituting another short statement, such as "Taxes on the rich should be increased." The revised statement is short, clear, easy to understand, and capable of support.

A common error is the subsumption of one point in another: "The basic industries tend to be monopolies, which should be owned by the people." In this statement, at least two points require support: (1) the idea that basic industries tend to be monopolies; and (2) the idea that monopolies should be owned by the people. These are separate, though related ideas, each of which requires a different kind of support. For simplicity and clarity, the statements should be separated and each kept short.

Points Should Be Clear and Vivid

Can you understand the following statement on your first reading? "In proportion as the customs and diversions of human societies are cruel and barbarous, so will the regulations of their penal code be severe." The English philosopher Herbert Spencer makes the same statement more clear and more precise with even fewer words: "In proportion as men delight in bullfights and gladiatorial combats, so will they punish by hanging, by burning, and by the rack."

The second statement is easier to understand than the first because Spencer substitutes *specific* words for *general* words. For "customs and diversions of human societies," he substitutes "bullfights and gladiatorial combats"; for "so will the regulations of their penal code be severe," he substitutes "so will they punish by hanging, by burning, and by the rack." By the substitution of specific words for general words, even general statements, at times, can be made interesting. Instead of "We can prevent revolution by voting the best persons into office," use "The ballot can stop the rifle and the bomb." Ralph Waldo Emerson, who delivered most of his essays as lectures before they were published, used this technique to make his ideas vivid. Take, for example, some ideas from his "American Scholar." Here is one passage from that essay as it might have been phrased by one less skillful with words than Emerson:

> Information accumulated by others involves the abeyant periods of one's productivity. This accumulation serves to increase the possibilities for the motivation of one's creative propensities. Books, which should be means to greater ends, often become no more than ends in themselves. The result is the pretentious collaborator who accumulates and publishes ponderous indexes of other people's contributions. Our institutions of higher learning can best meet the needs of society if they can accumulate the various contributions to human thought of creative minorities and the implication of that thought with the end in view that these works can be used to further implement additional discoveries and insights.

This version is more than twice as long as Emerson's statement:

> Books are for the scholar's idle times. They serve for nothing but to inspire. But the worship of the hero corrupts into the worship of his statue, and so we have the bibliomaniac, the bookworm. Our schools and colleges can

serve us best when they gather within their hospitable walls all the concentrated fires of genius and set the hearts of youth aflame.

Both compositions are on the idea that learning must inspire. Yet one is clear, vivid, concise; the other is verbose and dull.

Main points cannot always be stated vividly, of course, but they must be stated clearly. When you supply interesting examples, compelling statistics, and sharply worded quotations from legitimate authorities, your clearly stated point should be vivid. Aim first, therefore, for clarity.

COHERENCE

Audiences tend to become confused and to lose interest when a speaker's points seem to have no natural relation to each other. Whenever possible, the first point should somehow evoke the second; the second should evoke the third, and so on. A speaker may demonstrate the relationship among his main points by arranging them in chronological sequence. He may begin by discussing the harm a problem has caused in the past, go on to discuss the harm it does today, and conclude with the harm it may cause in the future. Or he may adopt a spatial sequence, showing how crime, bred by poverty in the ghetto, spreads through the city and finally invades the suburbs. Other possible patterns are problem solving, cause-effect, small scale–large scale. But one of the best (and easiest) ways to achieve coherence is by making points parallel to each other.

Parallelism. Main points should be parallel: that is, they should be of equal importance and cast in the same grammatical structure. The following statements are clearly lacking in parallelism:

I. If your ideas are parallel, you will find them easier to keep in mind and thus help you avoid forgetting them when you give the speech.
II. Parallelism makes it possible for audiences to remember the ideas of the speaker much more easily than ideas that are not parallel.

Although both statements are of roughly equal importance, the structure of each is faulty and less clear than it might be. Note how parallelism simplifies and clarifies each:

I. Parallel structure helps a speaker remember his ideas.
II. Parallel structure helps an audience remember the speaker's ideas.

Let us take one more example. Here are two statements that lack parallel structure:

I. The cost of crime represents both a direct and indirect expense to the taxpayer of which he is often unaware.

II. If we could rehabilitate most of those who have committed criminal actions and who are in prison, many of these same persons could turn into much more productive assets.

Here are the same ideas, now cast in parallel structure:

I. Crime wastes the taxpayer's money.

II. Crime wastes human resources.

Parallel structure emphasizes the relationship between two or more points. Consider the following outline where even subordinate points have been made parallel:

I. The basic industries tend to be monopolies.
   A. Telephone communications are a monopoly.
   B. Steel tends to be a monopoly.
   C. Transportation tends to be a monopoly.
      1. Fewer airlines exist each year.
      2. Fewer railroads exist each year.
      3. Fewer bus companies exist each year.

This outline, of course, is not ideal because it does not contain the supporting material that makes ideas vivid or valid. Our point here is only that parallel structure is appropriate in the outline as well as in the speech itself.

POINTS SHOULD FIT THE AUDIENCE

The points emphasized should be appropriate to the needs, the interests, the age level, and the knowledge of the audience. If you were to address an audience untutored in biology on the importance of that science, you would not choose to introduce this topic with the ideas that "ontogeny recapitulates phylogeny," for that idea requires a knowledge of biology and biological terms that the audience probably does not possess. Check your main points to be sure that they are within, or based on, the knowledge possessed by the audience. They should also fall within the interests of the audience, but the careful selection of supporting material may develop an interest where none previously existed.

Evaluation and Composition of Strategy

The following examples may help you to spot defects in strategy and to improve it. In order to improve your ability to analyze and compose strategy, do the following:

1. Read the example and carefully think about the strategy.
2. Analyze the strategy. What is effective about it? What is ineffective about it?
3. Read the criticism of the strategy in the text and compare it with your own.
4. Rewrite the strategic ideas so that they are improved.
5. Read the improved strategy in the text—your revision may be even better.

Consider the following strategy for a speech on the problem of prejudice:

I. Prejudice reduces the amount people earn, thereby cutting down on the amount they can spend and subsequently reducing the turnover of money; thus, low pay ultimately reduces our national income.
II. The ability of people of other races is often not recognized because they are stereotyped and, therefore, their ability is not seen and hence not developed, and all of us are the losers.

Both points are essentially true and, restated, may be shown to supplement one another. But at present, they are wordy, unclear, and certainly not vivid. Compare your revision with the following:

I. Prejudice reduces national wealth.
II. Prejudice reduces social wealth.

Now consider the following strategy for a speech designed to show that apathy is not a problem:

I. Although only 60 per cent of our people vote, even in a presidential election, we have chosen many great presidents.
II. Although in some nations, 90 per cent of the citizens vote, they have elected dictators such as Perón, Hitler, and Mussolini.

This strategy is unusual in that it attempts to convince an audience that certain conditions do not constitute a problem. If apathy is not a problem, we should recognize that fact because we should not be distracted by false or minor problems. But the statements present defects similar to those of the first pair: verbosity, lack of vividness, and lack of clarity. Compare your revision with the following:

I. When few vote, as in our country, we often choose good leaders.
II. When many vote, as in some foreign countries, they often choose dictators.

The revised strategy follows all the rules, for the most part. But no five—or fifty or five hundred—rules can contain all of the wisdom needed to speak well. In this case, we recognize that *if* a person could logically and vividly support both points, he would have a convincing argument. But in view of most of human history, the very notion that apathy is not a problem seems mistaken. In isolated cases, the two statements may be correct, but there is too much evidence to show that, from the time of Pericles to the present, apathy *does* constitute a serious problem: it permits government by minority, exploitation of the powerless, and corruption in government and business. Both statements are very shaky; although the speaker might support the first by pointing to such men as Lincoln, Cleveland, and Roosevelt, we have also had Grant, Harding, Coolidge, Hoover, and Nixon. The second point, however, cannot lead to the desired conclusion: the fact that 90 per cent of citizens in a country vote does not prove lack of apathy, for some governments punish those who do not vote. Under such circumstances, even the apathetic person will vote. Moreover, the second statement suggests that most people voted in a free election when Perón, Hitler, and Mussolini were "elected." If one is to show that apathy is no problem, the speaker might have made better strategic choices, such as the following:

I. Apathy does not exist.
II. Apathy cannot harm us.

The points are short enough and perhaps clear enough. But the first is impossible to demonstrate because it is false. Apathy does exist. The second may be the better point of the two, but there is too much evidence against it. Therefore, the best strategy for this speaker would be to revise his opinion, or choose another subject (especially since the points are inconsistent).

Consider the following strategy for a speech on the problem of starvation:

I. Starvation terrorizes those who are in danger of it.
II. Starvation paves the way for communist domination.

Not bad! The points are brief, parallel, and clearly related to each other. Moreover, the two points work well together because the first point presents starvation from the viewpoint of others who are suffering from the problem and attempts to arouse sympathy from the audience for the sufferers. But the second point relates starvation to a danger most of the members of the audience would recognize as a threat to themselves. Therefore, the first point appeals to the audience's sense of compassion for others, whereas the second appeals to its desire for security. As such, these points, especially together, are likely to influence a large number of people in the audience.

Now that you are quite adept at analyzing strategy, let us examine a more complicated specimen.

I. Hippies have existed in every culture.
    A. In the 1930s, America had the equivalent in the hoboes.
    B. Hippies are reacting to some important problems.
       1. Hippies recognize the lovelessness of big government, big business, big labor, and big education.
         a. Quote from a hippie poet.
       2. Hippies resent the facelessness that life in a modern city forces on one.
       3. Hippies react against the "success" goals of modern business culture.
         a. Statistics about business failures.
    C. But hippies will not learn to solve these problems by refusing to bathe, or by living a life in which they do not encounter the information necessary to solve the very problems they have located.

Let us examine the strategy in the outline. (See the Appendix on outlining, pp. 239–243.) The subject is a timely and important one. We must understand the hippies for they are part of our culture. Moreover, by understanding the hippies, we may gain insight into some defects of our culture and some insight into possible remedies.

Secondly, the points under "B," in which the speaker is attempting to point out that the hippies are responding to some significant problems, are clearly parallel. Each one elucidates a problem the hippies recognize; each one is stated in parallel grammatical form; and all the points are of comparable importance. Thus, these points have a relation to each other.

But there is little else of value in the outline. Every item in the outline consists of a general statement; if this speech were given it would seem dull to an audience. The first item is, we may assume, the introduction to this speech. As an introduction, it lacks any elements (except, possibly, the three parallel points in Section "B") that would help the speaker hold the attention of an audience; nor is there any material that would interest an audience that was not already genuinely interested in the hippies. The first suggestion would be that the speaker look for interesting anecdotes, vivid examples, and even gruesome illustrations to begin the speech. Two or three of these might furnish materials for an opening. Without concrete support, one has little possibility of making an acceptable introduction.

Furthermore, coordinate points should be made parallel, but Sections "A," "B," and "C" are not. "C" is too long, but could be revised to read "Although hippies are reacting to some of the important problems, they are not learning to solve them," which incorporates both a summary and a transition into the statement of the point.

Moreover, the first item (Hippies have existed in every culture) is not the point of the unit. The assumption that an item that comes first in time is necessarily a main point is a common flaw in student outlines. Item 1 a. (Quote from a hippie poet) is a marginal note, the sort of contentless outline entry that should be avoided. The poem itself, or at least its author and title, should appear instead.

Finally, some readers may be horrified that item "1" is supported by only one subpoint in violation of the tradition in English departments where, when one divides an item, it must be divided into more than one part; therefore, some say, if one has subpoints, there must be at least two.

But we do not look upon outlines as a series of divisions, and doubt that ideas can be divided into equal parts. Rather, *most rhetoricians regard an outline as a representation of the structure of the speech,* as a diagram of what ideas depend on other ideas. Furthermore, we must develop the habit of noting the support for a given item. Outlining, by our definition, will develop this skill. If a student has only one item to support a statement, maybe he should be urged to find more support, but he should not be urged to abolish the item, for it reveals the structure of his argument.

Examining examples of strategy will help you learn to evaluate strategy. Continue to evaluate strategy in your own outlines and in others' speeches. Later in this discussion, we offer more suggestions on strategy.

Tactics for Communication: Supporting Material

Poor strategy supported by strong tactics, Napoleon is reputed to have said, is better than the best strategy supported by poor tactics. The same is true in speaking. Good tactics will at least make an interesting speech; lack of vivid and valid supporting material will always result in a poor speech. Most of the speech should consist of supporting material —unless one writes as Emerson did. But even Emerson was often ineffective and misunderstood, a speaker to whom people listened because of his reputation. Rather than trying to emulate Emerson, the beginning speaker should include as much supporting material as he can find.

Most of the speaker's preparation involves locating good supporting material: good statistics, vivid and valid examples, intelligent testimony, interesting analogies, clear summaries, and worthwhile visual aids. You will have to read much to find good material; you will have to think carefully to recall experiences of your own; you will have to work hard to compose your ideas in vivid fashion. Good strategy will come with knowledge of the problem, but good tactics may not. Many a professor is well informed about his subject, but many professors fail to make their ideas interesting to others. Plan to devote as much time as you can to the location of supporting material, for with this material your speech will succeed or fail.

What kinds of support are most suited to presenting problems to audiences? How may these kinds of support best be used to make points interesting?

STATISTICS

Contrary to popular belief, statistics are not necessarily dull; indeed, carefully used, certain kinds of statistics add not only validity to a speech but color and life as well. Perhaps the problem is that statistics are easier to locate than any other kind of support; ineffective speakers, therefore, tend to overuse them.

Simple Mention of Statistics. Statistics can be used effectively to support general statements. Consider the following general statement and its support:

Despite [the] . . . increased interest in black capitalism, progress [in developing black capitalism] has been tortuously slow and has made little impact on the country's economy.

Forty-six black insurance companies, frequently cited as what black capitalists can do, have only two-tenths of 1 per cent of the insurance industry's total assets.

There are about 14,000 banks with assets of $477 billion in the country. Only 33 are black-controlled. And these have less than $300 million in total deposits.

A recent survey . . . revealed there were only 125 black manufacturers in the country, and 114 of those were cosmetic firms.

The largest of these cosmetics firms—Johnson Products Company of Chicago—is the only black-controlled corporation in the country listed on a major stock exchange.

Johnson Products' annual sales total $10 million.

Fortune Magazine's annual compilation of the nation's 500 largest industrial firms shows the 500th largest company had sales of more than $165 million last year.

Although they comprise [over] 11 per cent of the population, blacks own less than 1 per cent, or about 45,000 of the country's businesses.[1]

One simple statistic, even, can help. If you know that prominent ecologists believe that the pollution of the oceans may kill the phyto-

[1] *Pittsburgh Press,* October 24, 1972, Section C, p. 1.

plankton that produce most of the world's oxygen, and that, at the predicted rate of pollution the world has 36 years left, that fact may
persuade your audience.[2] When you know that in the United States one-
half of 1 per cent of the people control 60 per cent of the productive
capacity of the country and own 30 per cent of it, one is apt to think
differently about some problems in economics.[3]

Don't neglect to use statistics, but use them in interesting ways
that will command the attention of your audience.

Comparing Statistics.   We can influence the way in which an audience perceives statistics by comparing these statistics with other figures.
Comparisons can magnify or diminish the significance of a statistic. Consider the following example:

> Our national debt is over $400 billion. That amount is sufficient to pay
> the expenses of the Roman Empire during its entire existence; yet we accumu-
> lated that debt largely since 1939!

The comparison makes the debt look large. But another kind of comparison can make the debt appear small:

> A debt is a debt only in proportion to one's income, among other things.
> If you have a debt of $400 and an annual income of $1,000 you are at least
> solvent. But if you have a debt of $4,000 and an annual income of $1,000, you
> may be in serious trouble.
>
> If our national debt is around $400 billion, what is our income—our
> Gross National Product? The Gross National Product is now over $1 trillion,
> or more than three times the national debt. Moreover, we were able to survive
> quite well when, in 1947, the national debt was *greater* than the national in-
> come. In those days, we had a debt of $257 billion, but an income of only $225
> billion! We are better off than we were in 1947, because our income is much
> greater, even though our national debt is somewhat larger.

Still other comparisons can further diminish the apparent size of
the national debt. Sherrill calculates the total net assets of the government (land, oil on government lands, government buildings, and so on)
at over $17 trillion—fory-two times the size of our national debt.[4]

If we are worth forty-two times our national debt, why do some

[2] David Lyle, "The Human Race Has, Maybe, Thrity-Five Years Left." Pamphlet
Published by Planned Parenthood/World Population, 1967, p. 1.

[3] Ferdinand Lundberg, *The Rich and the Super-Rich* (New York: Lyle Stuart, Inc.,
1968), p. 21. The date applies to 1960. By 1970, the upper one-half of 1 per cent
probably owned 35 per cent and controlled over 70 per cent of our productive
capacity.

[4] See Robert Sherrill, "How Real Is Our National Debt," *Lithopinion* (Summer 1969),
14: 47–49.

say that we cannot afford to help the poor, the sick, the old, the student, and the disadvantaged? And why can't we afford to have the government stop its own pollution?

Sometimes a comparison of statistics can reflect an underlying sense of values. In 1968, the biggest year of the Vietnam War, the "body count" was 181,000 North Vietnamese. If the amount spent on the war that year is divided by the number killed, we find that each man killed cost us $154,000. Would it not have been wiser to have "bought" each man for, perhaps, half the amount it cost to kill him? During that same year, we spent $71 on the education of each of our nation's children. We spent, therefore, 2,156 times as much on killing as on education. The point is that by comparing one set of statistics with another we can increase or diminish their apparent significance.

Breaking Statistics into Comprehensible Units.   The United States spent about $130 billion on the war in Vietnam, but if that amount is to have its maximum effect on an audience, it must be broken down to more comprehensible amounts. We can bring the figure closer to comprehension by breaking the sum into units of $1,000 a day:

If you had started in business in the year A.D. 1 with $1 billion and managed your business so poorly that you lost $1,000 each day, you would still have been in business when the Roman Empire ended over four hundred years later. In fact, you would still have been in business when Columbus sailed from Spain in 1492. You would have remained in business when Lincoln signed the Emancipation Proclamation in 1863. You would still be in business today and you could continue to stay in business, losing $1,000 a day, for another seven hundred years! That's how much a billion dollars is. The United States spent $130 billion on the Vietnam War, and lost.

Interspersing Statistics with Other Material.   Even powerfully dramatized and vivid statistics, however, may become tiresome. Consequently, the intelligent speaker will strive for some variety in supporting material, interspersing statistics with examples, comparisons, and testimony. Moreover, the statistics that are relatively easy to find usually fail to reflect the human side of the problem—the way in which the problem harms, stultifies, or destroys those who encounter it. Statistics about starvation in India, about how many people live on the sidewalks of Calcutta, and about how much food is produced or imported *per capita* do not really convey the problem of starvation. Such figures provide you and your audience with an intellectual understanding of the problem, but they do not make clear what starvation is like to those who suffer from it. An intelligent speaker should try to convey both statistical knowledge and human knowledge. To convey the latter, perhaps no better device exists than the example.

EXAMPLES

An example, like a picture, is worth a thousand words. The example has more power than a general statement because it makes concrete what was abstract. It transforms general statements into people who suffer unjustly or profit unfairly. Some of the oldest and best-loved literature abounds in examples: in *Aesop's Fables* the story about a crow and his thirst epitomizes the value of intellect. Many of the tales from the Old Testament and parables from the New Testament are examples designed to enliven general statements. Thus the example can present us with a mental picture, a tiny drama, that can wake up an audience, clarify a point, or help us visualize a situation.

Why do we prefer the concrete to the abstract? The late James Jeans suggested that we prefer concrete things because during the first several million years of human existence, we needed to respond to the concrete things about us: to see the tiger ready to pounce, or the tiny animal that might make our next meal. Those who could perceive these concrete matters survived, passing on to their children a nervous system more adept at perceiving concrete than abstract matters. Only since the dawn of civilization, and especially very recently, has the ability to perceive abstractions been important. Whatever the reason, we still prefer and perceive more easily the concrete—the example, the picture, the play.

Examples are of many kinds, and we must examine some of the uses, the limitations, and merits of different kinds of examples. For our present purpose, we examine three kinds: (1) hypothetical examples, (2) real examples, (3) instances. Later, as we become more sophisticated about supporting material, we alter the classification.

Hypothetical Examples. Hypothetical examples are examples that are imagined. Surely no real fox ever went after the "sour" grapes, nor did a crow really fill a pitcher with stones to raise the level of the water so that he could drink: Aesop merely invented hypothetical examples. Perhaps there was no prodigal son nor good Samaritan, although there were, doubtless, many people similar to both. Any play is a long hypothetical example with one or more "themes" or general statements that the play makes concrete. Even the comic strip is a sort of hypothetical example, making a point by means of fictitious characters. In each case, a hypothetical example illustrates a point by the use of fictitious characters and situations. Much of the popularity and power of fiction and drama derives from the use of hypothetical situations that are illuminating or entertaining.

Hypothetical examples may be difficult to compose, for they require artistry, imagination, and the ability to write well. Consider the lack of these skills in the following hypothetical example:

Several nations now can produce atomic weapons. One day, through a mistake or an act of insanity, someone may launch an atomic attack upon us. What will happen to you that day? Will you be securely safe in a coal mine, and emerge unscathed from the bomb? Or will you be one of those who suffer for months as you grow weaker and weaker before dying? Or will you be in the center of things?

The student who wrote this passage has a good idea for a hypothetical example: he attempted to imagine the possibilities open to a person on the day the bomb falls. Yet, the example is no better than some strongly worded general statements. The speaker should have made greater use of his imagination to develop the illustration further. He might have described the devastation of buildings, parks, and districts familiar to the listeners; he might have imagined where the listeners and their relatives and friends would most likely be when the bomb went off. He might have imagined in greater detail the slow agonies that would have come to those who escaped instant death: the fever, the nausea, the loss of hair and teeth, and the gradual draining away of energy. Or he might have described what it would be like to be vaporized in an instant, even before one knew what was happening. But the example exploited almost none of these possibilities. A real example taken from the many descriptions of the bombing of Hiroshima would have been better. The invention of a hypothetical example takes time and creativity; yet the time is usually well spent, because the speaker then has a kind of miniature motion-picture that will make his point clear and vivid.

Some writers of speech books give strange advice, urging that one should never use a hypothetical example if a real one can be found. (One shudders to think what such advice, if followed, would have done to *Aesop's Fables,* the Bible, and Lincoln's speeches, which demonstrated his fondness for telling a story.) If what the authors mean is that one should never pretend that a hypothetical illustration is a real illustration —in other words, "Don't cheat," I, of course, agree. Still others insist that hypothetical examples must be based on what could have happened, even if it never did. Aesop, Plato, and countless others, however, did not follow such advice.

Real Examples. If an audience is to understand a problem from the standpoint of one who suffers from it, if an idea is to be made more clear or a clear idea more vivid, one of the best devices is the *real* example. The fact that fifty thousand Americans lost their lives in Vietnam is impressive, but far more effective in moving an audience would be one example of a young American soldier, his hopes, his fears, and the circumstances under which he died.

Although it may be clear, the following idea is not very interesting: *We have wasted much of our aid to other nations.* Yet, if one illustrates the idea, it begins to become interesting:

Men in power in Lebanon used our money to build a road from the capitol to the resort where many of them had estates. Such a road would not, of course, encourage commerce or communication, and was no more than a form of graft. But a kind of poetic justice unfolded: the leaders of Lebanon apparently let one of their friends build the road, and he must have cheated the government, because the cheap paving soon broke up. The road, winding up to the palaces of the rich, was filled with potholes and rubble. I often wonder what the citizens of Lebanon thought as they stood by the sign that announced: "This road was built for the people of Lebanon as a gift from the United States of America."

In fact, much that passes for aid to foreign countries is really aid to American business. The "aid" must, first of all, be shipped in American-owned ships. Secondly, it usually consists of American manufactured goods, often war goods—planes, tanks, guns, ammunition. How much good has our foreign "aid" done? Nothing much for foreign countries, but a good bit for American business.

In Cambodia, we built some superb two-story hospitals. But no Cambodian would use them. We couldn't even *coax* a Cambodian into one of them, because (as we found out after building them) the Cambodians believed that if a person were physically above them, he would have power over the persons below. Because we didn't take the time to understand the people, we wasted our money.

Locating real examples that will make the point clear and vivid will be one of the hardest tasks of the speaker. But once he has such examples, he can hold the members of his audience, and can lead them to understand a problem they perceived only dimly before.

COMPOSING EXAMPLES

Of course, not all examples are vivid and clear. There are ways of writing the same material so that in one way the example works well, whereas in others it may not. Vivid examples may generally result if one can use one or more of the following devices: (1) concrete description, (2) characterization, and (3) narrative. Let us discuss each.

CONCRETE DESCRIPTION

The use of images sets descriptions apart from other forms of composition. An image is a representation by symbols of something the senses could perceive directly. Thus a concrete description of a slum area would use words that represented what one *saw, heard,* and *felt* in a slum. The strongest words are images, for images are words that stand for sense impressions and arouse sense impressions in the minds of the audience. If one is concerned with poverty in America, or in Africa, he must describe that poverty; if he wishes his audience to drive safely, he should describe an accident; if he wishes the audience to stop pollution of the air and water, he should describe what such pollution does.

Let us take a specific example of imagery. Suppose one were giving a speech on the theme *Religious beliefs can be dangerous*. This subject may not seem to lend itself to imagery, but it does. The student may decide to select the following as one of the main points: *Self-righteously religious people often persecute those who differ with them*. With this main point, the student must now look for supporting material. His best source will be historical examples. One can immediately recall persecutions sponsored by Catholics, Protestants, Jews, Buddhists, and Muslims; indeed, it is a rare religion that has not both practiced *and* experienced persecution. One of the more senseless persecutions might furnish an example with which to open the speech. If we were to choose, say, the persecution of the Huguenots, we would go to the library to find the information that would help us describe this persecution. When we had accumulated enough material, we might decide to write about one episode in the persecution—one filled with images of sight, sound, and pain, and use that episode to introduce the speech. The final product is a reasonably vivid description:

Religious bigotry leads to the opposite of what all great religions profess: oppression instead of charity, distrust instead of understanding, hate instead of love. One of the bloodiest examples of bigotry was the attempt to destroy the Huguenots in the sixteenth century. Over thirty thousand of them were killed, and many were crucified.

You have never seen a man crucified, and probably never will. But if you had, you might have stood at the foot of the cross as it lay on the ground, and watched five soldiers do their work in less than five minutes. First, the soldiers held the victim on the cross. One soldier drove a wooden peg through the victim's right hand, while another soldier drove a peg through his left. Then a soldier drove a wooden peg through the victim's feet. Each peg had to be hammered hard until it sank deep into the wood beneath. The cross was then raised, and as the sun sank low in the sky, this cross, silhouetted in black against a crimson sky, stood with thousands of others as testimony to the piety of France, for all this was done in the name of righteousness and Christ.

There is almost no subject on which imagery cannot be used to advantage. A speech favoring tariff reduction can describe the way in which such reduction stimulates trade and business, and thus lends itself to the imagery of busy machines and factories. A speech advocating better study methods can describe the feelings of frustration, disappointment, and even terror in the student who fails. Some subjects, of course, lend themselves to the use of imagery more easily than others, but whenever a speaker uses examples, the possibility arises of using images to increase the vividness of the example. To write vivid imagery consistently, certain skills are needed. Imagery is a complex subject. Many works on English composition will furnish more detailed suggestions, so we will limit ourselves to two fundamental suggestions.

1. *Use the varieties of imagery best suited to the subject.* Imagery is more than a "picture," because the term includes not only things that can be seen but things that can be heard and felt. A reasonably useful and diverse classification of kinds of imagery should include the following:

> visual imagery (sight)
> auditory imagery (sound)
> gustatory imagery (taste)
> tactile imagery (touch)
> olfactory imagery (smell)
> kinesthetic imagery (movement)
> thermal imagery (heat and cold)
> organic imagery (internal sensations, such as elation, depression, nausea, or weakness)

2. *Describe only items that can be directly sensed.* Do not, in describing a slum, say "The houses were old and tumbledown." Such a statement is a conclusion drawn from perceptions, not the perceptions that *led* to the conclusion. Like all conclusions, it is a general statement. Much more vivid are the discrete bits of sense data that led to the conclusion: a broken window that is stuffed with newspapers, to keep out the cold; a screen door with the bottom of the screen rusted away, hanging on its one remaining hinge and banging in the wind.

In *The Light That Failed,* Rudyard Kipling has an artist describe painting as a process in which one sees with uncommon sharpness and then returns to his studio, where he remembers "better than he ever saw." The writing of images is much the same. One must note and remember the sense perceptions that lead to his conclusions. Instead of looking at a group of houses, one must look at *just one* broken window, just one board, or just one step, and describe exactly and only what he sees. Rather than saying, "The child was dirty," or "The street was filthy," describe the perceptions that led you to conclude the child was dirty or the street filthy.

CHARACTERIZATION

Vivid examples often can make use of characterization to enhance their effect. Some simple techniques will enable the speaker to use characterization to good effect.

1. *Depict a person with whom the audience can identify.* We identify with those who are like us: who have the same basic aims, background, customs, status, frustrations, and foibles. Thus the character must be represented as *similar to the audience* in one or more ways. This similarity can be simply and quickly established, as in the following example:

> Abdul is a Muslim and lives in a culture whose customs differ from ours. He wears an Arabian headdress and bows to Mecca. *But being about your age, he likes most of the things you like.* Of course, he doesn't own a car, but he has seen many of them. He doesn't go to school, as you do. He will remain illiterate and will work at menial jobs. But, like you, he gets hungry when he hasn't eaten. Like you, he will start a family; but, unlike you, he won't be able to support them. And, unlike you, he will see those starve who lack enough skill at thievery to escape hunger.

Far less effective was the same subject put in general terms without using Abdul as a basis of comparison and contrast. Let us restate the same idea without using identification:

> Muslims in the Middle East have a different culture and different customs. Their clothes are different, their religion is different. But they like, want, and need many things you do. They have seen cars, and they know about schools, although they may never have been in either.

Without the character with whom to identify, the passage is less apt to get a response from the audience. Often the response of readers to fiction and of audiences to plays and motion pictures is based partly on the change in attitude that occurs when the audience identifies with the leading character of the story, or rejects one who represents the opposite of what the author wishes the audience to accept. The character in an example with whom the audience can identify, either positively or negatively, may contribute to the vividness of the example.

2. *Depict a person who personifies the problem.* One may select or create a character who illustrates a way of life, a point of view, a characteristic. Literature is full of such personifications. Thus, Dickens' character Uriah Heep personifies false humility. Lady Macbeth personifies grasping, reckless ambition. Personification enables the writer to show how a general principle applies in a specific case. Through the characters in *Death of a Salesman,* and especially Willie Loman, we see how an ordinary man may live and die. We may not identify with the person, but we do get a concrete picture of the point of view he personifies.

Good characterization in a speech, therefore, requires that one find or create characters with whom the audience can identify or who personify concretely a problem, an attitude, a force, or a way of life.

NARRATIVE

Everyone likes a good story, and when a good narrative can be used in a speech, it will help to hold the audience's attention. A narrative usually involves the depiction of changes. In this sense, one might write a narrative of a city and depict its founding, growth, decay, and renewal. More strictly, narrative depicts change that results from the conflict of forces: man against man, man against fate, or man against himself. Such narratives increase the possibilities for capturing the attention of the audience, for they permit the use of identification, of personification, of concrete interpretation of a theme, and of intrinsically interesting actions.

The novels of Charles Dickens were persuasive: they resulted in legislation that recognized and protected some of the rights of children and the poor.

Uncle Tom's Cabin is not great literature, but it was persuasive literature, for it led millions of people to see part of the evil of slavery. It became one of the most popular novels in the English language. Today, the book is little read: the hero—Uncle Tom—who passively accepted whatever fate dealt him, who refused to resist those who mistreated him, and who even tried to love those who did, is not a person with whom the modern reader—black or white—can fully identify. But in its day, it was effective. In the days when we were less conscious of the evils of some forms of passivity, *Uncle Tom's Cabin* personified part of the evil of slavery in such characters as Simon Legree. Today we see Uncle Tom as personifying more than he seemed to in the 1850s and 1860s: *the evil of accepting an undeserved fate without protest.* I suspect that the book will not soon be widely read again. But let us not forget that the book helped to precipitate the Civil War and helped to keep England from supporting the Confederacy. How much would sheaves of testimonials and statistics have done? Perhaps not nearly as much as this hypothetical, vivid account that was filled with characters with whom readers could identify and with whose plight they could sympathize.

INSTANCES

Instances are a form of the real example, but involve only the naming of an example. Consider the following use of support by instances:

When a big dam is built, the waters backing up behind it may flood several thousand square miles of land. Every living thing not born to the water is drowned by it: trees, flowers, crops, animals, insects. Everything changes: the water's chemistry, the habitat of river fish, the kinds and numbers of aquatic plants, the life expectancy of disease-carrying insects and creatures

who customarily dine on them (not to mention those on whom they . . . dine
. . .), the weather, the wind, the flights of the birds, the pressures on the
earth's crust, the tendency, therefore, to earthquakes and landslides, the levels
and movements of underground streams and springs, the fertility and salinity
of the soil downstream, the depth, speed, and course of the river, the formation of the coast where it empties into the sea, the habitat of the coast where
it empties into the sea, the habitat of the coastal fish, the way of life for all
the people who used to be where the land was before the lake came.[5]

Yet if you are not interested in dams already, or in ecology, the
paragraph may be dull to you. Instances are limited in that they do not
add mightily to the interest an audience has in a subject. But when
interest has already been fanned, or when it already exists, they are
effective means of supporting a point. The instance will be of use *only*
when it is used to attack a commonly held belief, or to support an idea
that has already captured the interest of the audience. If neither of these
conditions exists, the instance should not be used.

But note the enormous amount of information the instances
furnish, and how efficiently that information is imparted. The great
merit of the instance lies in this presentation of an overwhelming
amount of information. But in precisely that merit lies the major weakness of the instance. Consider the following ideas supported by instances:

People often say that socialism leads to communism, but if that is so,
why are the socialist countries of the world those that are least in danger of
becoming communistic? The socialist countries are Norway, Sweden, Denmark,
The Netherlands, Canada, Belgium, England, New Zealand, and Australia; not
one of them is in danger of becoming a communist state.

But consider the nations that have become communistic: Estonia, Latvia,
Lithuania, Poland, Czechoslovakia, Hungary, Romania, Albania. All these
countries were previously capitalistic. Only two communist countries were not
previously capitalistic: Russia and China, which were feudalistic. In the face of
the evidence, how can anyone insist that socialism leads to communism?

Note that none of the instances was discussed. No one explained to
what extent any one of the nations is socialistic or capitalistic nor that
many communist countries became so against their will. Thus, the
instance, although it provides the hearer with a sense of having heard
an overwhelming amount of evidence, offers evidence that consists only
of names, and sometimes such evidence is not convincing.

Real examples, hypothetical examples, and instances can help
listeners to understand a problem, to understand how a problem affects

[5] Claire Sterling, "Superdams, the Perils of Progress," *The Atlantic* (June 1972), p. 35.

them as well as it does those who suffer from it. These devices are among the best a speaker has for presenting problems vividly.

TESTIMONY AND AUTHORITY

Everyone, at least in a state that aspires to be democratic, must understand problems and talk about problems that he has not directly experienced. He must read studies he has not made and judge them; he must cite or refute quotations from other speakers or writers; he must trust or reject statistics and examples compiled by others. The use of testimony and authority is indispensable in speaking about all matters that lie outside our direct experience.

Testimony refers to that which was said, whereas *authority* refers to the agent who made the statement. For example, Ralph Nader said that each year, 15,000 persons are killed by industrial accidents, 2.5 million are disabled, and 8 million are injured. At the same time, he says, we have only two thousand inspectors to check on safety in our industries but we manage to be able to afford two thousand eight hundred game wardens! [6] If we had worked in a factory, we might indeed have seen, or suffered, an industrial accident, but the statistics Nader furnishes allow us to realize the extent of such accidents, and to compare the number of people we have to protect industrial workers with the number we have to protect game animals. In this case, Ralph Nader and the magazine in which his article appeared are the authorities, whereas the statistics are the testimony. The authority is the source of the testimony, whereas the statements and data given are the testimony itself. We can nearly always make a better speech if we find and use materials by authorities and quote the testimony they give. Unless a speaker himself has performed expert studies on the matter about which he speaks, he will have to rely on authoritative publications, specialists, experts, and fact-finding commissions.

Qualifying the Authority. If an authority is to be believable, and if his testimony is to be accepted, he must be shown to *be* an authority. Qualifying an authority requires a brief, but well-designed demonstration that he is in a position to speak about the matters on which he is quoted. He may have performed a careful study of a problem, or he may have had direct experience with it. The speaker should attempt to establish the competence and credibility of the authority. The mere mention of the person's title—whether he be the warden of a prison, the director of a research institute, or the president of a university—is not enough: he may still be a very poor authority. If, on the other hand,

---

[6] Ralph Nader, How Can We Prevent Death and Disease on the Job?" *Lithopinion*, 6 (Fall 1971), 32–33.

the authority has himself instituted a new program in a prison and watched its effects, or designed and carried out some experiments on cancer-producing poisons, or made a survey of the opinions of faculty and students on the limitations of the university, then he may indeed be an authority. The experiences he has had rather than his titles qualify him as an expert and give him credibility as an authority. Whenever possible, the speaker must outline the experiences a person has had that give him that credibility.

Often one must show that the authority is unbiased, and that he can be trusted. We would not generally trust the testimony of a politician about his own achievements or that of a corporation scientist about the product of that corporation. When the charge of bias may be hurled at an expert, or a board of experts, the charge must be refuted; if the charge cannot be refuted, the testimony will not be persuasive.

What makes an expert, or any person, believable is *more* than a matter of having some experiences and being free of bias. Sydney Harris comes close to identifying what produces believability.

I had an English teacher named Miss Pope, who weighed no more than 90 pounds soaking wet and could have been pawed to death by a Pomeranian. She rarely spoke above a whisper, and she never commanded anything: she only suggested it.

There was never an unruly moment in Miss Pope's class, although there was plenty of freedom and humor. The biggest and dumbest louts in the room kept their peace and respected the learning process, even when they didn't know what was going on, which was most of the time.

The following class, by the way, was zoology, which was an utter shambles: the teacher ranted and threatened, the pupils paid no attention, and the louts would sometimes chase the teacher around the room with a window-pole (without exaggeration).

Why did Miss Pope have "authority," and the other teacher none? Both could send you to the principal, or flunk you, or get you put on suspension. And it was not that Miss Pope loved her teaching and knew her subject—many teachers are good at subjects, but bad at pupils.

It was here I first learned that all genuine authority is rooted in a moral base. Miss Pope embodied this axiom. You just knew that if you talked back to her, or were rude in any way, she would look at you with her steady blue eyes and the heavens would fall. . . .

It was not "fear," you understand, that we felt, as much as "awe." Fear is realistic, and can be coped with; awe is supernatural, and cannot.

And real authority partakes of the supernatural, because the moral realm which energizes authority is in no way material or physical. The ancient Hebrew prophets who castigated Israel stood naked to the winds, without a shred of power, yet their words irresistibly found their way into the Book, and all the potency of princes and priests could not prevail against them. Authority is a rare gift; it cannot be counterfeited by fraud or substituted by power. Moses had it, Jesus had it, all the great prophets and teachers have had it. We shall not be redeemed as a race until we choose for our leaders those who have been . . . imprinted with authority, over those who merely seduce us with easy promises.[7]

SOME DANGERS IN AUTHORITY

Every form of support, every kind of reasoning, has its limitations and, occasionally, its pitfalls, and testimony is no exception. Generally, for example, we tend to prefer the most recent testimony. Yet, probably Thomas Jefferson and John Stuart Mill knew more about democracy than most people alive today. Buddha certainly knew more about Buddhism than most of his followers, who distorted what was meant to be a protest against ritualism in religion and a rejection of superstition and outward signs of piety. Today Buddhism, at least among the masses, is one of the most ritualized religions in the world.

Furthermore, the believability of an authority must stem from his understanding, and his understanding is often hard to assess. The difficulty of assessing the understanding of an authority is particularly apparent in times of crisis. When old modes of thought are being overthrown, most "authorities" and "experts" are found to be wrong. When Pasteur discovered the germ theory of disease, there was only one authority—Pasteur himself—because the entire medical profession, with the exception of the admirable English physician, Dr. Joseph Lister, rejected for years the idea that a microscopic organism could cause illness and death. When the conventional "authorities" spoke of "laudable pus"—the infectious materials secreted from a surgical wound, which at that time were considered a sign of improvement—they were wrong. When Galileo spoke about falling bodies, he was right, and he was the only expert in the matter. Columbus and Darwin were, once, almost the only experts in their fields; no matter how many "experts" one quotes on the side opposing Columbus and Darwin, that side is still wrong. Therefore, we must recognize that sometimes most "experts" may be wrong. We must be sensitive enough to prepare ourselves to

---

[7] Sydney Harris, "Some Have It, Some Don't," *Pittsburgh Post Gazette* (August 12, 1972), p. 19. Reprinted by permission of Sydney J. Harris and Publishers-Hall Syndicate. Authority, of course, is a matter of one's ethos—discussed in Chapter 7, and is partly a psychological matter. The logic of authority is discussed in detail in a number of works, among the best of which is *Evidence* by Robert P. Newman and Dale R. Newman (Boston: Houghton Mifflin Company, 1969). See the Index of the Newmans' book under "Expertise," and the last four chapters on "Government," "The Press," "Pressure Groups," and "Professional Scholars" as experts, and on the conditions affecting credibility.

recognize these times. And we must treat all testimony from authorities not as dogma that must always be accepted but, rather, as only the best thinking available at the time.

Finally, we can help avoid following the "expert" who is wrong if we try to find out, not only the conclusions he offers us but the reasons for his conclusion, and compare his reasons with those of his opponents. Such a process takes time, but we dare not be wrong on the problems of war, poverty, caste, tyranny, and disease that face us today and that could destroy us tomorrow.

VISUAL AIDS

Visual aids—charts, diagrams, graphs, pictures, and objects—can often add clarity as well as vividness to a speech. Speakers so often misuse visual aids that a few suggestions may be in order.

First, the visual aid should be an integral part of the speech and not merely an attention-getting device. The speaker who begins an exposition of one of the causes of crime by pulling out a gun and firing it will hold attention; but the gun obviously has been brought into the speech *merely* to hold attention. The speaker is guilty both of using a trick to hold attention and of introducing his speech in a childish way that suggests that he has a mind to match the childish technique.

The object should add meaning to the speech, and should not be so sensational that it distracts attention from the speech itself. Also, the visual aid should be kept out of sight until it is needed, and put away after it has been used lest it distract the audience from the message. Finally, the speaker should practice the speech using the visual aid, until he can speak and use the device with dexterity at the same time. There are at least two dangers a speaker will face. The first is that while he writes on the board or manipulates the visual aid he has chosen, he will leave "dead spots" in the speech: moments when he finds it difficult to use the visual aids and talk at the same time. A speaker who has not practiced will be unable to do both at once; he is apt to lose the attention of his listeners if he has not learned to avoid "dead spots." Secondly, the speaker may find that, unless he has practiced the speech carefully, he will mishandle the visual aid. If he were explaining that there are three main parts to the typical booby trap, it would be most upsetting, if when he tried to show how it works, bolts dropped to the floor and springs shot out into the audience.

Finally, the visual aid must be large enough to be seen easily by all the members of the audience. Nothing is so ineffective as an object that cannot be seen beyond the first row. To be sure that the audience can see it without effort, the speaker should arrange to place the visual aid on a stand, pin it to a board, or hold it up. Visual aids should not be passed around the audience; the speaker will find it almost impossible to hold attention at a high peak while pictures are distracting the audience.

Visual aids are an addition to, not a substitute for, a good speech. No one doubts that sometimes an object can contribute clarity, as a graph does, or slides, or a blackboard. But some "educationalists" have apparently come to think that audiovisual aids are the essence of education. Jerome Bruner, who has almost made education interesting, criticizes the audiovisual approach to education:

> Films, audiovisual aids, and other such devices may have the short-run effect of catching attention. In the long run, they may produce a passive person waiting for some sort of curtain to go up to arouse him. We do not know. Perhaps anything that holds the child's attention is justified on the ground that eventually the child will develop a taste for more self-controlled attention—a point on which there is no evidence. The issue is particularly relevant in an entertainment-oriented, mass-communication culture where passivity and "spectatorship" are dangerous. Perhaps it is in the technique of arousing attention in school that first steps can be taken to establish that active autonomy of attention that is the antithesis of the spectator's passivity.[8]

SUMMARIES

No summary can add logical strength to a speech, but a clear, well-designed summary can bring together the parts of a speech and provide emphasis. Summaries are by far the easiest kind of support to use, and yet speakers, especially beginning speakers, use them too infrequently. The speaker can choose any of several kinds of summaries, among which are the following, arranged in order of effectiveness.

Cumulative Summary. When you wish your audience not only to be influenced by your major points but also to remember them, use a cumulative summary. After making each point, you should summarize all previous points. Therefore, at the end of your first point, summarize it; at the end of the second point, summarize the first point *and* the second point; at the end of the third point, summarize all three points, and so on. This kind of summary, properly designed and delivered, can *teach* the audience your major ideas.

Evidential Summary. Include in the summary the most significant evidence for the conclusion. For example: "Because 8 million people a year are injured in industrial accidents, while 2.5 million are disabled and 15,000 are killed, we need better protection for those who work in industrial plants." Such a summary carries more weight than one that merely restates the conclusion.

---

[8] *The Process of Education* (New York: Vintage Books, 1960), p. 72.

Repetition. If the speech has one single central idea that needs re-emphasis and that can gain impact through repetition, the speaker should plan to use repetition in the speech. To prevent the idea from becoming tedious, use different words to express the idea. Nevertheless, except in special circumstances (see, for example, Mark Antony's funeral oration in Shakespeare's *Julius Caesar*), this kind of summary is not as effective as the cumulative summary or the evidential summary.

Forecast. Any speaker who wants to be certain that an audience understands should state all his major points before he makes them. Then, by summarizing each point with an evidential summary, and having a cumulative summary throughout the speech, he will have made his speech about as clear as possible.

Final Summary. To repeat the major idea of the speech at the end of the speech is a simple matter; sometimes such a summary will help a large percentage of those in the audience to grasp an otherwise difficult idea. Nevertheless, the speech that is not understood until the last summary is somehow, somewhere, poorly designed. A final summary may clarify, and should be used, unless, of course, more effective summaries have been planned.

Use of Summaries

Summaries must be carefully planned and carefully worded. A mindless summary, delivered mechanically, inaudibly, or hurriedly will not be effective, whatever its kind or however great the need for it. The summary should be both clear and strongly stated. As the speaker delivers the summary, he should watch the audience carefully, not only to see if the audience grasps what he is saying and to see if it senses that he is summing up a major part of his speech but also to demonstrate that *he* attaches importance to what he is saying. A summary that does not convey this sense of importance is not worth giving. But with clear phrasing, strong statements, and a delivery that suggests the material being presented is important, a speaker will have used one of the best devices for attaining effective and persuasive communication.

Questions for Understanding, Discussion, and Research

1. Examine the strategy of any single speech, or of any social movement. Which strategies seemed successful? Which seemed unsuccessful? Why?

2. Good strategy is not often developed quickly or easily. Because its development requires time, and may require experimentation with different strategies, one can often trace the evolution of strategy in a speech or in a movement, or in a particular argument. Trace

the evolution of strategy in Lincoln's slavery speeches. What strategies did Theodore Roosevelt use to set forth his program for the country? Contrast the strategies used by Franklin Roosevelt to get elected in his first election with those he used in any subsequent election. Analyze the strategy of any of the following: the black movement, the Women's Liberation movement, the Chicano movement, the Red Power movement, the Gay Liberation movement. Analyze changes in strategy in any protest movement.

3. Analyze the supporting material in any contemporary political speech. How much was used? Was its quality good? Why do contemporary political speakers use few examples, statistics, and the like? How effective are these speakers? Do they generate much genuine interest among the voters?

4. Listen to a speech on any problem of the day. Describe its strategy and tactics. Evaluate its use of each.

Speech Assignment: see pp. 215–219.

4

Causation

To solve problems, sometimes we must understand their causes. A mistaken analysis of causes often ˙prevents problem solving. The ancient Egyptians knew that the earth was round and had measured its circumference four or five thousand years before Columbus was born. They also could perform certain kinds of brain surgery and solve many geometric and algebraic problems.[1] Yet even sophisticated people are in some ways unsophisticated. Just as we, the Egyptians often blocked themselves from making further progress by clinging to mistaken analyses of the causes of their problems.

Causal Mis-analysis

Egyptian medicine, for example, failed to determine the causes of most medical problems. If an Egyptian had a high fever, swollen glands in the neck, a headache, and smothering sensations in the chest, these four symptoms were not perceived to be related manifestations of a single disorder.

The Egyptian would go to a fever "specialist" for the fever, a neck "specialist" for the swollen glands, a head "specialist" for the

---

[1] Perhaps the most interesting source on the achievements of the Egyptians is Peter Tompkins, *The Secrets of the Great Pyramid* (New York: Harper & Row, Publishers, Inc., 1971).

headache, and a chest "specialist" for the smothering sensation. (Of course, we should not be too quick to condemn the Egyptian for stupidity because Western medicine began to make dramatic advances only about a hundred years ago.) Moreover, medical problem solving in Egypt was seriously limited by superstition.

That which precluded any progress toward real science was the belief in magic, which later began to dominate all the practice of the physician. There was no great distinction between the physician and the magician. All remedies were administered with more or less reliance upon magical charms; and in many cases the magical "hocus pocus" of the physician was thought to be itself more effective than any remedy that could be administered. Disease was due to hostile spirits, and against these only magic could avail.[2]

Causal Analysis

Those who communicate must form the habit of looking for causes and testing and checking the validity of these causes. Moreover, we who listen and read must demand good causal analysis and reject those who fail to furnish it. We still fail to do an intelligent job of analyzing causes of problems. The suburbanite who can't start his lawn mower may end by kicking it and swearing at it; the student who fails an examination may irrationally blame the teacher, or the teacher may fail to locate in his own teaching his share in the student's failure; the legislator who thinks that crime can be reduced by more severe penalties forgets that when a thief's hands were cut off for stealing a loaf of bread, stealing was more rampant than it is now. Americans—like all people before them—do a poor job of trying to understand the causes of the problems that beset them. Seldom does a politician describe the causes of the problems he discusses. Seldom does he design a solution that takes these causes into account. The voters fail to demand such causal analysis; hence, they don't receive it.

As soon as we are confronted by a problem—whether it be international, political, social, economic, or personal—we should look for the cause. When the cause of a problem is located, the solution is sometimes obvious. When the suburbanite finds that his lawn mower has corroded magneto points, he is on the way to the solution: they must be replaced. When the student realizes that he failed to recall and reproduce the material that he read, he will develop more efficient study habits.

Philosophers have addressed themselves to the problem of causa-

[2] James Henry Breasted, *A History of Egypt* (New York: Bantam Books, Inc., 1967) , pp. 85–86.

tion for thousands of years, and their formulations are many and varied. In the last few hundred years, most philosophers have been asking what may be a mistaken question: "What are the defects other philosophers have made in their analyses of causation?" Perhaps we should raise, instead, a question seldom asked and even less frequently answered: "How may the doctrines of causation be used to help us solve problems?" [3]

. Some philosophers have recommended that the concept of cause is archaic, because, they say, modern physics has abandoned the idea. But there is no reason to believe that problem solving for human beings must follow the pattern of physics. Furthermore, modern physics does *not* give up the idea of cause: The formula $F = M \times A$, where $F =$ force, $M =$ mass, and $A =$ acceleration, is still a causal statement, explaining what "causes" an increase in force and a decrease in acceleration. Thinkers who have advocated the abolition of causal thinking in the solving of human problems have not examined the implications of their position.

Many, though not all, problems can be solved when their causes are understood. Should we form the habit of searching for the causes of our problems, a revolution in thinking will have begun. The test of one's wisdom, Aristotle rightly asserted, was whether or not one could understand the causes of events. We need such wisdom to improve the quality of our life and, even more urgently, to survive.

Methods of Validating Causes

TESTIMONY

The testimony of an authority (see pp. 68–71) can, of course, be used to support a causal assertion. After Ralph Nader made his careful study of automobile safety, he concluded that one cause of the high accident rate was the faulty construction of cars. He had gone through the experiences necessary to qualify as an expert in the matter.

Although authorities who have studied the causes of a problem

---

[3] See "Causation," in the *Encyclopedia of Philosophy* (New York: Free Press and Macmillan Publishing Co., Inc., 1967), Vol. II., pp. 56–66. The bibliography cites most of the significant writings on causation and the text introduces the student to the varying concepts of causation and some difficulties of each. The problem of causation is not always a simple one, and for historians, it is most difficult. Louis Gottshalk (in *Understanding History* [New York: Alfred A. Knopf, Inc., 1966], p. 277) suggests giving up the general term *cause* in favor of more specific terms: *purpose, occasion, means,* or *motive,* wherever possible. Yet, for problem solving, it is useful, logical positivism to the contrary, to maintain one unitary concept of the conditions that bring about a problem: *causation.*

are useful to the speaker, their testimony has some undesirable characteristics. The thoughtful person will prefer to have the evidence that compelled the authority to draw his conclusion rather than only the conclusion itself. When the testimony of qualified authorities is necessary and desirable, it should be used, but even more effective is the material that gives the reason for the authority's causal assertion. If Ralph Nader says all automobiles are "unsafe at any speed," the audience should be given some of the evidence that led Nader to this conclusion.

ASSOCIATIONAL METHODS: THE CANONS OF CAUSATION

The demonstration of causal reasoning is aided by the Canons of Causation developed by John Stuart Mill. In 1843, Mill published his justly famous *System of Logic* in which he propounded his Canons of Causation, which were based on the work of the Scottish philosopher David Hume. Hume had been the first to note that causes could be inferred but not observed. For example, when ball *A* moves down the table and strikes ball *B*, setting *B* in motion, we observe only the conjunction of *A* and *B*. When *A* strikes *B*, *A* may stop and set *B* in motion, but the causes—inertia and momentum—are never observed. All that can be observed is the conjunction, the association, of two events. Although the example of the balls is not typical of all causes, Mill was impressed with Hume's discovery and set out to describe causal reasoning based on the idea that the association of two events is all one can discover when describing causes.

THN CANON OF AGREEMENT

Mill's Canons of Causation are actually common sense methods we all have used to discover and test causal notions. For example, if you were on a desert island with fifteen other people and suddenly five of the people became ill, you would immediately begin looking for the cause of their illness, and you would probably guess, first, that it might have been something they ate. You would therefore have assumed that the five had something in which their experiences agreed. You would have applied what Mill calls the Canon of Agreement. If you found that they had all eaten the same unusual kind of food, your hypothesis would be partly confirmed. Such partial confirmation is furnished by use of this Canon. Scientists, years ago, got a hunch that smoking cigarettes can cause death because people who smoked cigarettes died more frequently from heart disease and cancer than nonsmokers.

The Canon of Agreement can be stated as follows: *If two or more cases of the effect have one and only one relevant circumstance in common, that circumstance may be the cause of effect.* Thus, in the case of the five people who were ill, the fact that all five were breathing is not relevant; those who were not taken ill were breathing too. (If, however, the five had just been in a cave where they may have inhaled a dangerous gas, then the experience of breathing the gas might have been relevant.) The fact that all five ate a peculiar food *does* seem relevant, and it seems to be the one relevant matter in which their experience agrees; hence, the food *may* be the cause of their illness. Mill stated the Canon of Agreement as follows: *"If two or more instances of the phenomenon under investigation have only one circumstance in common, the circumstance in which alone all the instances agree is the cause (or the effect) of the given phenomenon."* [4]

To use the Canon of Agreement the following minimal conditions are suggested: (1) one or preferably more sets of closely similar data are required, each having the same effect; (2) each set of data should have only one significant circumstance in common.

We might argue that slow driving is a cause of accidents because of the following data: When the Nebraska Highway Department raised the speed limits on U.S. Highway 30, which goes through twenty-eight Nebraska villages and towns, the accident rate fell 34 per cent. When Illinois did a statewide test of the idea that *raising* speed limits might reduce auto accidents, auto accidents declined 36 per cent.[5] Here we have our two sets of data, each similar in that they were cases in which speed limits were raised and the effects measured; each, necessarily, had the same alleged cause—higher speed limits—and hence, each supports the hypothesis that raising speed limits may lower the accident rate.

Darwin accumulated volumes of evidence to show that competition for food and living space may cause natural selection. Freud accumulated examples to show that early childhood traumas may cause maladjustment in adulthood. Using the Canon of Agreement, one simply accumulates examples and statistics to show that whenever the suspected cause is present, the expected effect occurs. The Canon of Agreement, then, requires a search for a cause common only to those cases that manifest the particular effect, or it requires a search for a common effect wherever the cause is present. Thus the Canon of Agreement requires

---

[4] See John Stuart Mill, *System of Logic* (New York: Hafner Publishing Co., 1950), Book III, Chap. VII, Part 1. The best commentary on the Canons from the standpoint of problem solving has been done by Professor C. Franklin Karns in "The Usefulness of Mill's Canons of Causation to Rhetoric," *Pennsylvania Speech Annual,* 21 (September 1964), pp. 50–55.

[5] See Robert L. Schwartz, "The Case for Fast Drivers," *Harper's* (September 1963), pp. 66–67. Since the national speed limit has been set at fifty-five miles per hour, fewer accidents have occurred than before, but this effect may be because fewer people are driving fewer miles.

a speaker to accumulate examples and statistics to show that the cause and effect are associated in a convincing number of instances.[6]

To be able to understand the Canons of Causation, it is best that you search for examples of each Canon. Such examples are not hard to find. Many scientific discoveries began with a hunch furnished by the Canon of Agreement. Edward Jenner, in the late eighteenth century, discovered a rumor to the effect that milkmaids never caught smallpox. This discovery led to the further discovery that the milkmaids all had caught a certain kind of cowpox that was not particularly harmful but that caused immunity to smallpox. This observation led, in turn, to Jenner's invention of the vaccine that has nearly obliterated smallpox from most of the earth. Dr. Walter Reed noticed that yellow fever patients all lived in buildings without screens and hypothesized that, possibly, mosquitoes carried yellow fever. The same kind of discovery led to the discovery of the cause of malaria. All of these discoveries came about as a result of a hunch first furnished and first tested by the Canon of Agreement. The Canon provides a bit of support for an hypothesis and may lead to its confirmation.

Sometimes, no evidence exists except that furnished by the Canon of Agreement. In such cases, the conclusions must always be tentative, because they may be wrong.

Drawbacks in the Use of the Canon of Agreement.   When other methods of causal analysis are feasible, they should be used, for the Canon of Agreement can lead to error. Note the following:

Whiskey	and	water	causes	intoxication
Scotch	and	water	causes	intoxication
Gin	and	water	causes	intoxication
Vodka	and	water	causes	intoxication

The only element common to the series is water, yet no one would suggest that water causes intoxication. The data seem to conform to Mill's Canon of Agreement perfectly, but in this case, the Canon would lead to a wrong conclusion.

A common factor may not be a cause, but an inert, accidental, irrelevant element in a situation. In the data given, water is an inert element not leading to the effect. Common factors, therefore, are not always causal. The state in which people have the longest life expectancy

---

[6] Mill insisted that the phenomenon have *only* one circumstance in common; such a condition, however, *never* exists. All phenomena are, after all, entities that share several circumstances. Nevertheless, when a *seemingly relevant* circumstance seems to be the significant thing two or more data have in common, that circumstance *may* be the cause. Thus, this Canon results only in a possibly wise guess as to the cause.

is South Dakota; it is also the state with the fewest doctors per capita. Unless our practice of medicine is hopelessly bad—and some people would insist that it is—there is no relation between these two factors. In the same way, towns that prohibit the sale of alcoholic beverages have lower crime rates than those that do not, but such towns are also usually wealthy towns, or towns with very stable populations; hence, the lower crime rate may result from factors other than the prohibition of the sale of liquor. Furthermore, a common but unnamed factor may be present in what appears to be different, discrete factors. Whiskey, scotch, gin, and vodka, of course, all contain a common factor: alcohol.

THE CANON OF DIFFERENCE

John Stuart Mill devised another method that would help correct the difficulties inherent in the Canon of Agreement: the Canon of Difference. If, on that desert island, you had found that the five people who were ill had all eaten the same food, and if you therefore suspected that the food had caused their illness, you would test this hypothesis by finding out if any of those who were well had also eaten the food. If some had, the hypothesis would be shaky; but if they had not, the hypothesis would have been strengthened. In either case, you would have been using the Canon of Difference.

The Canon of Difference can be stated as follows: If you can remove the alleged cause and find that the effect does not occur, then the removed element is probably the cause of the effect. Or, as Mill put it: *"If an instance in which the phenomenon under investigation occurs and an instance in which it does not occur have every circumstance in common save one, that one occurring only in the former, the circumstance in which alone the two instances differ is the effect or the cause, or an indispensable part of the cause of the phenomenon."* (Mill, Book III, Chap. VIII, Part 2.)

To return to our illustration of whiskey, scotch, gin, vodka, and water, we could have used the Canon of Difference to rule out water as a cause of intoxication, thus helping to correct an erroneous conclusion. The Canon of Difference can be applied in two ways. First one could eliminate the whiskey, scotch, gin, and vodka and consume only water, and one would find that intoxication did not result. Or, had the water been eliminated and each of the alcoholic beverages consumed in turn (although one might not have been able to record the results) it would have been plain that, even in the absence of water, intoxication resulted.

The Canon of Difference is a check on the hypothesis to which the Canon of Agreement leads. Dr. Walter Reed confirmed that the mosquito was the carrier of yellow fever by asking for volunteers who were willing to be bitten by the variety of mosquito he believed carried the disease. He gathered the mosquitoes in glass jars and put the open mouth of the jar on the body of the volunteers until the volunteer reported he had been bitten; they all came down with yellow fever, whereas the members of the control group, who were kept inside screened buildings, remained well. Thus when the suspected carrier, the mosquito, was present, yellow fever was contracted; when the suspected cause was removed, yellow fever did not result. The Canon of Difference, therefore, is the method of the experiment, the method of scientific control.[7]

The Canon of Difference must first be preceded by the Canon of Agreement, in which the suspected cause is present and the effect occurs. The suspected cause must then be removed in closely similar cases, and the effect should not occur. The method can be very simply, if somewhat inaccurately, stated: *If the suspected cause is present, the effect should be, but if the suspected cause is not present, the effect should not occur.* Even primitive men apparently used the method, for early agriculturalists found that large seeds produce large heads of grain, whereas small seeds produce small heads, and therefore concluded that the size of the seed partly determines the size of crops. Roger Bacon noted that whenever light passed through a mist, a rainbow resulted, whereas whenever either the mist or the light rays were not present, there was no rainbow. To determine the effectiveness of a certain drug, scientists will administer the drug to some patients, and a placebo—a sugar-coated pill containing inert ingredients—to others, and can determine whether or not the drug causes certain effects.

Drawbacks in the Use of the Canon of Difference. The Canon of Difference, however, does give rise to certain difficulties; certainty is so elusive that one must always exercise care, for not only the average citizen has been led astray by mistaken use of the Canon of Difference, but so, too, have scientists and other brilliant men.

Consider, for example, the inferences drawn from the data of the famous case of "Martin Kallikak," the fictitious name of an actual Revolutionary War soldier who fathered the illegitimate child of a feeble-minded girl. From this union 480 descendants were traced. Of these descendants, only forty-six were known to be normal; the other 434 were feeble-minded, or prostitutes, or alcoholics, or criminals, or a

---

[7] For simplicity, we have combined John Stuart Mill's Canon of Difference with his Joint Canon. Both methods may be found in Mill's *System of Logic,* which contains the following definition of the Joint Canon: *"If two or more instances in which the phenomenon occurs have only one circumstance in common, while two or more instances in which it does not occur have nothing in common save the absence of that circumstance, the circumstance in which alone the two sets of instances differ is the effect, or the cause, or an indispensable part of the cause of the phenomenon."* (Mill, Book III, Chap. VIII, Part 4.)

combination of several of these. Kallikak later married a girl from a respected family. From this union, 496 descendants were traced, of whom only five seemed to show signs of abnormality, whereas the remaining 491 were normal; many were successful businessmen and eminent professional people. The data are probably accurate, although some questions might be raised about what the observer—who published the study in 1915—chose to call *normal* and *abnormal*. One might also wonder if the legitimate side of the family, being more able financially, might not have had more opportunity to cover up its errors. Still, let us assume the accuracy of these statistics, and ask what inference can be drawn from them. The Canon of Difference seems, at first sight, to have been used here, and the inference that many social scientists drew from the study was that intelligence and character are hereditary: the "bad" genes on the illegitimate side of the family produced abnormal descendants, whereas the "good" genes on the legitimate side of the family produced normal and productive descendants.

Yet this inference is not warranted. The illegitimate side of the family did produce abnormal offspring, but this side of the family also had an abnormally bad environment. A child whose parents are thieves may have criminal tendencies, not because he was born with them but because his environment provides him with knowledge of thievery and with an atmosphere that does not condemn, and perhaps rewards, thievery. The child of professional people has opportunities that the child of thieves or prostitutes would never know.

Thus, Kallikak descendants with "good" heredity also had a "good" environment; and those with "bad" heredity, a "poor" environment. There is no control here, and therefore the Canon of Difference is *not* used. One must maintain a skeptical attitude, continue to probe, to accumulate information, and to search for criticism. There are no simple answers—and that statement, itself an oversimplification—is also partly wrong.

The necessity of looking for the unexpected can be illustrated by an interesting experiment on longevity. It once appeared that starvation led to longevity among rats. Rats that were fed normally lived 650 days, but those that were denied food one day in every four lived 667 days and those deprived of food every other day lived 708 days. The simple conclusion seems obvious and inescapable: fasting lengthens life.

But, again, the simple conclusion must be viewed with suspicion, and soon after the data were published, scientists found that the situation was more complicated than they had originally thought. Starvation did produce an increase in life span, but only if the starvation occurred before the rat had reached maturity. Once maturity had been reached, deprivation decreased the life span. The increase in life span in the first instance came about because starvation postponed the development of maturity. Because a rat does not begin to age until after he has reached a point roughly equivalent to the onset of late adolescence in the human being, the postponement of that stage can increase the rat's life span. Such starvation probably could not lengthen the life of a human being. Even if starvation may prolong life, the reduction of nutrition might influence the development of intelligence, and it is quite likely that starvation would not produce a secure and productive psychological attitude. Few would care to add a few years to life at such cost.

Thus, what appears to be a good use of the Canon of Agreement and the Canon of Difference may lead to an unjustified conclusion. There is no road to certainty, yet the Canons can help us reject uncertainty, provided that we use them intelligently and keep our minds alert.

THE CANON OF CORRELATION [8]

The Canon of Correlation simply notes that as the cause increases, so, too, should the effect increase. On that desert island, those who ate less of the poisonous food should be only slightly ill, whereas those who ate more should be quite ill, and those who ate a large amount should be very ill. If the degree of illness varied in proportion to the amount of the food eaten, then the hypothesis that food had been the cause of illness would be further strengthened.[9]

The Canon of Correlation supports the idea that smoking cigarettes is a cause of heart disease, because medical reports demonstrate that the more one smokes, the greater is the danger:

Amount Smoked per Day	Increase in Risk from Heart Disease
½ pack	29%
1 pack	89%
2 packs	115%
Over 2 packs	241%

[8] Mill named this Canon the Canon of Concomitant Variation, but contemporary students are more familiar with the term *correlation*, used here. The Canon of Residues is omitted because it can seldom be used in public affairs. Nevertheless, its statement is worth producing here: "*Subtract from any phenomenon such part as is known by previous inductions to be the effect of certain causes, and the residue of the phenomenon is the effect of the remaining causes.*" (Book III, Chap. VIII, Part 5.) But in human affairs we can hardly ever be sure we have considered all possible causes, and this method is, therefore, seldom useful.

[9] Mill's statement of this method is as follows: "*Whatever phenomenon varies in any manner whenever another phenomenon varies in some particular manner is either a cause or an effect of that phenomenon or it is connected with it through some fact of causation.*" (Mill's Book III, Chap. VIII, Part 6.)

Of course, it is possible that the people who have a psychological need to smoke are also those who are susceptible to heart disease. But there is no strong evidence to show that this outside factor causes both smoking and heart disease, so smokers might be well advised to stop smoking.

The Canon of Correlation may also be used negatively. As a simple example, drilling holes in a board will reduce the weight of the board; the greater the number of holes, the less the board will weigh.

The Canon of Correlation helped to ascertain the cause of recent earthquakes in Denver, Colorado, which historically had experienced very few. The Army's Rocky Mountain Arsenal near Denver had drilled a well twelve thousand feet deep to serve as a repository for poisonous chemical wastes. After four million gallons had been poured down the hole, Denver had its first earthquake in eighty years. As more material was poured down the hole, the number of earthquakes increased. When the Army stopped pouring the liquids down the hole, the earthquakes began to decrease, and now have stopped. Thus, correlations may some-times—but not always—locate a cause.

To use the Canon of Correlation, one must have phenomena in which the amount of the effect varies as does the cause, either positively or negatively.

Drawbacks in the Use of the Canon of Correlation. There are limits to all correlations. For example, raising speed limits is usually positively correlated with a reduction in accidents, but there is some point at which the speed limits may become so high as to encourage dangerously fast driving. Similarly, one's health may be positively cor-related with the amount of vitamins he consumes; but after a certain point, some vitamins, particularly A and D, begin to act as a poison.

Some time ago, a study of the causes of aging indicated that literacy might be a cause of early aging. The more literate a country or state was, the fewer people it had that lived to be over a hundred. The follow-ing presents some of the data:

Area	Illiterates per 100,000	Centenarians per 100,000
Bulgaria	66	60
New Zealand	2	1
Alabama	12	10
Utah	1	0.4

Data used in the study were drawn from each state in the United States and many of the countries of the world. And it seemed possible that literacy, which brings one knowledge of the troubles of the world, places one in demanding jobs, and conveys knowledge of the suffering of one's fellow man, is conducive to an early death.

But there are difficulties with the evidence. Nothing in the study, for example, shows that illiterate people are the same people who live to a ripe old age. But there is another reason that, if you wish to live for a long time, you should not drop out of school, forget how to read and write, and try to become as illiterate as possible. How can illiterate people accurately calculate their age? Many of them, besides not being able to read or write, cannot count. In many countries, accurate birth records are not kept. Hence, there is no way of being sure, when some old people say they are over one hundred years old that they really are centenarians.

APPLICATION OF THE CANONS OF CAUSATION

The Canons of Causation must be used with awareness of the kinds of errors to which they have sometimes led. Even when suspected causes and effects occur together, the relationship may not ᴗ a causal one. For example, the time given by one watch closely correlates with the time given by another, yet the one watch does not cause the other to run. (If one watch stopped, the other watch would continue to run.)

But what about matters in which the suspected cause cannot be so easily eliminated? For example, we know that the price of eggs in the United States correlates with the amount of snow that falls in Siberia. Using the Canon of Agreement, we could show that whenever snow increases in Siberia, the price of eggs in the United States rises. Using the Canon of Difference, we can show that when there is no snow in Siberia, eggs cost less. We could apply the Canon of Correlation, and find that the deeper the snow in Siberia, the higher the price of eggs in this country, and the less snow in Siberia, the lower the egg prices here. The data would all be correct and we would have applied all three Canons, but if we concluded that snow in Siberia caused egg prices to rise in the United States, we would be making a common mistake in the use of the Canons. Often what appears to be causal is the result of an outside factor. Watches run simultaneously because of an outside factor: they were made to do so. In the case of the eggs and snow, the outside factor is the amount of sunshine and warmth, the lack of which causes both snow in Siberia and high egg prices in the United States. Whenever, therefore, you find a striking correlation, even when all three of the Canons of Causation seem to verify a causal connection, look for a hitherto unsuspected cause that may account for both the suspected cause and the apparent effect.

The association between the reading of comic books that depict violence and the amount of violence in America has led some to suspect that comic books may cause the violence. Perhaps they do, but some sociologists believe that both are caused by an outside factor. Life, particularly in poverty areas, is so frustrating and inhumane that it makes one want to slash out at the environment, to "rip off" the establishment. Life in high-crime areas may cause both the real violence and the vicarious violence of comic books. Indeed, such books may act as a release for violent feelings. The banning of comic books might produce even more violence.[10] Thus, further use of the Canons of Causation may reveal that what seemed to be cause and effect were really effects of some outside force.

Another potential error in using the Canons is the mistaking of the cause for the effect. The rooster, for example, may think that its crowing causes the sun to rise, but we know that the sun's rising causes the rooster to crow. As with all causal thinking, the cause and the effect do not carry labels, and, therefore, sometimes we mistake the effect for the cause. Early in this century, a study of genius was performed in which the biographical details of a thousand geniuses—including Leonardo, Bach, Shakespeare, and Locke—to see if a common factor might be the cause of their genius. (The author of the study was, of course, using the Canon of Agreement.) Only one significant common factor was found: serious psychological maladjustment. Since there were very few exceptions to this pattern—only a dozen or so out of the thousand geniuses studied—it seemed reasonable to conclude that genius is caused by serious maladjustment. The implications are quite clear: there is a fine line between genius and insanity, and if we want more geniuses, perhaps we should not try to cure neurotic and even psychotic behavior; perhaps, in fact, we should "help" people develop maladjustment. Regrettably, however, the study contains an error: maladjustment is not the cause of genius, but the result. A genius responds to certain problems—whether in art, science, philosophy, literature, or politics—with more intensity than the average person. The problem holds his imagination and batters his nervous system. And when he finds a solution, he knows that most of society will not accept the solution except after a long struggle, or until, perhaps, after his death. Perhaps, then, it is genius that causes maladjustment, rather than maladjustment that causes genius.

One must also remember that the association of two events may sometimes be accidental. The following data suggest a pattern that a president of the United States elected to office at the beginning of a twenty-year period will die while still in office:

---

[10] The matter is not quite so simple: studies of the effect of violence in motion pictures have established that justifiable violence (as when a "good" man gives the "villain" his just deserts) tends to *increase* violence; but unjustifiable violence (performed by the "wicked" on the "good") tends to *reduce* violence.

1860: Abraham Lincoln
1880: James Garfield
1900: William McKinley
1920: Warren Harding
1940: Franklin Roosevelt
1960: John Kennedy
1980:   ?

Unless one is willing to assume that there is something about twenty-year cycles that causes the death of these presidents, the startling pattern is an accidental one.

In using the Canons, therefore, one must remember that what seem to be cause and effect may both be the results of an outside factor, that what seems to be cause may actually be effect and vice versa, and that the data may be the result of an accident. By keeping in mind these three common dangers, we may make more intelligent use of the Canons of Causation.

A TEST OF UNDERSTANDING

Vitamin C is alleged, by Linus Pauling, winner of the Nobel prize in chemistry and biology, and later of the Nobel Peace prize, to reduce the possibility of catching a common cold.[11] He makes frequent use of the Canons of Causation to arrive at his conclusion. Set up, using each of the three Canons, a test of the hypothesis that large doses of Vitamin C will prevent the common cold. Begin with the Canon of Agreement, then use the Canons of Difference and Correlation to set up situations in which you might test the hypothesis. After you have done so, read the following footnote.[12]

Connectional Methods

By the time one drinks enough alcohol to feel its effects, the alcohol has already killed about ten thousand brain cells. Those who drink alcohol suffer brain damage (the Canon of Agreement), but those

[11] See his *Vitamin C and the Common Cold* (San Francisco: W. H. Freeman, and Co., Publishers, 1970), esp. Chap. 5.
[12] For Vitamin C to be effective, Linus Pauling says, its level in the body must be kept constant by small doses taken throughout the day since Vitamin C can be excreted in a few hours. According to Pauling, different people require different amounts of Vitamin C; some people need only half a gram a day to avoid colds, whereas a few need as much as sixteen grams a day. Set up the Canons in such a way as to take these factors into account. By the way, if you use animals in your experiments, the results would *not* apply to human beings. Animals can produce their own Vitamin C, but human beings cannot.

who do not drink generally do not suffer such damage (Canon of Difference). Moreover, the amount of brain damage suffered is proportional to the amount of alcohol consumed (Canon of Correlation).

But why does alcohol kill brain cells? *The Canons show us only that cause and effect are associated; why* they are associated is another matter. To understand why a certain cause produces a given effect, we must describe the conditions that produce the effect.

Alcohol makes the red blood cells "stick together" so that they tend to clog the capillaries, thus starving the cells of the body. Unlike other body cells, nerve cells of any kind, including brain cells, never regenerate, although other nerve cells may take over the function of the dead cells. (Of course, although the thousands of cells destroyed by one bottle of beer are gone forever, the normal brain has 17 billion cells, and even ordinary living causes the death of a few thousand cells each day.)

This method is properly called the connectional method and contrasts with the associational methods exemplified by the Canons of Causation. The Canons *demonstrate that* an alleged cause produces (or does not produce) an effect by showing that the cause and effect are (or are not) associated. For example, we might set up each of the Canons of Causation to demonstrate that Vitamin C causes a reduction in the number of colds a person has (provided he distributes the amount of Vitamin C he takes throughout the day). But nothing in the Canons would tell us *why* it helps prevent the common cold. Clearly, the associational methods show only *that* a cause is operating. Connectional methods can explain *why* a cause is operating by describing the conditions that produce the effect. Linus Pauling explains why when he shows that one function of Vitamin C is to keep the cold virus from penetrating the cells of the body where the virus can multiply, and that Vitamin C decreases the permeability of the body cells to the virus, keeping it in the bloodstream where it will be destroyed by the body's resistance mechanisms. Using these connectional forms of causal statement, one can understand why some people may not find that taking Vitamin C helped prevent colds: if one takes a gram of Vitamin C each morning (a low dosage for those who are subject to colds), he may have almost as many colds as if he had taken none. Vitamin C is excreted from the system within three or four hours. Once the Vitamin C is gone, its protection is lost, and the cold virus can enter the body cells and multiply. Taking another gram of Vitamin C the next morning will not help, for it will be too late. The level of Vitamin C must be maintained throughout the day. Here again, we are describing the conditions that produce the effect.

SIMPLE CAUSES

Freshly poured concrete hardens even under water. Contrary to popular belief, concrete does not "dry"; in fact, drying would weaken concrete and severe drying could cause it to crumble into dust. Concrete, rather, crystallizes; it can harden even better under water than in dry air because water is required in the process of crystallization. Here we have a single causal assertion together with a description that accounts for the assertion: concrete hardens under water because water is essential to its crystallization.

Connectional statements must not be too simple, too bare of evidence, or too lacking in explanation. Connectional statements require support. For example, we can assert with some certainty, "Rome may have fallen partly because Romans had lead poisoning." Yet the statement is not very convincing, especially because of the traditional belief that Rome fell because of moral decadence, poverty, and corrupt government. Nevertheless, medical anthropologists have recently examined the bones of Romans who died during the fall of Rome, and they find that the bones of wealthy Romans contain enough lead deposits to warrant a diagnosis of lead poisoning. Wealthy Romans seem to have consumed an unusual amount of lead, probably because they stylishly kept their wine in lead casks or flasks. The wine dissolved small bits of lead, which, over a number of years, were enough to poison those who drank the wine. The poorer Romans, who could not afford such luxuries as lead casks, do not seem to have had the same problem, but the wealthier Romans are known to have shown some of the symptoms of lead poisoning: lack of energy, inability to reproduce, and, ultimately, insanity. Now, after this explanation, one might legitimately assert: "The drinking of wine from lead casks may have been an important and, until recently, overlooked cause of the fall of Rome, because wine dissolved enough lead from the flasks in which it was kept to cause the symptoms of laziness and, eventually, of insanity among the rulers of Rome."

If a simple causal assertion is made, it should be accompanied by explanation, amplification, and supporting evidence. One generally should limit oneself to a minimum of unsupported statements, because they are generalizations and, therefore, tend to be dull and unconvincing —unless the audience is already interested in them, which is relatively rare.

MULTIPLE CAUSES

Protagoras, the ancient Greek who at the age of ninety was persecuted for his beliefs, was the first to recognize that many causes always enter into any particular event. He argued with Pericles about the causes of the death of a spectator at a javelin-throwing contest. The wind, it seems, changed the direction of a javelin so that it accidently flew toward the spectators and pierced the heart of one. Protagoras pointed out that there were many causes of the death of the innocent bystander, and each was a true cause: the wind, the cardiac arrest caused by the javelin, the carelessness of the director of the games in allowing spectators to be too close, the carelessness of the javelin-thrower in not taking the wind into account, and perhaps even the failure of his teacher for not imbuing him with the proper caution. One could add other causes: the desire of people for adventure that necessitated artificial means of creating adventure and the desire of young men to excel in sports. All these were causes of the death of the spectator, and all were equally valid causes. Protagoras, therefore, established the idea that events have no single cause, but often have many causes, and that each multiple cause is equally "true."

DISCREET CAUSAL STATEMENTS

One event may have different causes in different cases. Most of our problems today are not caused by one single factor that can be stated in a single simple sentence. There is no single cause of divorce, or of crime, or of riots, or of poverty, or of war, or of caste. Most of our problems are caused by many factors, but each of these factors can be understood and removed. Consider, for example the causes of riots as outlined by a federal Commission created to study the riots following the assassination of Dr. Martin Luther King, Jr., in 1968:

White racism is essentially responsible for the explosive mixture which has been accumulating in our cities since the end of World War II. Among the ingredients of this mixture are:

Pervasive discrimination and segregation in employment, education and housing, which have resulted in the continuing exclusion of great numbers of Negroes from the benefits of economic progress.

Black in-migration and white exodus, which have produced the massive and growing concentration of impoverished Negroes in our major cities, creating a growing crisis of deteriorating facilities and services and unmet human needs.

The black ghettos where segregation and poverty converge on the young to destroy opportunity and enforce failure. Crime, drug addiction, dependency on welfare, and bitterness and resentment against society in general and white society in particular are the result. . . . Yet these facts alone cannot be said to have caused the disorders. Recently other powerful ingredients have begun to catalyze the mixture:

Frustrated hopes are the residue of the unfulfilled expectations aroused by the great judicial and legislative victories of the Civil Rights movement and the dramatic struggle for equal rights in the South.

A climate that tends toward approval and encouragement of violence as a form of protest has been created by white terrorism directed against nonviolent protest; by the open defiance of law and federal authority by state and local offi-

cials resisting desegregation; and by some protest groups engaging in civil dis-
obedience who turn their backs on nonviolence, go beyond the constitutionally
protected rights of petition and free assembly, and resort to violence to attempt to compel alteration of laws and policies with which they disagree.

The frustrations of powerlessness have led some Negroes to the conviction that
there is no effective alternative to violence as a means of achieving redress of
grievances, and of "moving the system." These frustrations are reflected in
alienation and hostility toward the institutions of law and government and the
white society which controls them, and in the reach toward racial consciousness
and solidarity reflected in the slogan "Black Power."

A new mood has sprung up among Negroes, particularly among the young, in
which self-esteem and enhanced racial pride are replacing apathy and sub-
mission to "the system."

The police are not merely a "spark" factor. To some Negroes police have
come to symbolize white power, white racism, and white repression. And the
fact is that many police do reflect and express these white attitudes. The atmosphere of hostility and cynicism is reinforced by a widespread belief among
Negroes in the existence of police brutality and in a "double standard" of
justice and protection—one for Negroes and one for whites.[13]

The tragedy of the riots is heightened by a paragraph at the end of the
report:

I read [the] report . . . of the 1919 riot in Chicago, and it is as if I were reading the report of the investigating committee on the Harlem riot of '35, the
report of the investigating committee on the Harlem riot of '43, the report of
the McCone Commission on the Watts riot.

I must again in candor say to you members of this Commission—it is a kind
of Alice in Wonderland—with the same moving picture reshown over and over
again, the same analysis, the same recommendations, and the same inaction.[14]

As long as knowledge of the causes of our problem is confined to a
few people and ignored by most citizens, we will suffer from the degradation, the torture, and the danger of these problems. If, however, we
can learn to understand our problems and their causes, and if we can
communicate that understanding to others of this generation, we might
yet save ourselves.

CHAIN OF CAUSES

Aristotle added more than a bit to the possibility of analyzing causes
by pointing out that each cause itself has a cause, and so on to an

---

[13] From the *Summary of Report,* reprinted from the Bantam Books edition of the
report of the *National Advisory Commission on Civil Disorders* (New York: Bantam
Books, Inc., 1969), Part II, Chap. 4, pp. 10–11.
[14] Statement by Dr. Kenneth B. Clark, Ibid., Chap. 17, p. 31.

infinite regress. Each of the causes mentioned in the investigations of riots have causes, too, and these causes—each of them—run to an infinite regress. Similarly, when a man dies of a heart attack, the immediate cause of that heart attack may have been the constriction of the blood vessels that feed the heart muscle. What caused this constriction? Fatty deposits that were high in cholesterol resulting from the food he ate. Why did he eat such food? Partly because it was the style to do so. But why was it the style to each such food? Because it was expensive and showed one's wealth. Why should one make a show of one's wealth? To prove that one is superior to other human beings. And so on to infinity. As any child of five knows, one can ask "Why?" to every reply that is given and go on forever, or, at least, until Mother says "Why don't you go outside and play?"

If each cause runs to infinity, the problem of analyzing causes may seem to be hopelessly complex but, on the contrary, is actually simplified. A chain of causes may be broken at any point and the ultimate result prevented. The man's heart attack might have been prevented had he developed an ascetic way of life, refusing to respond to the pressures of society to display wealth, or had he realized the dangers of a rich diet and eaten more sparingly, or had medical science developed a drug that dissolved the accumulation of fatty deposits.

A chain of causes is often less difficult to trace than a single cause or ordinary multiple causes. For example, a meteorologist from the University of Wisconsin once visited India, and because of his interest in weather, flew over India to observe its atmospheric conditions. At no point, however, could he see much of India because of the enormous amount of dust in the air. He discovered, however, that the vast Rajputana desert of India had as much moisture in the air as the area over the Congo or the Amazon—enough moisture to turn the desert into a rain forest, if it could be "wrung out" of the air. What prevented the rain from falling where it was so desperately needed? If the "impediment" could be removed and rain induced to fall, a fertile area would be created more than large enough to make India self-sufficient in food. The following chain explains the causes:

1. Air filled with particles of dust is heavier than ordinary air.
2. Heavier air tends to settle, and to become warmer.
3. Warmer air holds more moisture than cool air.
4. Warmer air holds so much moisture that rain does not fall.[15]

[15] Adapted from Reid A. Bryson, "The Research Frontier," *Saturday Review* (April 1, 1967), pp. 52–56. As we will see, this causal analysis led to a solution (see pp. 109–110).

Some kinds of causation, therefore, clearly constitute a kind of chain, each link of which must be present for the effect to occur. If even one link is removed, the chain is broken.

FUNCTIONALLY RELATED CAUSES

Sometimes, we can describe causation so accurately that we can express the formulation mathematically. In such a formula, a variation in any one of the factors will cause a corresponding variation in the opposite side of the equation; we call these factors functionally related causes.

Let us consider a functionally related cause, expressed in formula, that can be used to account, in part, for high and low prices, for periods of depression and periods of inflation: $P = \dfrac{\$ \times T}{G}$ In this equation, P is the price of a product; $\$$ stands for the amount of money in circulation; T stands for the number of times that money changes hands; G is the amount of goods produced. Suppose prices were too high and you wanted some sensible ways of lowering them. The price can be lowered by anything that lowers the numerator of the fraction or that raises the denominator. So, if we could decrease the amount of money in circulation, we could slow inflation; but one consequence is that money would be more scarce, and food, housing, and shelter would be more difficult to buy. Or we could lower the price by decreasing the turnover: employing rationing, for example, so that everyone could buy only certain amounts of scarce commodities. Of course, the more popular way to reduce inflation would be to increase the number of goods, but the danger would be that prices might drop so low that it would be impossible to recover even the cost of production. Nevertheless, in the regulation of these three factors—the amount of money in circulation, the number of times that money turns over, and the amount of goods available—lies the solution to the problems of inflation and deflation.

One should note that there are exceptions to this formula, and that it certainly does not cover the whole of economic life. For example, large corporations are no longer subject to the law of demand and supply implied by the formula. Some corporations are powerful enough to set prices regardless of demand, and are even able to influence the prices of raw materials.[16]

Nevertheless, once in a while in human affairs we do find statements of causes that represent functionally related factors. Regrettably, we cannot say that crime equals a certain amount of X factor times a

---

[16] See John Kenneth Galbraith, *The New Industrial State* (New York: Signet Books, 1968) , Chap. X, esp. p. 121.

certain amount of Y factor divided by a certain amount of Z factor, and we probably never will be able to make such statements. But when such statements can be made—as in economics, for example—we should make use of them.

THE METHOD OF CONSEQUENCES

One of the more sophisticated methods of locating the causes of events is the search for consequences we would expect to occur provided a suspected cause is operating. Sherlock Holmes, for example, suspects a certain person of committing a crime. If this person did commit the crime, certain causes should be present: he should have had an opportunity; he should have had a weapon, or the means for committing the crime; and there should be signs that those means were used.

Let us use an example involving a chain of causes. We suspect that ice ages are caused not so much by cold weather as by warm weather, as the following chain of causes suggests:

1. The great glaciers that once covered much of the Northern Hemisphere have been melting slowly for about eleven thousand years.
2. As these glaciers melt, the level of the oceans slowly rises.
3. As the level of the oceans rises, the narrow stretch of sea between Greenland and Europe deepens, permitting the warmer Gulf Stream to flow into the Arctic Ocean.
4. As the Gulf Stream flows into the Arctic Ocean, it melts the Arctic ice cap.
5. As the Arctic ice cap melts, it releases moisture for additional snowfall, and more snow falls on the entire Northern Hemisphere that can be melted in the summers.
6. As the snow accumulates, glaciers form, and the level of the oceans drops to the point at which the Gulf Stream can no longer enter the Arctic Ocean.
7. Since the warm Gulf Stream is shut out from the Arctic, the Ocean freezes over, less snow falls, and the great glaciers begin to melt.
8. As the glaciers melt, the level of the oceans slowly rises and the cycle begins over again.

How can such a theory be tested? Naturally, we can't use the Canons of Causation because we can't go back in time. But we can look for some consequences of each link in the chain of causes; if these consequences exist, they tend to confirm the theory. If the theory is correct, we would expect to find that the oceans were lower eleven thousand years ago; indications are that the earth's oceans were some four hundred feet lower at that time. If the theory is correct, we would expect that the ice cap on the Arctic Ocean should be getting thinner and thinner; it is, at present, the thinnest that it has been since we began taking measurements of it in 1890. If the theory is correct, we would expect more precipitation eleven thousand years ago than now; in fact, at that time the Sahara was not a desert, but a grassland capable of supporting considerable animal life. If the theory is correct, we should expect to find that relatively little snow has fallen in the Northern Hemisphere during the last eleven thousand years; indeed, most of the snow in the remaining glaciers was laid down several thousand years ago. If the theory is correct, we should expect to find that the oceans are rising; in fact, they have been since we began measuring them a century ago.[17]

The tracing of consequences is perhaps the most sophisticated of the methods of studying causation, and the most seldom used. In some respects it is also the most dangerous, because it is impossible to know when enough consequences have been found to confirm the theory or that each of the consequences found may not be the result of some other factor. The rain in the Sahara might have been caused by a shifting of wind currents over the area. The thinness of the Arctic ice cap may not be significant: measurements began only a few decades ago. More snow might have accumulated in the Northern Hemisphere simply because the weather has turned colder. And so on. But all methods for studying causation entail some risk, and occasional risk does not negate their occasional usefulness.

The ideal, of course, would be to be able to use the Canons to demonstrate that a cause is operating, and then use the methods of association to explain why it operates. We can seldom expect the ideal, but we ought to inquire into the causes of the problems we face and to note when a speaker does or does not analyze these causes. We also ought to encourage and support speakers who make intelligent causal analyses and reject those who do not.

Questions for Understanding, Discussion, and Research

1. Give examples of cases from the past and in the present in which people misunderstood the causes of one or more of their major problems.
2. Using Mill's Canons, what data would you need to discern the causes of the following: laziness, good teaching, self-actualization,

---

[17] See for example, Betty Friedan, "The Coming Ice Age," *Harper's* (December 1958), 39–45, which describes the research of Maurice Ewing and William Donn.

bravery, open-mindedness, racism, intelligence, happiness, longevity, cynicism, radicalism, and the opposite of each.

3. Mill's Canons are most useful in locating a single factor; that single factor, however, need not be the total cause, nor the most important cause of the problem. The Canons can locate a partial cause of a problem. Show how the Canons might be used to locate a part of the causes of any of the problems described on p. 220.

4. Think of a problem that you confront. How can you discover its causes?

5. How can one be certain that connectional causal statements are accurate?

6. How can our society increase the amount and quality of causal thinking in our communication?

7. What factors account for the virtual absence of causal thinking in our communications?

Speech Assignment: see pp. 219–221.

5

Solutions

The horse collar may not seem important, but its invention may rank with that of the wheel. Before the invention of the horse collar (about the tenth century), animals pulled wagons and plows by means of a yoke around their necks. If animals pulled too hard, or too heavy a load, they choked; hence, animals could pull only about two or three times their weight. But after the invention of the collar, the strain fell on the animal's shoulders instead of its neck, so that it could pull up to fifteen times its weight.

With the expenditure of little more animal power and no more human power, man had seven times as much energy as he had before, or, ultimately, access to seven times as much wealth. A farmer could plow more land, mill more grain, and transport heavier loads to market. Animals now more than paid for their keep; food surpluses became available; people could eat better and be stronger. Life as a whole became more rewarding than it had been for centuries.

The prosperity that began in the tenth and eleventh centuries helped end both the poverty and the desolation of the Dark Ages in Europe, and ushered in the far richer civilization of the medieval period. Even so seemingly simple a solution as the invention of the horse collar may help to bring about new bursts of energy and confidence, and enable life to begin at a higher level. Since solutions are so important, speakers, analysts of communication, and students of communication must develop a rhetoric of solutions.

Solutions for Survival

The failure to find solutions to problems means that life continues to be plagued by the same problems, the same miseries, and the same limited possibilities. In our own time, some rewarding breakthroughs have been made. In the United States, for example, although the work-day has been reduced by one third since 1900, production has more than doubled. Man lives twice as long as he did two hundred years ago. The first airplane flew only about seventy years ago; now it is the chief means of transportation over long distances, and spaceships travel to other planets. Our successes have given us hope.

But we have fewer grounds for optimism on the great problems that have brought about the decline and destruction of every previous civilization; on these problems, we have made surprisingly little progress. Even though most American homes have electricity and television sets, we have not adopted palatable solutions to the age-old problems of war, poverty, caste, and tyranny, although we have made at least tem-porary gains over the problem of disease. Our culture today is threat-ened by failure to find solutions to these most crucial problems. We must not let our technical progress obscure our failure to eliminate the classi-cal problems. If war, poverty, caste, tyranny, and disease are not solved, it will console us little that (provided we do not have a power shortage) we sit in our air-conditioned living rooms—proud that we have devel-oped gadgets for heating and cooling, for spraying and painting, for cut-ting and welding, for filming and televising the final cataclysm.

Poverty is increasing rapidly in the world, and although we are prosperous, we must not forget that we are grossly outnumbered by those who are not: each year, starvation turns more and more people into living skeletons, and estimates suggest that 1 million a day are dy-ing now. Caste, prejudice, and racism are rampant, so that goods and power are distributed not on the basis of merit or justice but on the basis of irrelevant criteria. The twentieth century is the most tyrannous in history, and nothing suggests that the twenty-first will be better. Though a few nations have reduced the incidence of disease, in most of the world, life expectancy is not over forty years, and the World Health Organization estimates that one person in three needs medical care. If we are to survive, we must give more intelligent thought to solutions than have any people before us. Without solutions to our major problems, we will perish; and, perhaps, if like others before us, we do not solve the problems of our people, we may deserve obliteration.

All problems are like diseases in that they cause pain, drain en-ergy, and eventually destroy. The most important reason for studying solutions is that each unsolved problem represents a lethal danger. Survival depends on solution.

THE ROLE OF RHETORIC

John Dewey, America's most influential educational philosopher, is credited with the discovery that thinking does not begin until one is confronted with a problem. Dewey did not take into account, however, that many people will not work with a problem nor recognize it as such until they believe it can be solved. Humanity often merely resigns itself to its fate, not perceiving its present existence as something that can be changed—not, in other words, perceiving its present state as a problem to be solved.

American efforts to increase agricultural production in Greece and Turkey illustrate the way solutions enable people to recognize a problem and respond to it. During recent centuries, Greek farms yielded so poorly as to offer only a bare subsistence. Although these farms were small, with proper care their yield could be multiplied. The first step was to persuade a few of the farmers to go through their fields removing the abundant stones and rocks. This partial solution to unproductivity was usually met with derision by the other farmers, but the American advisors were able to persuade one or two farmers in a given area to follow their advice, and thus to offer these farms as examples. When the rocks were removed, the farmers were persuaded to abandon the custom of sowing seed left over from the previous harvest, to purchase the best hybrid seed, and use appropriate fertilizers. The yield from these farms increased nearly five-fold. The neighboring farmers were impressed, and began to perceive that low yield was a problem open to solution.

Since solutions give hope that life need not be accepted fatalistically, they stimulate not only thinking but also argument, debate, and discussion. In the words of the Declaration of Independence, men are more likely "to suffer, while evils are sufferable, than to right themselves by abolishing the forms to which they are accustomed." Poverty, for example, is as old as man, but never before has the problem been so much discussed. Even popular magazines take note of the problem. A few years ago, John Kenneth Galbraith's *The Affluent Society* even became a best seller. Editorials, film documentaries, and panel discussions by economists deal daily with the problem of poverty. Why so much discussion of poverty? Poverty in our country is not as bad as it was a hundred years ago, but poverty is discussed because the solutions within our grasp help us to recognize the problem and give us the confidence that poverty is not an eternal fact of life but a problem that can be solved.

Solutions are of special importance to students of communication because they generate discussion and argument. But solutions generate discussion not only because they bring hope but also because they represent a demand for action. If a bill establishing a negative income tax is proposed in Congress, it must be passed or rejected. A problem can be ignored, but a proposed solution calls for a vote, and thus a bill represents a point of decision and requires action. Since solutions require some sort of decision, they often give rise to more thinking, more speaking, and more action than perception of the problems themselves can.

Solutions are important also because they are more central to speaking than are either values or problems. To solve a problem we do not need to agree on the nature of the problem or the values that lead us to define it as a problem. We need only agree on the solution. We may agree, for example, on sending fertilizer to a foreign country. Some who agree may be concerned with the problem of poverty abroad. Some who agree may hope thereby to stimulate markets for American products. Others will agree because they believe international trade binds nations together, and furnishes more employment at home. Senator X may support the fertilizer bill in order to win Senator Y's vote for another bill. Whatever the reason, solutions become the center of argument, the focus of debate.

Although solutions have a central place in the theory of rhetoric and communication, nearly all rhetorical works have neglected the rhetoric of solutions. Now we must inquire into the rhetoric of solutions with special vigor.

THE CREATION OF NEW PROBLEMS

"The cause of our problems," said Eric Sevareid, "is our solutions." This remark, interpreted at the simplest level, means that our solutions are so unintelligent that they intensify our problems. But, on the other hand, the sentence may have a deeper meaning. In a progressive culture, one's solutions are—and should be—the cause of one's problems: a culture developing as intelligently as possible will invent solutions, but these same solutions, though they may obliterate or reduce the problems for which they were designed, will raise new problems.

One problem, for example, that our country faced during most of its history (except during periodic depressions) was a shortage of labor. We sometimes "solved" that problem stupidly and cruelly, as when we imported African slaves to work on the cotton plantations and Chinese to build the railroads. Sometimes, however, we responded brilliantly, as when we devised machinery that made it possible to produce more goods at lower cost. But that solution brought with it new problems. A man's labor now could produce more goods and was therefore worth more: any work stoppage added to the cost of production by idling expensive machines. Labor became a power in the economy and in politics. Strikes, organizational struggles, and jurisdictional disputes stemmed in part from the brilliant attempt to invent machinery to do the work of men. Moreover, the mass production made possible by the machines requires mass consumption, and intensified the evil of unemployment and depressions. Thus, even the most brilliant solution often leads to new problems.

Arnold Toynbee insists that the process by which man finds a solution to a problem, and the solution itself begets new problems, is the mechanism of progress.[1]

At any rate, to seek a world without problems or to expect to evolve perfect solutions is not realistic. What we can seek, however, is the kind of world in which our problems can be changed from terrifying to tolerable, and perhaps from tolerable to stimulating. Thus the test of a solution is not whether it raises new problems (for it will), but whether or not we prefer to live with the old problems or the new. Strikes and boycotts are sad problems, but they are preferable to the problems of living in a subsistence economy.

Of course, industrialization may prove a curse. At this writing, 102 giant corporations now control 48 per cent of the assets of manufacturing firms in the United States, and take 53 per cent of the profits. The more powerful a corporation (with some notable exceptions) the more it tends to control government, to avoid taxation, to pollute the environment, to be able to operate beyond the law, and to be out of touch with human needs. But the point is that the success of a solution lies in the extent to which the new problems are more tolerable than the old. The poverty that afflicted the world before industrialization was a greater problem than the problems wrought by industrialization, at least so far.

THE ROLE OF CREATIVITY

To discover or invent solutions requires a certain amount of creativity. All of us must invent solutions to our personal problems, and to the problems posed by our own specialties. Perhaps a few geniuses will invent improved solutions to the great classical problems, but one cannot devise "six steps to creativity," or "ten ways to develop inventive ability." The product of creativity, by definition, is that which is unexpected. The unexpected cannot be commanded by a few rules; the surprising will not appear by mere application of simplistic directions.

[1] Arnold Toynbee, *A Study of History*, abr. by D. C. Somervell (New York: Oxford University Press, 1947), Vol. I, pp. 199–208. The problems brought about by a solution are usually, Toynbee insists, internal.

Moreover, some distrust for the supposed "rules of creativity" found by modern research is warranted, for the concern of much of the research is with puzzle solving rather than problem solving. The creativity required to solve puzzles is different from that required to solve problems. Nevertheless, some sensible advice can be given about the kinds of procedures that seem to reduce creativity and those that increase it.

Although most solutions stimulate thinking, probably the best thinkers remain "problem-minded" rather than "solution-minded." To remain problem-minded, one must see the significance of the problem in new ways. One can try to imagine its effect on different kinds of people in different times and places. One can try to represent the problem and its different aspects in diagrams, graphs, cartoons, pictures, and abstractions. One can search for additional causes of the problem, some of which might suggest an appropriate solution. One can reflect on the problem, letting thoughts go where they will. Even after one finds a solution, one can use the device of forcing oneself to develop a second or third solution.[2] Probably the best advice is to stay away from solutions for a while and to immerse oneself in the problem instead.

Categories of Solutions

FALSE SOLUTIONS

Most cultures fail to solve a great problem because they actively resist solutions. When an establishment or a "dominant minority," controls most of a culture's wealth and power, it fancies it would be harmed if the poor were led out of poverty, if the caste system were fractured, if wars were prevented, or if tyranny were ended. In most civilizations, this dominant minority has been very small: in ancient Egypt, for example, it consisted of less than 0.1 per cent of the society. Thus, cultures fail to solve problems because those who suffer often have little power to solve them, and those who have power do not suffer, and hence do not recognize the urgency of the problems.

In the decline of Rome, we can see reflected the processes of false solutions. Rome did not permit discussion of the problem of poverty. No one spoke of the poverty in Rome; no one suggested solutions to it. Instead, the attention of the masses was turned to bread and circuses. The poverty grew into what Arnold Toynbee describes as an "enor-

---

[2] See Ray Hyman and Barry Anderson, "Solving Problems," *The Creativity Review,* n.d. (Precept IV, P. 3). The authors insist that forcing oneself to look for a second solution increases the number of creative solutions. The idea fits well with the notion that good solutions are repressed and must be forced into consciousness.

mity," a massive tumor that drained more and more energy from the culture until the culture was destroyed.

Students of communication must recognize the mechanism of false solutions, which generally manifest themselves in three stages: first, the establishment refuses to permit solution of a problem and may prevent discussion of it; second, the problem grows into an enormity; finally, the culture is wracked by revolution or fades into oblivion. Doubtless, the ancient Romans who worshipped Rome thought themselves patriotic. But had their patriotism taken another form—had they recognized the problems of their people and worked toward a solution—Rome might have survived.

Some of the same techniques are at work in our own country. Perhaps the reader could supply his own illustrations of repressed problems that have led to weakness or revolution. An example of diversion from a problem happened when Ralph Nader demonstrated that automobile accidents were caused, in part, by the unsafe design of automobiles.[3] The manufacturers themselves are at fault; although they can design a safer car, they do not. When Nader's book became popular, General Motors produced a film on auto safety that stressed two causes of accidents: the individual driver and the faulty construction of roads. The film, obviously, was an attempt to divert attention from auto construction as a cause of accidents. In a less successful attempt at diversion, General Motors hired detectives to follow Nader in the hope of discovering something about his character or habits that could be used to discredit him. The detectives found nothing; the plan was exposed; Nader was awarded damages of over $450,000.

But one can find the same techniques of repression and diversion in higher places and on problems even more important than auto safety. The high price of fuel and the energy crisis, at this writing seem at least partly "arranged" by the big companies. Whenever one finds such false solutions, he performs a significant service to his country by exposing them, for repression and diversion reduce our chances for survival.

Workable solutions to the classical problems are possible, and many already have been devised. The world, for the first time, probably could end—or at least greatly reduce—each of these ancient dangers. Thus we

[3] See *Unsafe at Any Speed* (New York: Pocket Books, 1965), rev. ed., 1971. Nader points out that the National Safety Council is controlled by the auto manufacturers in Detroit, as is the American Automobile Association. These two guardians of public safety never discuss the possibility that many accidents are caused by something other than driver error or poor road design, thus diverting attention from one major solution to accidents.

need not create solutions to these problems. We will, however, be responsible for selecting those solutions that will produce the best results. We will need to know something about the kinds of solutions that are possible and available, and some of the characteristics of each.

Symptomatic Solutions

We can treat a problem by locating and eliminating its cause, or we can simply treat the symptoms of the problem. Neither solution is inherently superior; each kind has advantages and dangers. We might devise symptomatic solutions and causal solutions for any of the major problems that confront us today. We might treat the problem of crime symptomatically by deciding to increase the amount of light on streets in high-crime areas. Or, if we realized that one reason for recidivism is that former convicts have difficulty finding jobs, we might try to reduce crime by assuring that every man in prison learned a trade and had a job on his release. In this case, we would be dealing with the causes of crime and reducing or removing them. Thus, many problems can be treated either symptomatically or causally, and sometimes one way is best and sometimes the other. Regrettably, we usually treat crime only symptomatically: we put better locks on doors, turn on more lights, hire more policemen, and install burglar alarms. Seldom do we inquire more deeply into the problem.

How could one treat the problem of poverty symptomatically, and causally? Try to devise some solutions of each kind. They need not be brilliant; they need only show that you understand the distinction between them. Among the symptomatic solutions are relief or doles, a guaranteed annual wage, unemployment insurance, Medicare, and Social Security. Among the causal solutions are the redistribution of wealth, and the increasing of the purchasing power of the unaffluent majority (which results in the need for more goods, which raises employment, and so on).

How could we treat the danger of Communist expansion? (Try to answer the question before reading further.) The most certain way to separate causal from symptomatic solutions is to ask, "What are the causes of Communist expansion?" After answering the question, we more easily may devise causal solutions. Clearly, one of the causes of Communist expansion has been widespread poverty: Communism seems to have little appeal in times and places in which people are prosperous. Therefore, causal solutions to the expansion of Communism would strengthen the economy of poorer countries. Symptomatic solutions, however, would usually be attempted *after* the fact: the United States might invade if a Communist takeover seemed likely, or it might withdraw recognition or refuse to trade with a country that had embraced Communism.

Sometimes, a solution may be difficult to classify or may be partly symptomatic and partly causal. For example, a dole is only partly symptomatic: it is applied after unemployment occurs, but it does slightly increase the purchasing power of the poor. Nevertheless, many solutions are clearly symptomatic or clearly causal.

ADVANTAGES OF SYMPTOMATIC SOLUTIONS

Symptomatic solutions usually can be applied more easily and quickly than causal solutions. To discover why one has a headache requires testing dozens of hypotheses, and the headache would probably have disappeared long before all the hypotheses were investigated. Taking aspirin is faster, even though it treats the symptoms in ways we do not still completely understand. When a little boy plays an irritating prank, a parent may administer quick symptomatic treatment to the seat of his pants. But if the child has a habit of playing with matches, symptomatic treatment (though it probably would work) might be less appropriate than an attempt to discover the cause of the child's desire to light matches. If the child's playing with matches were found to be a symptom of his hostility toward his parents, treatment might entail psychoanalysis of the child *and* the parents. Causal treatment is more often much slower than symptomatic treatment, and sometimes impossible.

The simplicity of treatment characteristic of most symptomatic solutions leads some to attack them as superficial and ineffective. If, for example, more light is introduced into a high-crime area, some argue, the would-be criminal merely moves to a darker area; if more policemen are put on subways, then muggers move to buses. Are symptomatic treatments as worthless as they are easy to apply?

A careful study of the question fails to support the idea that if the symptoms are reduced in one area—such as crime in the subways or in a lighted area—these symptoms necessarily erupt in another—on buses or in darker areas.

We must analyze the value of shortcuts more precisely: Some shortcuts "work" for society in . . . that they reduce the societal cost of the problem . . . but not the personal costs. For instance, between 1955 and 1965 the number of patients in state mental hospitals declined from 558,922 to 475,761. This decline . . . [resulted from] massive use of tranquilizing drugs. . . . [S]ociety's costs are much reduced (the cost of maintaining a patient in a state mental hospital is about seven dollars a day; on drugs, an average of fifteen cents) . . . . But, obviously, heavily drugged people are not effective members of society or happy human beings. Still, a device or procedure which offers a reduction of costs on one dimension . . . without *increasing* the costs on others, despite the fact that it does not "solve" the problem, is truly useful—almost by definition. . . . *Often our society seems to be "choosing" not between symptomatic . . . treatment and "cause" . . . treatment, but between treatment of symptoms and no treatment at all.* Hence, in the examination of the values of many short-cuts, the ultimate question must be: is the society ready or able to provide full-scale treatment of the problem. . . ?[4]

Moreover, the cost of certain symptomatic treatments is so low that these treatments can hardly be ignored: the cost of seat belts in auto-mobiles is approximately $87 per death averted. But the cost of a causal approach to the problem (driver education, for example) is $88,000 per death averted.[5]

Gun control is a simple symptomatic treatment for crime, yet its simplicity should recommend it, particularly because of the peculiar nature of most murders:

> Out of 9,250 so-called "willful" killings which took place in the United States in 1964, only 1,350 were committed in the course of committing some other crime such as robbery or a sex offense. The others, 80.1 per cent, were committed among friends, neighbors and one's family, by normally law-abiding citizens, in the course of a quarrel or following one. Obviously, if deadly weapons were harder to come by, the chances of these quarrels being "cooled out," or of a third party intervening, would have been much higher and most fatalities would have been averted.[6]

The possibility of symptomatic solutions should not be discarded; rather, the quickness and ease with which they may be applied should lead us to consider them with great care. Perhaps, instead of abolishing symptomatic treatment, we should consider applying it more often.

In the late eighteenth century, Dr. Edward Jenner discovered the vaccine that prevents smallpox. He was unable to identify the cause of smallpox (viruses were not discovered until the twentieth century), yet we were able to free ourselves of the plague of smallpox as early as 1800. Intelligent treatments can be devised, even though we may not know—or may not agree about—the cause of a problem.

During the Great Depression, many economists seemed uncertain

[4] See Amitai Etzioni, "Shortcuts to Social Change?" *The Public Interest*, Number 12 (Summer 1968), 47–50. Copyright © by National Affairs, Inc., 1968. By permission of the author. The author points out that despite the sharpness of the attacks on symptomatic shortcuts, there is not enough information available to *know* whether or not certain widely recommended shortcuts work or not. The lack of information, however, does not seem to have reduced the severity of the disputation on the matter.
[5] Ibid., pp. 49–50.
[6] Ibid., p. 51.

of the causes, and many of those who were sure disagreed. Nevertheless, the New Deal was able to propose a number of symptomatic solutions, effective enough so that no subsequent administration has effected their repeal. They are now probably a permanent part of our economic situation.

Thus, symptomatic solutions often can be applied quickly and easily, whether or not we understand the causes of a problem. Nevertheless, such symptomatic treatment often has disadvantages that should be carefully considered.

Disadvantages of Symptomatic Treatment. One can imagine a world burdened with problems—economic, political, personal—but inhabited by people who did not feel the weight of these problems because they were given huge doses of tranquilizers. Such symptomatic treatment would not remove problems but would, rather, be a source of danger. Symptoms warn us of approaching danger, and if we mask the symptoms, we fail to see the danger. In a sense, the problems of the Third Reich were masked by the Nazis' parades, their use of the Jews as scapegoats, and later by their spectacular military victories during the early part of World War II. When problems are masked, the condition worsens. A society may spend so much energy repressing instead of solving problems that not enough is left to meet an emergency, be it a barbarian invasion, a sudden plague, unexpected famine, or the slow depletion of agricultural or natural resources. A vicious cycle results: a symptomatically treated problem requires increasing repression so that energy could have been used for growth is used up. Meantime the problem may worsen, requiring that more energy be wasted in repression and in paving the way for final breakdown. All civilizations have spent too much energy ignoring symptoms and too little in solving problems.

For example, we now understand some of the economic and sociological causes of crime, but our approach remains symptomatic: we increase police forces and police power; we increase penalties; we appoint more judges and create more courts. Seldom, however, do we embark on programs that attack the causes of crime. In the meantime, crime seems to increase and to require more repressive measures, so that we are drawn into a vicious cycle.

We often have treated our economic problems symptomatically, providing unemployment benefits, Social Security, health insurance for the aged and the destitute, and welfare. Nevertheless, the real economic problem—that too many of our people have neither economic power nor economic reserves—seems to elude us. But who hears of plans to boost the purchasing power of the majority of Americans or plans to increase the wealth of most of our people? Fortunately, the growth of our wealth (until recently) has slowly reduced the relative number who suffer poverty, but we should try to devise ways to increase their wealth and to make their existence more secure.

Some argue that symptoms serve as stimulants to achievement. Poverty does serve as a stimulant to some, but it weakens and destroys many more. If poverty is as stimulating as some rich people say it is, why don't *they* take what they have, give it to the poor, and receive the benefit of this stimulation?

Nevertheless, symptoms may act as incentives, provided they are not so intense as to weaken those who suffer. And symptoms do have a value in that they warn of a condition that is dangerous.

Of course, symptomatic solutions sometimes gratify a desire for vengeance. When a man commits a crime, it seems appropriate that he should suffer for it. We desire to make those suffer who have made us and others suffer, and we lose sight of what should be our real goals. Does the traffic policeman who orders you to draw over to the curb seem intent on solving the problem of traffic safety? Or does he seem to be acting out his desire for vengeance on a world that assigns him a job that is either dull or dangerous and rewards him with only a modest salary? One hardly blames him for his feelings, yet he does not seem to be problem-oriented in his address to you—any more than you may seem concerned with your own safety, or that of others. Like the parent who has had a frustrating day at the office and overpunishes his child for committing a minor offense, we have masked our desire for vengeance behind our approach to several problems. The desire for vengeance will almost always blind one to the best solutions.

Therefore, because symptomatic solutions often ignore the causes of the problem, and permit those causes to increase, and because such symptoms sometimes coincide with an unconscious desire for vengeance, we should try to see if there are not more intelligent solutions available.

CAUSAL SOLUTIONS

Sometimes no solution can be developed until the causes of the problem are discovered. In India, where the entire Gross National Product of the country is only $70 per year per person, starvation has many causes. One recently discovered cause, however, may lead to the most productive solution yet devised. Recall from Chapter 4, the chain of causes that produces drought in the Rajputana Desert of India:

1. Over India, suspended particles—which exist in greater quantities than over the smokiest, dirtiest cities in the world—come from the deserts in India.
2. Such suspended particles cause the air to settle.
3. As air settles, it warms up, and can hold more moisture.

4. The more moisture air holds, the less rain falls, and the dryer the land becomes.

Thus a major cause of drought in India is the ever-present dust from the deserts. Nevertheless, the air above India's deserts contains more moisture than exists above the tropical rain forests of Panama, the Amazon Valley, or the Congo. That water-laden air, however, produces no rain. How can one arrive at a possible solution if one has this information?

Suppose one could persuade grass to grow on the surface. . . . Grass seed could be planted over the whole area (let's say spread by an airplane), and after the rains the grass would take root and anchor the soil. With the soil anchored, there would be less dust. With less dust in the air, the air would sink less. With less sinking, there would be more rain. More rain would support more grass and more grass would hold down more dust.[7]

But sowing grass over the whole of India would be expensive, even though it might be an excellent investment. There is a less expensive way to utilize our knowledge of causes and produce a workable solution:

The grass alone won't do the trick unless man is willing to cooperate. We learned that much in Wisconsin, on our dairy cattle farms. When we let the cows range freely in the pastures, they wore the ground to such a degree that the forage thinned. Now we pen the cattle and carry the hay to them.

When I visited India the last time in January 1967, I noticed that a group of Indian scientists were trying a variation of our Wisconsin philosophy. A few miles outside the city of Jodhpur, they built a fence around forty acres of the Rajputana Desert. The wire of which the fence was made was strong enough to hold off goats and men. Within the enclosure, nothing was planted. The fenced earth was not even watered. Yet, at the end of two years, the experimenters . . . found wild grass growing all over their forty-acre plot. Seeds carried by the wind had taken root and, in the absence of eroding feet, put forth progeny that not only survived but multiplied.[8]

Before 1500 B.C., this desert area was a vast agricultural empire. But probably overcultivation and overgrazing turned the land into a desert. If man has inadvertently changed the climate in this once-productive land, man should think of changing it back. Solutions to the drought that afflicts much of India can be found when we understand the causes and let them direct us to possible solutions.

Even when we identify the cause of a problem, of course, we cannot always solve the problem causally. But *we cannot make the decision to use causal solutions or to use symptomatic solutions until we have first studied the problem to discover its causes.*

---

[7] See the description of these conditions reported by Reid A. Bryson in "The Research Frontier," *Saturday Review* (April 1, 1967), 52–55.
[8] Ibid., p. 55.

NARROW-SPECTRUM AND BROAD-SPECTRUM SOLUTIONS

The concepts of narrow-spectrum solutions and broad-spectrum solutions are based on an analogy with medicine. Some medicines will attack only one disease; measles vaccine, for example, will prevent only measles. Others attack a broad spectrum of bacteria: penicillin can deal with streptococcus, pneumococcus, staphylococcus, and other bacteria. Just so, some solutions may attack only one problem, whereas others may attack many. Just as all cultures have generally depended too heavily on symptomatic solutions, so have they tended to prefer the narrow-spectrum solution and failed to consider the possibilities of using broad-spectrum solutions. Generally, a governing body will enact solutions that are designed to deal with a particular problem considered in isolation, as when, to prevent crime, they increase penalties. This symptomatic, narrow-spectrum solution can solve—if anything—only the particular offense in question. Yet legislatures enact separate laws to deal with crime, with poverty, with civil unrest, with sanitation and disease, without ever realizing that if we devised a genuinely good solution to poverty, that solution would also take care of many of the manifestations of disease, civil unrest, and perhaps even low-grade education, and low productivity.

In the *Republic,* Plato comes to grips with two problems that face our own culture: How may we keep the ignorant from making laws? How can we keep selfish interests from ruling a nation? The questions are good ones, for ignorant rulers cannot arrive at informed answers and can be easily deceived into supporting programs that are not in the best interests of the nation. Selfish rulers will use the resources of the nation to their own advantage. Though Plato's questions were good, his solution was poor. For both problems, he recommended what may seem, at first, to be a broad-spectrum solution, but which turns out to be a relatively narrow-spectrum solution: He recommended that only those who have been educated in a long and arduous process, lasting perhaps forty years, should be permitted to rule. These philosopher-kings, however, would not be permitted to own property, and therefore would not profit from their power. Their long education would instill in them a certain sense of values, so they would be above graft and have little love of material goods. (How candidates would be selected is not made entirely clear.) In this way Plato would end the danger of rulers who were either ignorant or selfish.

Democracies, as poorly as they work, have attempted a more ambitious, broad-spectrum solution: they have decided to solve the problem of keeping the ignorant out of government by attempting to educate the entire citizenry. When all are educated, when information is freely published and freely discussed, then the ignorant cannot rule. The solution is so ambitious as to be almost unworkable, yet with the gradual extension of education, with enormous pressure to improve its quality and relevance, with the increase in the publication of information and the increase in literacy, there is hope. The immensity of the solution precludes "instant" success, but its broad-spectrum possibilities make it still the best—and perhaps the only really workable—solution to the problem of preventing the ignorant from dominating government.

Universal education can attack other problems as well. It can help to give people a knowledge of their problems and help to suggest solutions; it can refine one's sense of values; it can increase the productivity of a nation. It can do so much that no man yet has described the possibilities inherent in universal education. The present state of education falls far short of the goal; nevertheless, one can respect the ambitious quality of this broad-spectrum solution.

Democratic states have been working toward another broad-spectrum solution to the problem of keeping the selfish from ruling. We can keep special interests from dominating a government by giving each man one, and only one, vote. This kind of equality at the ballot box has never been completely achieved in our country, but the idea is there, however shamefully slow we have been in applying it. When each man has equal power, the rule of special interests ends, and, at the same time, this equality encourages equal opportunity to secure such desirable ends as a broader economic base for prosperity, and protection for consumers.

One of the most striking attempts to use a broad-spectrum solution was the attempt of the people of Manus Island to restructure their culture.[9] The insecurity of the people of Manus was illustrated by their homes, which were built on piers that jutted into the island lagoon; in such a home, a family considered itself relatively safe from outsiders, who were considered untrustworthy and threatening. Life seemed to offer little to the young adults, and most of them left the island as soon as they were old enough. But after World War II, a young citizen of Manus who had caught the idea of democracy from his association with American soldiers during the war, began urging the people of Manus to overthrow their old way of life and redesign all their institutions—religion, education, economy, and political system—to meet one supreme value: brotherhood. For people to effect so thorough a revolution—and to have it work—is surprising and heartening.

Although broad-spectrum solutions are seldom used, they should be carefully considered in times when so much is tragic and unjust. Al-

---

[9] Margaret Mead, *New Lives for Old* (New York: William Morrow & Co., Inc., 1956).

though legislatures, city councils, and school boards are inclined to narrow-spectrum solutions, philosophers, theologians, and a very few great statesmen recommend broad-spectrum solutions. We should pay more attention to the latter than we have.[10]

INDIVIDUAL AND GROUP SOLUTIONS

Two opposing theories, each partly true, exist in contemporary psychology and sociology: the theory of individual determinism and the theory of group determinism. The former, the older, asserts that the properties of groups depend on the kinds of individual who joins the group: the Ku Klux Klan is intolerant because it consists of intolerant individuals; the United States Marines are brave because brave individuals join. According to this theory, to reduce crime, we must work with individuals who are apt to commit crimes or who have committed crimes, training them to earn an honest livelihood and helping them to develop a sense of values that will deter them from dishonest living. To improve our country, we must improve the morality of the individuals in the country; when individual morality is improved, then the nation itself will show improvement. To create a peaceful world, individuals must become peaceful. And so on.

According to the theory of group determinism, promulgated early in this century by George Herbert Mead, individuals acquire certain characteristics when they become members of certain groups. Thus, a person who joins the Ku Klux Klan tends to become less tolerant: if he is not to suffer severe social disapproval, he must display the attitudes of the group; when he attends group meetings, he is exposed to programs, speakers, and ideas that reinforce his intolerance. He is *expected* to be intolerant, and this expectation tends to produce intolerance. When a member reflects the aims of the organization, he is rewarded; when he does not, the organization punishes him. Hence, groups we join mold us in ways of which we are not always aware.

To improve the quality of students in a class, according to the theory of individual determinism, the poor students should be replaced by better students. The newer theory suggests that if one merely acts as

---

[10] At least one analysis of narrow- and broad-spectrum solutions, which the authors term *incremental* and *large change*, respectively, endorses only small changes: Societies, it goes without saying, are complex structures that can avoid dissolution of intolerable dislocation only by meeting certain preconditions, among them that certain kinds of changes are admissible only if they occur slowly. Political democracy is often greatly endangered by nonincremental change, which it can accommodate only in certain limited circumstances. David Braybrooke and Charles E. Lindbloom, *A Strategy of Decision* (New York: Free Press and Macmillan Publishing Co., Inc., 1963), p. 73. Their analysis, however, is poorly supported.

if the students were better, they will become so. Consider the experience reported in *Pygmalion in the Classroom*.[11] Two experimenters represented themselves to various high schools as coming from Harvard University with a new kind of psychological test capable of determining which students were "late bloomers." They tested the students, and those students declared to be "late bloomers" were put in a separate class. Results at the end of the year clearly showed that the "late blooming" students did much better than the slower students.

In truth, however, *there is no such test,* nor can one be devised. The experimenters had arbitrarily designated some students as "late bloomers." Nevertheless, when a teacher merely thought a student was about to do better, that student made significant gains. The mere fact that the teacher thought, however wrongly, that students were "smart" or "dumb" influenced the success of the child. Thus, the teacher's perception of the nature of the group changed the group.

Some of the implications of group determinism are undoubtedly interesting and worthy of more extensive experimentation.

We can apply group determinism in many ways: To change a juvenile delinquent, we might discourage delinquency and encourage socially acceptable behavior by putting the juvenile in athletic groups, Boy's Clubs, and other activity groups that will change his way of thinking and reacting. To create people who are peaceful, we might construct a world government under which no country would have a standing army or weapons other than those necessary for police protection; when no country has either an army or the vast munitions necessary to fight a war, war cannot exist. To change individuals, perhaps we must change society first.

Group determinism and individual determinism both have merits and limitations. The problem is not to decide which is true but, rather, to decide which is more useful in a given situation. Most important, we may be able to develop more solutions to problems if we use both kinds of solution consciously rather than we could when, unconsciously, we were restricted to only one. Finally, we should recognize that in most cultures, group determinism is at work making people Romans or Greeks or Chinese or Aztecs, whereas the power structure of these cultures consciously uses only the individual approach to problems, holding individuals responsible for crime, for bravery, and for invention. Perhaps it is time we tried to exploit the possibilities of reconstructing individuals by changing the groups to which they belong, and use group determinism to increase creativity, to ensure problem solving, to produce

---

[11] Robert Rosenthal and Lenore Jacobson (New York: Holt, Rinehart and Winston, Inc., 1968) . See esp. Chap. 2.

more gifted children, and to reduce the fear, distrust, and hate that plague all peoples.

PREVENTION VERSUS TREATMENT

States and nations usually confine their solutions to those that treat already dangerous situations. Nevertheless, we ought to be on the outlook for solutions that will prevent such situations from arising. We deal largely with acutely intolerable situations, partly because citizens tend to distrust government. We have never learned that government, controlled by people who are protected by bills of rights, can act in a preventive way. Many times in our history, we could see problems developing, yet did nothing to deal with them. At any time since 1910, we could have predicted that our cities would suffer because of inadequate and dangerous housing, archaic transportation systems, and unwholesome environments. Yet today, as the cities sicken, we do little to treat the problem, even as we did less to prevent it.

Our distrust of government is probably sound, but it must not keep us from solving problems before they become so large as to defy solution. Almost any problem could have been solved when it was small. We must form the habit of looking toward the future and dealing with problems that we know will arise rather than dealing only with those that already seem unmanageable.

"VILLAIN" AND "SOCIAL FORCES" SOLUTIONS

Sometimes a single person or single group seems to be a major source of harmful problems. Certainly Hitler, who led millions to their deaths in World War II, was such a source, as was Stalin, who starved to death millions of his own countrymen and terrorized the rest. There are villains in history, and the world is better when they are removed.

Nevertheless, we tend to think of the world's problems as if villains were the *only* cause, and to forget the social conditions that made possible the villain's rise to power. If Hitler had been assassinated in 1938, it is altogether likely he would have been replaced by a person manifesting the same anti-Semitism, the same rabid desire for conquest, the same tendency toward tyranny; his replacement could have been a person of even greater depravity for, hard as it is to imagine, some of his henchmen were even worse than Hitler himself. If Stalin had been assassinated in 1925, he would probably have been replaced by someone who also believed in a stern, narrowly nationalistic dictatorship and who was equally bent on the quick collectivization of farms, the development of large armies, and the repression of dissent.

Villains indeed exist, but the conditions that put the villain in the seat of power are the prerequisites for the evil he works. Without hopelessness, poverty, apathy, and unsolved problems, villains could not take over. If we are to prevent the rise of greater villains in the future, we must concern ourselves with solving problems, for the surest way to be safe from such men is to reduce or eliminate poverty, to prevent wars, to smash systems of caste and prejudice, and to extend freedom. But to see all problems as residing in a villain has only limited usefulness; we must find solutions that prevent or remove the social forces on which the villain capitalizes.

NEWER AND OLDER SOLUTIONS

Mankind has frequently used symptomatic, narrow-spectrum, individual, "treatment," and "villain" solutions. Civilizations have not consciously tried causal, broad-spectrum, group, or "social forces" solutions. If we behave as have previous cultures, we will certainly be destroyed. We must break with history and try some of the newer solutions.

The Rhetoric of Solutions

STRATEGY

Even though solutions tend to generate discussion of a problem, one should generally not present a solution without first vividly describing the problem. The apathetic or uninformed members of the audience will not be interested in a solution unless they are convinced one is needed. If, on the other hand, they are fully aware of the problem, then one may proceed directly to consideration of solutions. Even then, however, a few powerful examples of the problem and some well-chosen statistics can increase the audience's desire to find a solution. Therefore, a speaker can raise attention and interest if he begins with a strong, though brief, depiction of the problem.

CLARITY

Once the audience is convinced that a problem exists, the speaker must present the solution clearly. Some exceptions to the desirability of clear presentation of solutions, however, should be noted. In some political campaigns, for example, candidates prefer to remain vague. In 1960, when John F. Kennedy campaigned against Richard M. Nixon, he did not present either lengthy or detailed solutions to the problems the nation faced. Rather, he preferred to have the nation identify him with a "progressive" approach to problems. "Let's get this country moving again" was the major theme of his campaign. He did not say exactly what he would do for the cities, for foreign affairs, for the poor, for education, or for much of anything else. Nor was Richard Nixon particularly clear when he won the elections over Hubert Humphrey and George McGovern. Most presidents have not been particularly clear in their campaigns. Revolutionary laws were enacted by Congress under Franklin Roosevelt in 1933, but in the 1932 campaign, few of his proposals were mentioned. Perhaps, when one is running for office, it is more intelligent to call attention to major problems, leaving solutions to a later time, lest a good problem solver lose the election.

Comparatively few speakers are running for high office, and if no one ever spoke of solutions, few solutions would be adopted. Our culture and times may need a few speakers who vaguely identify themselves with problems, but we also need speakers who can make sound solutions clear and psychologically compelling. If ability to make solutions compelling is one of the needs of our time, then let us address ourselves to that problem.

CONFIDENCE AND THE SOLUTION

To enact a solution, we must hope that the solution will work, and be reasonably certain that it will. When people are faced with increasingly severe problems, they tend to repress their concern—and even their recognition—of the problems. On the other hand, *confidence that a solution is possible may often be a prerequisite for a problem-solving response.* Confidence removes inhibitions and initiates thought, speech, and action. Nothing is more inhibiting to an individual than a lack of confidence, and nothing will destroy a solution more quickly than the feeling that it won't work.

But what produces confidence? The kind of confidence that is most desirable and, certainly, most intelligent is not unwarranted confidence. Prohibitionists in the early part of this century had the unwarranted hope that forbidding the sale of alcoholic beverages would solve the problem of alcoholism. Surely this confidence gave them the energy to work for the Eighteenth Amendment to the Constitution, but their confidence was misplaced, for Prohibition probably increased the demand for alcohol. We aim, rather, at an intelligent confidence, best described by Wordsworth, who said: "True confidence abides in him alone, who, in the quiet moment of his inward thought, can still suspect, yet still revere, himself." Blind dedication to a solution may result in its adoption, but may also result in disappointment. We prefer that which is less blind, and more certain to solve problems; namely, "Wordsworthian" confidence.

We have already suggested some ways in which this kind of confidence can be generated. The speaker can build confidence in his ability to present a solution by showing that he understands the problem. Vivid presentation of the problem not only prepares the audience to want a solution but also suggests that the speaker knows what he is talking about, that he understands the problem. Further confidence in the speaker can be developed if he shows that he understands the cause of the problem—when such understanding is possible. Finally, the audience can develop Wordsworthian confidence if the speaker shows that he is aware of the difficulties and limitations of the solution. Nevertheless, the major way of developing an audience's confidence is to demonstrate that a solution will work. When an audience believes a solution will work, this confidence will release the inhibitions that make an audience repress its response to a problem, encourage thought and discussion about the problem, and encourage people to accept the solution—and to work for it.

THE USE OF ANALOGY

The most important use of the analogy is to demonstrate that a solution will succeed because a similar solution has worked before in a similar situation. As we will see, analogy is not, as logicians have insisted for hundreds of years, a weak form of argument. The following is an analogy, but nothing about it suggests that it is unreliable: "Vaccination against smallpox will prevent smallpox in you because it has in millions of others." That analogy is more than 99 per cent certain. The problem of analogical reasoning is not that is is by nature weak, but that there are some weak analogies. There are weak examples, weak statistics, and weak arguments of all sorts, but nothing inherent in the analogy makes it inferior to other forms of argument.

As with all forms of support, mistakes are possible with analogies. No known system of logic or of thinking guarantees error-free conclusions. But the analogy is particularly important because *only by using the analogy can we make use of the experience of others and profit from that experience.* If the use of seat belts reduces injuries in automobile accidents for most people, it will probably do so for you. If a particular device reduces water pollution in Pennsylvania, that same device may reduce water pollution in other states. Were analogical thinking not worthwhile, we could not apply successful solutions from person to person, city to city, state to state, or one part of the world to another. The problem, then, is to learn to use analogy in order to increase the confidence of an audience that a solution will solve a particular problem.

But the analogy has a more important function than that of making the experience of others in similar situations available to us. *The analogy is a test of relevance.* The world is full of facts, but relevant facts are fewer, and more pertinent to problem solving. History can be considered as a huge testing ground for solutions. The classical problems we face confronted all people in the past. What did the Greeks, the Romans, the Chinese, and others do in response to these problems? How successful were their responses? The whole of history can be looked upon as a gigantic laboratory for the study of human responses to the great problems. Too frequently history becomes a mass of facts and interpretations of facts, with little relevance to students. (A recent poll revealed that high school students considered history the most irrelevant of their subjects.) But history can be among the most relevant of studies if it is viewed as a testing ground for solutions. Whenever there is a clear analogy between the problems and solutions of another culture and those of our own, history is relevant.

More surprisingly, history can be relevant even when there is no analogy. If, for example, a particular solution seemed to work in Rome, but conditions in Rome were essentially different from ours, those differences may make the solution invalid for us. The study of whether or not a solution might work in our own circumstances when it did in other circumstances is itself relevant. Or if a particular solution did not work in Rome, conditions in our own times might be so different that a sound argument might be made that it would work for us. These concerns warrant the use of analogy. The analogy may be the most useful of all kinds of arguments because it conveys to us the experience of others.

SOLUTIONS AS CAUSES

Any solution implies a causal argument because a solution is always a proposed cause of a better condition. For example, if we propose putting more policemen on the streets to reduce crime, we are treating crime symptomatically, but we are proposing a cause of reduced crime, and are working with causes even though our solution is directed at symptoms. If we propose to reduce injuries and fatalities from automobile accidents by recommending the use of seat belts, we are not attacking the underlying causes of accidents; nevertheless, our solution is causal in the sense that if applied, seat belts will cause fewer fatalities and fewer injuries. All solutions are, therefore, causal. The analogy, properly used, takes note of the causal nature of all solutions. Because the analogy is causal, one should incorporate, whenever possible, the use of the Canons of Causation.

The Canon of Agreement. The Canon of Agreement can be restated for solutions in the following way: *wherever a similar solution was tried, the problem lessened. The task of the speaker is to discover places where the solution worked.* For example, the use of better police protection as a solution to crime seemed to work in New York City: in one high-crime district, where the number of policemen was increased from 284 to 613, the number of crimes dropped from 1,100 to 450. There were

70 per cent fewer holdups, and no muggings at all.[12] Better police protection seems to have worked in New York City. Thus, the first step in using the analogy is to show that where the solution was tried, the problem lessened. This kind of presentation gives the audience confidence that a solution will work and, at the same time, demonstrates that logical reasons exist for the workability of a solution. Moreover, we see that the Canons of Causation, which are thought to be of use only in analyzing the cause of a problem, are likewise applicable to its solution.

The Canon of Difference. We may restate the Canon of Difference in the following way: *where the solution was not tried, or the opposite of the solution was tried, the problem remained or worsened.* To illustrate the method, we might propose, as a solution to the problem of traffic safety, the raising of speed limits. We can support the idea by showing that the opposite of the solution increases accidents. When Governor Ribicoff of Connecticut ordered a crackdown on speeders—a procedure that, in effect, slows down drivers—the number of injuries from accidents in his state *increased* 22 per cent.[13] If slowing down drivers increases accidents, letting them speed up may decrease accidents.

Let us take another example of the Canon of Difference. Gun control is clearly a symptomatic solution to the problem of crime, especially murder. But Philadelphia tried a gun control law, and it seems to have worked. In Philadelphia, guns cannot be sold to drunkards, to felons, or to the insane. During the first nine months that the gun control law was in operation, twenty-five convicted burglars, thirteen convicted robbers, twenty-two persons who had committed aggravated assault, two rapists, two habitual drunkards, and two murderers—a total of 139 persons—were prevented from buying guns. In those nine months, there were 17 per cent fewer murders in Philadelphia than in the previous nine months. But during the same period, in the rest of the nation murder increased by 9 per cent. In some cities the murder rate increased enormously: Phoenix, 32 per cent; Houston, 59 per cent.[14] If murder rates decrease in areas that have gun control, but increase in areas that do not, then gun control may be a tenable solution to the problem of murder. Moreover, we can show that Dallas, which has no gun control law, has a murder rate five times higher than New York City, which

---

[12] See Richard Doughtery, "The Case for the Cop," *Harper's* (April 1964), 129–133.
[13] See, again, Robert L. Schwartz, "The Case for Fast Drivers," *Harper's* (September 1963), 65–70. Although the recent limitation on speed to fifty-five miles per hour was accompanied by fewer accidents, the newly gained safety may be because fewer miles were driven.
[14] Reported by Carl Bakal, "Do Gun Control Laws Really Work?" *Saturday Review* (April 1962), 22.

has a gun registration law.[15] The Canon of Difference can be used to show that a proposed solution works, and that the lack of such a solution worsens the situation.

The Canon of Correlation. The Canon of Correlation can be restated in the following way: *a small amount of the solution should produce small results, whereas a greater amount of the solution should produce more results.* Suppose we propose, as a solution to the problem of prejudice, forced association among those of different races? We can show that forced association tends to reduce prejudice. When the United States Merchant Marine was desegregated by presidential order, psychologists were much interested in the effect on prejudice. Before the order went into effect, a poll taken among members of the Merchant Marine revealed that 54 per cent were opposed to integration. After seamen had shipped out twice on an unsegregated basis, the opposition to desegration fell to 25 per cent; after five voyages, it had dropped to 9 percent.[16] When none of the solution was applied, prejudice was high; when a bit of solution was tried, prejudice seemed to be reduced; when a larger amount was tried, the prejudice against desegregation seemed markedly reduced.

The Canons of Causation prove useful in demonstrating that a solution has worked elsewhere, that lack of it (or its opposite) fails to work or worsens the problem, and that a small amount of the solution produces some results, whereas more of the solution produces more results. Thus, the Canons of Causation are necessary to the use of analogy. They are not, however, enough.

Evaluation of Solutions

In searching for solutions, we must carefully evaluate their workability. Often, the merit of solutions has been overstated:

In 1965, when President Johnson dedicated a two-stage sewage-treatment plant on the Potomac River, he promised his audience that its completion, together with the construction of several others like it, could make swimming in the Potomic River a happy public pastime. Actually, the conditions of the Potomac that make that river less than swimmable today include not only untreated . . . sewage, but extensive growth of algae, which no one fully knows how to control, extensive silting and turbidity, which is equally untouchable by current technology, and unevenness of stream flow, which . . . affects the concentration of pollution. In short, the president was promising an achieve-

---

[15] See C. W. Griffin, Jr., "The Rise of Nopanaceism," *Atlantic* (September 1966) , 76.
[16] See Ira N. Brophy, "The Luxury of Anti-Negro Prejudice," *Public Opinion Quarterly,* 9 (1946) , 456–66.

ment beyond the capacity of any equipment yet designed. Although it is painful to say so, the Potomac River may *never* be a good place for swimming.

If one were to establish attractiveness for swimming as the standard of successful water depollution, as the president did in the case of the Potomac, one would expose the national commitment to the . . . risk of a popular disappointment.[17]

One does not attract adherents to a solution, in the long run, by presenting it as a panacea. But the fact that a solution is not a panacea should not obscure whatever workability it has. For example, the structural safety of automobiles can be increased greatly. The president of General Motors, however, insisted, "Safety is a highly complex problem, and there are no simple solutions or pat panaceas."[18] But if a solution produces a significant improvement at relatively little expense, the fact that it does not solve the entire problem should not prevent its adoption. C. W. Griffin calls this propensity to condemn a partial solution *Nopanaceism.*

But the Nopanaceist seldom claims that your proposal won't achieve *your* goal; he claims that it won't achieve *his* goal. And since he will accept nothing less than a panacea, his goal, by definition, is impossible.[19]

We should not make exorbitant claims for solutions, nor should we be distressed if a solution does not entirely solve the problem. If we can save *some* lives, lessen *some* prejudice, reduce *some* poverty, prevent *some* diseases or *some* wars, we should.

USE OF ANALOGY: DESCRIBING THE CONDITIONS THAT PRODUCE
AN EFFECT

We should try not only to demonstrate that a solution has worked elsewhere, but also to explain why it worked. For example, after we have shown that increasing the number of policemen in an area of New York City decreased crime in that area, we can go on to explain that the crime rate is reduced because the presence of sufficient policemen increases the possibility that the robber or mugger will be apprehended, and no man commits a crime when he thinks he may be caught.[20]

If we wish to argue that higher speed rates might reduce traffic accidents, we should describe the conditions that produce this surprising

[17] Roger Starr and James Carlson, "Pollution and Poverty: the Strategy of Cross-Commitment," *The Public Interest* (Winter 1968), 105–106.
[18] C. W. Griffin, Jr., op. cit., p. 76.
[19] Ibid., p. 76.
[20] One should note a contemporary exception to this rule: nonviolent (and violent) protestors often wish to be caught and imprisoned, and are most apt to protest when police are present.

result. First, slow driving is irritating and frustrating; an irritated driver is more accident-prone than one who is relaxed. Secondly, fast driving occupies the attention of the driver more completely than slow driving does; the attentive driver is less susceptible to accidents than the driver whose attention wanders.

We have seen that gun controls do reduce crime. If we were to describe the conditions that explain this effect, we would point out that the gun is probably the "safest" instrument for committing a murder; without a gun, an angry man must run greater risks. Without a gun, he would be more apt to "cool off," or to express his anger in a less murderous way—with his fists, for example.

If we were to describe the conditions that result in reduced prejudice among people who are forced to associate together, we might say that we often fear or hate those we do not know, but when we get to know them (as we must when we are forced into close association) we realize that they have many of the same aims, needs, and sorrows as we do. Since we tend to like those who are like us, often, we find that those different from us have a unique and pleasant charm and style. Therefore, forced association reduces prejudice.

In all of these cases, we have strengthened the analogy by furnishing explanations of why they worked. We cannot always find or develop such explanations, but when we can, the appeal of our solution is strengthened.

The crucial and most characteristic part of the analogy is the similarity of situations. One must show that the situation in which the solution worked is similar to the one for which it is proposed.[21] If we recommend that the same techniques be used to reduce crime in Pittsburgh as were used to reduce crime in New York City, we must also show that Pittsburgh and New York City are essentially similar in regard to crime prevention. We might argue that the presence of more policemen reduced crime in New York because the policemen increased the risk to the would-be criminal, and that if police make crime unsafe in New York, they can do the same in Pittsburgh. Here we have not embarked on a long "proof" that New York and Pittsburgh are the same, nor is there need to do so. The essential matter is to show that the reason a large police force reduces crime in New York also would be present in Pittsburgh. On the other hand, the presence of more policemen

---

[21] Most rhetorics, in describing the use of the analogy, say that the two situations must be alike in all significant respects. But what respects are "significant?" No guidance is given. Such guidance is possible, however, when the causal nature of analogies is grasped. Without sensing that nature, no test of "significance" is possible. With it, such a test is apparent.

probably would not have reduced campus unrest in the 1960s because campus protesters sought confrontation with the police and sought arrest to attract attention to the problem. We must be certain that the factors that account for the success of the solution in one situation are also present in the situation for which the same solution is recommended.

Suppose we recommend, on the basis of the evidence from Connecticut, that speed laws on open highways be increased slightly. Connecticut is different from many other states in various ways. But the differences are not relevant. What is relevant is that those factors that made the solution effective in Connecticut are found in all the states: slow driving is irritating, and rapid driving may occupy more of the driver's attention. Therefore, the experience of Connecticut is relevant to any other situation where these factors occur. In presenting the analogy, the speaker must show that the situations are analogous only in this one respect. Thus, gun control could be advocated as a solution to only part of the problem of crime; gun control would have no effect on embezzlement, on counterfeiting, or on espionage because the reason gun control is effective is that it forces "cooling off." This "cooling off" would not influence the incidence of these other crimes.

We must, in using analogy, show that the solution worked elsewhere, and show that the situation in which the solution worked and the one in which it is proposed are alike in that each manifests the factor that made the solution work. Thus when we describe the conditions that produce the solution, we lay the groundwork for the analogical part of our reasoning. The solution will be analogous if the causal conditions that make the solution work in one place also are present in the one for which the solution is proposed.

There is one exception to the need to demonstrate this analogous relation. When the solution works in a widely diverse series of places, one establishes the idea that it works wherever it is tried. In such cases, we need not demonstrate the analogical nature of the situations. If we show that better street lighting reduces crime in slum areas, in suburban areas, in business districts, in small towns, in rural areas, and in wealthy areas, we need not show that the conditions in these areas are similar to those in the one for which we are proposing the solution. Such diverse data establish the idea that the solution works under all, or nearly all, conditions, and this idea is sufficient.[22]

---

[22] Some rhetoricians would insist that what we have called an analogy is really an example. The analogy is a form of the example; whenever we use analogy, we are also using examples. When we use diverse examples—because we are assuming that the conditions in the slum, the business district, and the small town pertain to the place for which the solution is proposed—the analogical content is implied though unstated. One can call this an "example," but more is implied than mere example.

Solutions: Other Methods

The analogy is a most convincing method because, properly used, it demonstrates to an audience that the recommended solution has worked well under similar conditions. The analogy is argument based on precedent. We can usually find some sort of precedent. Some similar, if not identical, situation has occurred somewhere before. If the problem of disposing of radioactive waste did not exist before 1945, we did have the similar problem of disposing of dangerous chemicals or of garbage and sewage. If we never had a federal world government, the experience of the Thirteen Colonies that formed a federal union might be a similar situation through which to argue for a world government. Nevertheless, there are times when no precedent exists, or in which no precedent can be found. At such times, we must examine other means of arguing for a proposed solution. In any case, a speech gains strength and variety if it relies on several kinds of support. Let us explore some lines of argument that may be used to support a proposed solution.

ELIMINATION OF CAUSE

Even if one cannot demonstrate that the solution has removed the cause in a similar situation, one can show that it is likely to do so. Most of us want clean streams, lakes, and rivers. We are not likely to have them, however, because the kinds of sewage plants that will remove all bacteriological pollution would cost about $200 billion. We could reduce the cost of treatment if we could reduce the quantity of water requiring treatment. At present, nearly all water—including rainwater— is run through the same sewers. But rainwater contains only about 2 per cent of the pollution present in the sewers. To treat the combined rain and sewage of a city requires a plant four times larger than one that would treat only sewage. At present, when heavy rains occur, we simply bypass the treatment plants, letting both rainwater and raw sewage pour directly into the streams. We could treat all raw sewage adequately if we built separate storm sewers so that the rainwater, with its negligible amount of pollution, ran directly into the streams. The cost of these separate sewers would be only about $30 billion, and the building of these separate sewers would relieve much of the unemployment in the large cities. We cannot solve the problem of stream pollution unless we understand that heavy rains force our present systems to bypass treatment plants.[23]

[23] The interested student is referred to the meticulous study of Starr and Carlson, previously cited. The article illustrates a causal solution without recourse to analogy, and for that illustration (as well as information about pollution) the article is worth study. Moreover, the study is broad-spectrumed in that building separate storm sewers is considered not only as a solution for pollution but also for unemployment.

Let us take another case. We have mentioned that in the Rajputana desert dust causes air to settle, that settling air warms, and that warm air holds more moisture, reducing rainfall. Reducing the amount of dust would eliminate one cause of drought in many areas of the world. One does not need to rely on precedent but only upon an understanding that a proposed solution such as reseeding desert areas or fencing them in so as to prevent human and animal traffic might work because they remove the cause. If we can, in addition, show that such a solution has worked elsewhere, we strengthen our case; but if we cannot find such a precedent, we can find the cause of the problem and demonstrate that we can remove that cause.

PREVENTION OF SYMPTOMS

Many good solutions are symptomatic. We have successfully reduced the number of inmates in mental institutions by the use of tranquilizers, and the amount of crime by the use of better lighting and more policemen. Nevertheless, these measures have serious limitations. Somehow, we must find and remove the causes of mental illness, and the causes of crime, as well as the causes of our larger problems. Symptomatic solutions for most problems, and for the classical problems of war, poverty, caste, tyranny, and disease are merely stopgap measures. A curfew may stop rioting, but it does not solve the problem that started the riot, and that problem will surface again. Strict enforcement of laws may curb crime, but the causes of crime remain. Unless we wish to spend our energies on repressive enforcement, we must solve whatever problems drive men to crime. Symptomatic solutions are like a dose of morphine: they relieve the pain temporarily, but they do not cure the malady. Until a cure is discovered, however, treatment of the symptoms is essential. When we need such treatment, let us use it, but let us always try to look beyond to a cure.

APPROPRIATENESS FOR VALUES

The drive to abolish poverty in our country is motivated partly by the fact that poverty does not fit our values; that is, our sense of justice, our sense of the value of human life, or our revulsion at human suffering, especially preventable suffering. Our attacks on the problem of poverty, such as welfare, Social Security, and unemployment insurance are partially symptomatic solutions and cannot really solve the problem of poverty. But these, too, were justified and adopted because they fit our values: that no person should be destitute, especially in a rich country; that all should be offered help until they no longer need help. Very often a speaker should take some time to show that the solution fits the values of the audience.

TESTIMONY OF EXPERTS

In using testimony, one must show that the authority is worth listening to. Merely naming an "authority" and his title is usually ineffective. Instead, describe the experiences he has had, the education that helps qualify him, and the studies he has done that make his solutions more worthy of acceptance.

COMBINATION OF APPROACHES

For logical and psychological reasons, a solution that can be supported in a variety of ways is more apt to be accepted than one supported by only one method. If one way fails to convince some members of the audience, another may work. The speaker should try to become aware of all the possible ways in which he can support a solution, and select those that are most appropriate to his subject, to his audience, and to himself. If all of these approaches are used well, he probably will have an unusually strong case. *If he can show that the solution has worked well elsewhere, that it can remove the cause, or treat the symptoms of the problem, that it fits our values and is supported by experts, the audience will be more likely to accept the solution.*

Nevertheless, the speaker should select only those justifications for a solution that can be presented in an interesting way, and that will touch the minds of his audience. The speaker should look for the best way of supporting a solution; if he finds one such way, he should use it and perhaps forget the others. But in human affairs, few arguments can be considered irrefutable. Variety in the kind of support given a solution is generally more effective than only one approach.

ON THE HOPE FOR SURVIVAL

Faced as we are by the problems of our time, and in full knowledge that no civilization before us has ever solved them, can we hope that Western culture will not be destroyed? The question is important, for if we lack hope in our chances for survival, we will gradually fall into an uncreative fatalism that will increase our chances for failure. If our hopes are uninformed and unrealistic, we will easily become discouraged by a few failures. Neither fatalism nor unwarranted optimism will lead to successful solutions to the problems we face.

WAR

Of all our problems, that which poses the greatest threat of instantaneous and irreparable destruction is war. Although mankind has fought about eight thousand wars in the past seven thousand years, until 1945, *we have used only two solutions to war.* The most frequently used solution is the balance of power among states. At present there is a precarious balance of power between the Soviet Union and the West, but balances of power are known to work for only short periods of time—roughly twenty-five or thirty years. The other solution is the conquest of the world by what Arnold Toynbee calls "a universal state." The Roman Empire, the Chinese Empire, and the British Empire are examples of attempts at such solutions. The universal state seems to keep peace for longer periods, but is probably not possible in our time; moreover, the idea of one nation ruling the rest of the world is repugnant to us; nor could one nation govern the entire world wisely. But the important fact is that in all of human history, only two basic solutions have been used, and neither has long been successful.

No individual in his right mind would use, over and over, solutions that didn't work. Edison, for example, examined and tested thousands of kinds of filaments when he was developing the electric light. Had he use one and watched it fail again and again, he would have been not an inventor but an eccentric.

Instead of using the same two solutions over and over again, let us try others. For example, we might try to tie the world together economically, much as France and Germany are now tied together, so that the welfare of one nation demands the welfare of others. A solution such as the European Common Market, or the European Coal and Steel Community, ties nations together economically. By increasing trade across national boundaries, we might tie the world together, or, at least, tie together the major powers of the world, so that each profits from the skills and products of the rest, and all can sell goods profitably to one another and thus achieve mutual prosperity. There are literally hundreds of ways such economic interdependence can be effected. At any rate, we must try a solution different from the two unworkable standard solutions. Trying almost anything new would itself be more sane than continuing in our present course. There is hope for a solution to even the problem of war, provided we address ourselves to searching for it.

POVERTY

Two thirds of the people of our world do not have enough to eat. Yet a former secretary of agriculture, Orville Freeman, has said that if we used the best *known* methods of agriculture on the land currently being farmed, the world could feed itself. If, in addition, we sponsored serious research, we could increase that yield by developing more hardy grains, more efficient species of animals for food, new techniques for desalinization of water (to irrigate arid areas), and new ways of getting food from the sea. Poverty has existed in every culture before ours largely because the world did not have the means necessary to feed, house, and clothe people. But for the first time in history, we can systematically invent new means of production. In limited ways, we already have. In the United States, agricultural surpluses have easily been produced, and (until we faced the shortage in the 1970s) much of our land had been retired from production because we had increased our yield at the rate of 4 or 5 per cent each year. If all the world farmed as efficiently as The Netherlands, we could support a population ten times the present population of the earth. Paul G. Hoffman points out that some nations are already growing economically at a rate faster than the United States ever did: Mexico, Japan, the Philippines, Ivory Coast, Tanzania, and Thailand.[24]

He also says that within ten to fifteen years, Greece, Spain, Lebanon, and Taiwan will have reached the "take off" point—that point at which wealth becomes self-sustaining and continues to grow—and will no longer need economic aid. In twenty-five years, Brazil, Chile, Turkey, Pakistan, South Korea, Tunisia, and Ceylon will reach this economic turning point. Large areas of the world are rapidly reducing the problem of poverty, and there is demonstrable hope that a conscious attempt to alleviate poverty by economic research and mutual aid can work. We are closer to possessing the knowledge required for mastering poverty than ever before in history.

Much of mankind, then, is passing into a new era of consciously trying to solve the problems that have defeated man before. We have reason to believe that Bertrand Russell is correct when he says, "Neither misery nor folly seems to me any part of the inevitable lot of man. And I am convinced that intelligence, patience, and eloquence can, sooner or later, lead the human race out of its self-imposed tortures provided it does not exterminate itself meanwhile." If our speakers can devise or find solutions to our problems, we may survive and begin a new era in human history. If they can't, we may face oblivion.

Questions for Understanding, Discussion, and Research

1. In your opinion, which solutions were the most significant in human history? Why?
2. Most solutions raise new problems. Illustrate this fact by describing the new problems brought about by any of the major solutions in our history. Which solutions represented an advance (i.e., a tolerable level of new problems), and which brought about a decline?
3. Take a particular personal problem that confronts you, and try to find a solution for it. After you have devised one possible solution,

[24] Paul G. Hoffman, "The Rich and the Poor," *Saturday Review* (September 17, 1966), 23.

force yourself to invent other solutions before you settle on working with any one. When did the solution that appears most desirable come to you? Relate your experience to the class.

4. Give examples of false solutions used by any presidential candidate
or administration. Why are these solutions false?

5. Name some symptomatic solutions you would like to see applied;
name some in use you would like to see abandoned. Explain.

6. Give original illustrations of each of the following solutions: symptomatic and causal, individual and group, treatment and prevention, "villain" and social forces.

7. Analogies go by different names. In literature, they are often called
similes and *metaphors;* in psychology, *models.* Cite some familiar
analogies (e.g., the brain is a telephone switchboard) that show
the analogy is a way of understanding our world.

Speech Assignment: see pp. 221–224.

6

Values

As a pair of praying mantises mate, the female begins to devour the male alive. Her first step is to turn her head around and bite his head off. His loss, however, does not change the pace of his mating, for he proceeds as if nothing happened. During the mating process, a single female can consume as many as seven apparently happily aroused males. The stick-like hideousness of the mantis and its behavior may make us shudder—and thank whatever forces keep them away from us. But perhaps the insect world is not factually more horrible than the one we have created for ourselves. After all, *man is the only creature who has made himself an endangered species, and man is the only species that can destroy all other life.* For our own sakes, we are fortunate that insects cannot comprehend how astonishingly more horrible we can be than they.

Values and Survival

Behind man's potential for destruction are the values that some men hold: the dogged need for dominance, regardless of the cost or danger to others; the pathological unwillingness to observe the rights of others; the psychopathic willingness to seize these rights; the mindless indifference to those who need help. Man can survive, and probably will for a long time, but his security and ultimate survival will be uncertain until he has developed a different set of values and expressed them.

131

The need to find values that will make survival possible is reason enough for studying them.

Rhetoricians and specialists in communication should understand values because values influence our perception and recognition of problems, our recognition of causes, and our selection of solutions. Moreover, our values influence our life-styles and the degree to which we may be suited for survival. Therefore, specialists in communication should be able to analyze values, to criticize them, and to discern ways of persuading others to maintain or to change them.

LIFE-STYLES

To search for arguments against one's own life-style is an unusual but wholesome activity, and develops one's sense of proportion and sense of humor. It is fun to find good arguments against one's life-style. Western culture, for example, is based on the premise that problems can and should be solved. But among the best arguments against problem solving are those found in the most ancient of all Chinese classics: the *Tao Tê Ching*.[1]

Among the most important teachings of this strange and beautiful masterpiece is "Do nothing, and you will achieve all." Most likely, we were raised to believe "Do nothing, and you will have, and be, nothing." The idea that inaction can be productive seems absurd to us, but it does not seem so to the Taoist. Probably no fewer than a billion Chinese, over the centuries, have found sense in the idea that inactivity is among the most productive ideas of man. If we stretch our minds, we can begin to see a glimmer of sense as we look at similar Taoist teachings. "Because the wise man never contends, no one can contend against him." Even our own culture knows that "It takes two to make a quarrel," a somewhat similar idea; but no Western idea is quite like the Taoist idea of inaction, which is called *Wu-wei*. "Consider the water," says the Chinese sage, "It offers you no resistance if you want to put your strong hand in it. But your strong hand should be like the passive water, and then it, like the water, might raise up great forests and wash away whole mountains. Which is stronger: the passive water, or your strong hand?" And again, "If you discard some of your wishes, then you can have them all." What does Lao-tzu mean by such things? We cannot be sure, but he might mean that one ought not to try to solve problems, for then they are beyond solving, or one ought not go looking for problems, for then he will surely find them.

---

[1] The title cannot be translated, but roughly means *The Way of Living*. The author of the *Tao Tê Ching* was supposedly an ancient sage named Lao-tzu who lived in China over two thousand years ago.

Suppose you adapt, in your imagination at least, some of these ideas on inaction to the next speech you are to give. Lao-tzu might suggest that you not work on the speech, that you neither read nor force yourself to think about it, but simply say that which comes without effort. What would be the results of so doing? In some cases, perhaps, you will compose a delightfully original and thoroughly natural speech, superbly suitable to your nature, the occasion, and the audience; probably you will be free of stage fright. You may already have learned that you can get so worked up over a speech that you paralyze yourself; at least, a Taoist approach would keep you from crushing yourself with the anxiety that blocks your creativity, interferes with your preparation, and stuns you with stage fright.

But take care. Instead of following immediately the few quotations you have read from the *Tao Tê Ching*, doing what you think they mean, you will be safer if you try to understand them better before you try to follow them. Our values are different from those presented by Lao-tzu, and to comprehend his values takes some effort. You could start by reading the *Tao Tê Ching*, for it is a very short work consisting of only eighty-one verses of great beauty, no one of which fills even a single printed page. Perhaps you will stumble onto more than one of the forty or more English translations of this short work and see how, strikingly different from one another they are. You could read some works about Taoism, such as Holmes Welch's *The Parting of the Way*.[2] After you have studied and thought about Taoism a while, you might try it out. If you wish to embark on a more serious study of Taoism, the officially sanctioned commentary on the *Tao Tê Ching* is available.

[It is] a bible of 1,120 *volumes*—not pages—compiled over a period of fifteen centuries. Many of the books that compose it use an esoteric vocabulary which only initiates were meant to understand, and in some cases the last initiate may have died a thousand years ago. . . .[3]

The point is not that Tao ("The Way") is difficult to understand so much as that values that are different from our own may be difficult for us to understand, and yet they can be partly understood and may prove more than merely interesting. Almost anyone can go a long way toward understanding Taoism by merely reading the eighty-one verses. Taoism is a whole way of life, and if we are to believe the Taoists, it is *The* Way. Nevertheless, the *Tao* is not easy to understand, as the very first sentence assures us: "The Way that can be spoken is not The Way."

[2] Originally published in hardcover (Boston: Beacon Press, 1957) and now available in paperback, entitled *Taoism: The Parting of the Way* (Boston: Beacon Press, 1965).
[3] Welch, op. cit., pp. 88–89.

We should remember that others' life-styles may seem strange, absurd, repulsive, or ridiculous, but when we try to understand these life-styles, they no longer seem so. Sometimes, too, our familiar life-styles are romanticized. Western cowboys, for example, existed in great numbers only for a few decades, and lived a life most of us would consider intolerably unvaried and dull. Yet we mythologized the life-style of the cowboy, and neglected the more promising life-style of the American Indians. We assumed that Indian chiefs were like European kings, but no chief had the power to sell the land of his people; the chief, rather, was more a respected spokesman. Never reflected in our cowboy-and-Indian films is the description sent by Christopher Columbus to the king and queen of Spain:

> So tractable, so peaceable, are these people, that I swear to your Majesties there is not in the world a better nation. They love their neighbors as themselves, and their discourse is ever sweet and gentle, and accompanied with a smile; and though it is true that they are naked, yet their manners are decorous and praiseworthy.[4]

Our values blinded us to the merits of the Indian, and only recently have we begun to understand his brilliance. "Among some of the Indian chiefs of American history . . . there is an eloquence, dignity, and precision of speech worthy of the ancient Greeks. . . ."[5] Perhaps we were vaguely aware of the oratorical tradition of the Indians, but how much more often do we find the Indian portrayed as possessing a vocabulary restricted to the monosyllabic "Ugh"? Only our own inability to appreciate his values made him seem stupid. The American Indian was not intellectually depraved, but *we* were for not being able to fathom his values. These values, based on respect for the land and love for nature (rather than mastery over nature) are more suitable for survival than our own. The great difficulties of appreciating the values of those who differ from us, our frequent unwillingness to try to understand such values, and our hostility to any values except those with which we grew up make us miss ideas and perceptions of other life-styles. Yet these styles might be a source of help, comfort, delight, or serenity. By missing the values of others, we miss ideas that might enhance our own lives.

One would expect that this sort of parochialism would not be found in great citadels of learning, but our universities are not only

---

[4] Quoted in Dee Brown, *Bury My Heart at Wounded Knee* (New York: Holt, Rinehart and Winston, Inc., 1972), p. 1.
[5] Michael Novak, "One Species, Many Cultures," *American Scholar* (Winter 1973), 115–116. Copyright © 1973 by the United Chapters of Phi Beta Kappa. By permission of the publishers.

unconcerned with appreciating a variety of values but are hostile, perhaps somewhat unconsciously, to all but certain values.

Not long ago, the humanities meant, not humanity, but Western civilization. More than that, it meant Western civilization as seen through English,
Protestant, upper-class eyes. Not many of the graduates of Harvard, Princeton,
and Yale now in their fifties learned very much in their college days about the
other cultures of the world—about Buddhism, or Slavic history, or Jewish
family life, or Chinese civilization, or Latin America, or the history of slavery.
What they were instructed in as "liberal arts" was not quite fully liberating;
what passed before their eyes as "the humanities" was, rather astonishingly, a
mirror image of their own ethnicity.[6]

No one should dispute the "ethnicity" of our universities, for
Novak is correct. When our universities talk of the "liberal arts," they
do not mean "an understanding of the nature of freedom and of how
freedom may be preserved and extended." And when they talk of "the
humanities," they mean foreign languages, literature, art, music, and
philosophy, and seldom concern themselves with the question "What
makes a person a *human* being?" And even in the studies about Western
culture, we do not study Scandinavian or Russian literature, history, science, or art, although such studies are clearly part of Western culture.
Where does one study Greek literature after the fourth century B.C.? Or,
as Novak forces us to admit, where can one study Slavic writers and
heroes? Are we certain that they are so unimportant as to be ignored
by all of us? To ignore Spanish literature and African civilizations, to
skip the activities of the entire subcontinent of India while we major
in Greco-Roman, Judeo-Christian, and Anglo-Saxon ideas almost exclusively is to miss something: we miss reinforcing the idea that America
is supposedly creating a new society in which no one value or idea will
rule, and where there is room for differences and love of them. As Novak
points out, if such be our purpose, we have not succeeded yet:

The great Slovak names Svatopluk, Janošik, Benovsky and Stéfanik mean
little to most Americans. But this is only to say that an ordinary American
education is remarkably ethnocentric. About one third of our population is of
Anglo-Saxon ancestry. Yet so far is our nation from filling its own pluralistic
destiny that our education is entirely Anglo-American. . . .[7]

Many of our present perplexities arise from two confusions: one is a
misperception of class; the other, a misperception of culture. Some young
blacks from Hough [Cleveland] may not be literate, but that does not mean
that the basic human voyage is closed to them. Both the *Autobiography of
Malcolm X* and *Soul on Ice* are classically Greek and Christian. . . .[8]

[6] Ibid., p. 114.
[7] Ibid., pp. 113, 115.
[8] Ibid., p. 115.

The study of other life-styles and the values that support them is good, if only to cure our own provincialism. But we seem hardly to make the effort, or even to know that the effort is worth the trouble. Other life-styles and the values behind them may lead us not only out of our provincialism but to the very system we want. Would you like to live in a culture where everyone lived well and yet no one worked over four hours a day? The Incas lived in this way. Would you like to abolish crime and insanity. Cultures exist today whose values create a life-style in which crime does not occur and no man goes mad. These life-styles come from certain "savage" cultures. Which is savage—the culture with no murder, no suicide, no thefts, and no psychoses, or the arrogant, polluted, proud culture that has all of these faults? The study of other values may at least cleanse us of the provincialism that has blinded us to much that is good.

FREEDOM

Moreover, by learning to appreciate other values, we help to enhance our own freedom. Freedom involves the ability to select from a relatively unrestricted set of alternatives. But when the basis of our choices is restricted by our values, our freedom itself is restricted. If we have accepted the conventional values of our time, we will continue making conventional choices. These conventional choices may be fine, if the values we hold are the best values for us. Often, we feel most comfortable with the values with which we grew up. But merely feeling comfortable with a value is no guarantee of its quality. We should learn to expand our sense of values, and to analyze our own values and those of other times and other places. Just as the unschooled savage cannot choose to be an engineer or a detective because he has never heard of these professions, so we, with our conventional values, may not choose the kinds of life created by other societies. *Our own freedom requires that we become aware of other values and that we learn to evaluate them.*

To paraphrase Justice Oliver Wendell Holmes, Jr., perhaps the best test of values is their ability to survive in the competition of the marketplace. If we disdain a sympathetic look at other values, there is no competition among values, and no test of our own. If we have adopted a poor sense of values in our childhood, we will probably never realize it, and never have the freedom to choose something better; we will remain chained by an unexamined value system and whether it is the best for us or the worst, we can never know. To secure our own freedom, therefore, we must extend our values and compare them to others.

PERSONAL GROWTH

Only by expanding one's knowledge of values can one grow, at least intellectually and emotionally. We each come from environments that are somewhat limited and each of us tends to adopt the values implicit in those environments. Thus we grow up with the values of our parents (or we react against their values and choose those that seem opposite). Now if these are the best for us all's well. But our acceptance or rejection of childhood values is often unconscious, unsophisticated, and likely, therefore, to be unintelligent. Even if we do not change our values, we must learn to empathize with those who have different values, or we remain somewhat provincial. Try to empathize with that which brings joy to a Chicano family or brings joy to a family of a different socioeconomic class or to an individual with a different life-style, or to a family of a different racial or religious background. *Different* is the key word. Different from what? Different from our own, of course. The aim is to learn to appreciate whatever we can in the values of those who differ from us. Let us try to capture the values behind the great periods of growth and development of the Golden Age of Greece, of Renaissance Europe, of precolonial West African civilizations, and of ancient Indian civilizations. Others' values may be good, too, for we have no natural monopoly on the best values. Moreover, we did not grow up recognizing the values implicit in music or painting, or good fiction, or religions that differ from our own, nor did we have much understanding of the value behind certain periods and movements in science, poetry, music, or art. If we are to grow, we must try to understand the values behind these arts and behind the varied movements in each period of culture. By understanding the widest array of values possible, we renew the possibility for growth.

Values and Problem Solving

THE IDENTIFICATION OF PROBLEMS

Values are important because they are especially significant in problem solving. They help to determine the problems we perceive as well as those to which we are blind or unresponsive. With one set of values, we believe in alleviating suffering; with another, we may cause suffering. Values are like light:

Light can play strange tricks. In ordinary light, certain kinds of rocks appear grey; but when fluorescent or ultraviolet light is turned on them, the dull greys are replaced by iridescent blues, yellows, greens, and reds. In sunlight, a green sweater appears green, but in pure red light, it looks black. Like the light, values and value systems color our world and give it brightness or dullness. By the light of various values, civilizations find the unique paths they follow and from that light cultures are given their distinctive hues. The light cast by these values, moreover, either reveals our problems to us, or blinds us to them. But like the light, which is itself invisible until it strikes an object,

our values and value systems also remain invisible . . . until they are reflected in a decision. Because of the pervasive influence of values, we cannot
speak intelligently without understanding something of their nature.[9]

With a strong belief in the sanctity of human life, we are shocked
at the hunger and starvation in the world; with values that are based
only on the most narrow view of our own individual welfare, we ignore
the problems of millions of people.

Values are not, of course, the only determinant of the problems
we see and to which we respond. You are a student; do you think a
millionaire banker would be able to name the problems you confront
daily? Would you be able to judge the problems on which he spends
his day? Not only do values determine the problems we see but so do
the *circumstances in which we find ourselves,* so that it is hard for us to
feel—even if we can partly state—the problems a coal miner feels, just
as it would be hard for a coal miner to respond fully to the problems
that plague you. We might be able, indeed, to state many of the problems faced by one of another race, or one who is blind, or one who is
ill, but to *feel* them as these others do requires more empathy and
knowledge than most of us possess. Nevertheless, the problems we see
are a function not only of the values we hold but of the circumstances
in which we exist.

THE SEARCH FOR SOLUTIONS

As a cynical professor once remarked: "There are two ways to cure
malaria; one is to kill all the mosquitoes, which is rather difficult; the
other is to kill all the people, which is not." This professor's attitude
toward human beings is fortunately not shared by enough people in
the medical profession to gain acceptance for his solution to the problem
of malaria; besides, he was probably only showing his own "creativity"
and, regrettably, he could do so only by being shockingly sour. Our
values have much to do with the solutions we accept, just as our values
condition the problems to which we respond. As time goes on, our
values sometimes change, and open new solutions to us and prevent us
from using old solutions once preferred. So although once slavery was
widespread in the South—and, much earlier, found even in New England—today our values are such that we would almost unanimously
reject slavery. At one time, our values permitted us to imprison a whole
family for the debts incurred by one of its members, and to hang a man

---

[9] Otis M. Walter and Robert L. Scott, *Thinking and Speaking: A Guide to Intelligent
Oral Communication,* 3rd ed. (New York: Macmillan Publishing Co., Inc., 1973) , p.
231.

for petty stealing. But our values have changed and we no longer even consider such "solutions."

The changes, however, are not always for the best. When we fought the Revolutionary War, and even the Civil War and the Spanish-American War, we (usually) would not accept the idea of bombing, shelling, and attacking civilians. Of course in the Mexican War, we fought our way down to Mexico City to the Castle of Chapultepec—the Mexican equivalent of our White House—and massacred a group of high school boys who were protecting their capital. In the Vietnam War we dropped about ten times more explosives over North Vietnam than were dropped on Europe and the South Pacific in World War II. Since the 1940s, we have—although not everyone approved—accepted the destruction of whole cities in Europe, in Japan, and in Southeast Asia. What are the values that account for our unwillingness to use civilians as targets in the Revolution and our willingness—even eagerness—to do so in World War II and in the Vietnam War?

Sometimes, people with the same values may arrive at different, even opposing solutions. For example, one may favor legislation to stop the exploitation of laborers by large industries because he believes in freedom, and because he sees how such exploitation limits the laborers' freedom. But another person may be against such laws because he also favors freedom, and such laws limit the freedom of management. Both parties favor freedom, but one is concerned with freedom for the employer; the other, with the freedom for the employees. "What is freedom for the sheep is not for the wolf." One might suspect that neither really holds the value of *freedom;* each person values, instead, the good of management or the good of labor, and "freedom" is brought in to make each side look more persuasive. Be that as it may, there is nothing deterministic about values. When one knows the values a person advocates, one cannot always predict exactly which solutions he will endorse. Yet if we knew the values he privately held, we could come close to knowing the problems that concern him and the solutions he might favor.

Many of us apply our values inconsistently, or apply them only under certain limited conditions. Or as more frequently happens, we have *public* values in which we endorse whatever society expects us to believe, and *private* values that we may keep to ourselves but more strongly influence our decisions. In knowing a person's values, we cannot predict his behavior, because we can usually never know how consistent he will be nor how closely his private values coincide with his public values. But when we wish a solution adopted, it may be wise to show that the solution fits one or more of the values of those whom you want to accept the solution.

Underlying not only every problem we perceive but also every *solution* we accept are one or more values—public or private. If we were all good Puritans, we probably would not see freedom from routine or the lack of joy as problems. We might either ignore these matters or consider them devices of the devil. To the extent that we embraced problems that gave us mastery over the environment (or, at least, a temporary feeling of mastery), we may lead beyond survival: though damning Puritanism is popular today, Puritanism itself is a perfect recipe for the survival of an isolated and threatened group, and for building an empire, if an empire is what we want. But the advantages and disadvantages of Puritanism are not crucial here; the point is that we would select different problems to solve and different solutions for these problems if we were Puritans, than if we were Cavaliers.

THE IDENTIFICATION OF CAUSES

Our values influence us to select not only certain problems and solutions but also certain causes as well. One often thinks that causes are somehow objective, not subject to choice, but this is not so. As Protagoras showed, there are many causes of every event and each cause is "true." In addition, Aristotle showed that each cause also has a cause, and that cause has another cause, and so on to an infinite regress. Now if there are perhaps an infinite number of causes for each event, we sometimes select those that fit our sense of values better than others. Suppose a man drives to a political meeting and, on the way home, drives into another automobile and is killed. The political meeting was one link in the chain of causes that resulted in his death, but it does not occur to us to abolish political meetings, even though such an abolition might prevent some traffic accidents. We are a political people and value political discourse too much to seriously consider this kind of cause; because this cause conflicts with the value we attach to political activity, we hardly recognize it as a cause. Even the causes we select depend, in part, on our values.

SUMMARY OF THE SIGNIFICANCE OF VALUES

We must develop values that will save mankind, that will keep us from being self-endangered, values that will remove our mindless unconcern for the interests of others and our mindless unconcern for even our own best interests. We need to learn to understand, even when we do not care to accept, the values behind other life-styles, some of which may be better for us than the one we were born into. We need to increase our own freedom by extending the range of values we can appreciate so that we have a stronger basis for our choices. Our own personal growth requires that we expand the values we can understand and enjoy. Of course, values partly determine the problems we recognize and those we respond to, just as they partly determine the causes we select and the solutions we accept. All these reasons require us to look for values that are new to us and to understand better those we already hold. Let us begin the search for values that can save us from destruction, nourish our growth, and, finally, transform us into beings that can survive and that truly deserve survival.

Defining Values

Tools change our life. The discovery of fire gave us the means to keep warm, to cook food, to refine and forge metals—and to create conflagrations. If the wheel had never been invented, what in our world would still work? Even the horse would be of limited usefulness, for he could not be hitched to a wagon. But perhaps, if we had no wheel, we might survive, for no planes could come to bomb us, no refineries could turn out rocket fuel (and pollution), no motors could run, and even bicycles would be useless. No one disparages tools, unless the tools are tools of thought. A definition is just such a tool, and as a tool, definitions are poorly understood by those who use them and often even by those who write about them.[10] Definition is not a dull tool, and its cutting edge is more than sharp enough to excise, from a dull thought, a penetrating idea. Admittedly, dictionaries are no fun to read. But, then, dictionary definitions perform only one of the functions of definitions, and for our purposes, that function is usually not important. You will not have to read widely in *Webster's* to define values well, and if you do so read, you are almost sure *not* to define them well. Yet, definitions are tools that can change thought.[11]

[10] In the English language there is only one small book about definitions, and it is mostly concerned with questions other than the one we ask: Richard Robinson, *Definition* (Oxford: Oxford University Press, 1954). Robinson's book occasionally touches on how definitions change beliefs, attitudes, and values, but his real concern is in codifying what philosophers, particularly logical positivists, have said about definition.

[11] Surely the perceptive student will ask, "If definitions are so important as tools of thought, why haven't you defined *problems* or *causes* or *solutions* or *values* or, for that matter, *definitions?*" There are, here, no definitions of these concepts, but though definitions are useful tools of thought we need not always use them. We did define *liberal arts* (see p. 6). But we did not define many of the key concepts in this book because the meanings ordinarily assigned to these terms are quite sufficient. Suppose you consider two questions: "What are the worst problems humanity faces today?" or "Are the problems of humanity the same that they were a thousand years ago?" You will not find it necessary to reply "What do you mean by *problem?*" any more than I would respond with "What do you mean by *mean?*" To respond to the question "What causes inflation?" with the question "What do you mean by *causes?*" would strike the listener, rightly, as ridiculous. Whenever our common sense notions are understood, definitions are not necessary. The problem comes when we *think* we understand but don't. Then definitions may perform a service.

THE TYRANNY OF DEFINITIONS

In the 1890s, *psychology* was defined by Edward Bradford Titchner as "the study of consciousness." Titchner "enforced" this definition as if it were a creed to be defended, and permitted none of his students to study any aspect of the human being that did not fit the definition. His students possessed the same arrogance, and, for the most part, the same interests. And so for decades, psychologists studied the sensations of the human being, particularly his visual and auditory sensations. Titchner was a brilliant man, and despite his dogmatism, psychology made some strides. But his dogmatism also prevented the study of many aspects of the human being that are clearly recognized as significant today. Freud, who might be said to have implied that *psychology* was "the study of the unconscious," was not taken seriously by most psychologists until about fifty years later. The study of the psychology of learning, the psychology of adjustment, and the psychology of abnormal personalities were outside the Titchnerian definition, and remained neglected until it was superseded by other definitions. The meaning of *psychology*, as expressed by the definition of the word, influenced what psychologists studied, and restricted the value of the study of psychology. The most frequently used definition in the twentieth century, *the study of human behavior,* also influenced psychologists, some of whom turned psychology into a narrowly behavioristic study so that man was looked upon almost as if he were a white rat. This narrow behavioral approach is gradually being replaced by broader studies of the human being.[12]

But we need not go to technical studies of academic fields of learning to see that what we mean by a term may change our behavior. Take *love,* for example. If we think we are in love merely because we feel a strong physical attraction toward someone, we may take the feeling more seriously than we would if we merely recognized it for what it is: physical attraction. But since physical attraction is apt to fade, and if we are convinced that such attraction is the essence of love, when it fades, we are apt to think that we are no longer in love. Someone once defined *love* as "the feeling that you cannot imagine life without the other person." If we accept this definition of *love,* we are apt to find a more permanent relationship. In either event, what we mean by the term *love* may well change our attitudes and behavior toward dating, marriage, and life and living. The meaning we attach to certain values changes or

---

[12] For an interesting refutation of narrow behaviorism, see Joseph Wood Krutch, *The Measurement of Man* (Indianapolis: Bobbs-Merrill, 1954), and A. H. Maslow, *Motivation and Personality* (New York: Harper & Row, Publishers, Inc., 1954). The most intelligent view of behaviorism itself, and one seldom followed—partly because the book is hard to understand—is George Herbert Mead, *Mind, Self, and Society,* ed. by Charles Cohen (Chicago: The University of Chicago Press, 1934).

fixes our attitude toward them, and changes our behavior. Let us explore the techniques of definition so that we may become more aware of hidden meanings and of ways of changing those meanings usefully.

TECHNIQUES OF DEFINITION

One way of looking at definitions is to consider them as classifications, as Aristotle did. To classify a term, it must be found to fit into at least two categories. The first category any definition must express is the *genus,* or the largest useful category in which the term can be placed. Thus *psychology* is a *study; love, a feeling; democracy, a condition of government.* Each of these phrases is too large to convey a precise meaning, because there are studies other than psychology, feelings other than love, and conditions of government other than democracy.

A good definition, therefore, must also express a *species,* indicating how the term differs from other members of the same genus. Thus *love* becomes *a feeling that one cannot imagine a satisfactory life without the other person; psychology, the study of human behavior; democracy, a condition of government in which majority will can be expressed and carried out with protection for minority rights.*

The traditional advice about using a genus and species in definitions is sound advice for the most part. Nevertheless, the advice lacks an important contribution that Plato made: [13] Plato recognized that ideas were, or could be, transforming. His main interest, throughout most of the *Dialogues,* was to locate the meaning of a value that would transform people and even nations into something better.[14] To give a definition of a value means to look for a meaning of the value that would most likely lead to the transformation of men and nations. This transforming meaning is the most important meaning to Plato, but it is not always the most important.

Sometimes we want to know how people use a term. We may wish to know, for example, how people use the term *nonviolence.* Is *nonviolence* simply "acceptance of whatever befalls one without protest?" If so, Jews who were killed in Hitler's Germany were nonviolent, and

[13] Plato himself, in the *Dialogues,* seemed to anticipate Aristotle, for he seemed to be seeking for a genus and species in definitions. See, for example, *Gorgias,* 449–51; *Meno,* 72. Aristotle only stated these two implications of Plato.

[14] A definition, in ordinary language, of what *ethical* can mean is contained in Henry Nelson Wieman and Otis M. Walter, "Toward an Analysis of Ethics for Rhetoric," *Quarterly Journal of Speech, 43* (October 1957), 266–70; reprinted in Ethics and *Persuasion,* ed. by Richard L. Johannesen (New York: Random House, Inc., 1967), pp. 130–38. Also reprinted in *Selected Readings in Public Speaking,* ed. by Jane Blankenship and Robert Wilhoit (Belmont, Calif.: Dickenson Publishing Co., 1966), pp. 220–26. The article was meant only to evolve a definition, but apparently no one noticed that fact.

to no purpose. But if *nonviolence* is used to mean "resistance without the use of violence," then it has a meaning that is more useful. In this sense, nonviolence is in fact a powerful weapon; it was the main instrument used to free India. When we wish to know how people are using a word, we should not expect, necessarily, a transforming meaning.

Sometimes, one cannot use a classification, nor can one find a transforming meaning for a definition. In such cases, one may use the more modern (but not always the most useful) operational definition. Operational definitions have two forms. First, one may define a thing by explaining how to create or produce that which is being defined. If one could explain how to produce *love,* one would have followed this first method of operational definition. Second, one may define operationally by stating the characteristics of whatever is being defined. One might define love by listing characteristics we attribute to it, such as devotion to each other, a desire for the presence of each other, and a feeling of well-being with each other.

Three distinct modes of definition are most useful in problem solving: the use of *classification,* in which one attempts to state the genus (or largest classification) in which a term may be placed and the species (or the way in which that term differs from other members of the same classification) ; the search for and use of the most *transforming meaning* of the term, as suggested by Plato; and, finally, stating either the means by which the item being defined may be produced, or the properties it has. No one seems to have noted that these three kinds of definitions are not mutually exclusive, and most discussions on definition quibble about which kind to use. Aristotle's advice applies only to wording or composing a definition; Plato suggests only a worthy aim for a definition; the operational definition merely suggests a method of deriving a definition (especially useful in the physical sciences). One can construct a definition that incorporates all three: a statement about a transforming idea, using a genus and species that explain how to bring this idea about. Thus, one might define *justice* as "a situation in which each person receives all he needs for his fullest development, and in which he contributes whatever he can to the development of others." It has a clear genus: Justice is a *situation.* It has several clear species and subspecies, all of which entail the rest of the definition. Therefore it is Aristotelian because it is based on classification. But it is also transforming because it furnishes an ideal toward which to work, as Plato would have definitions do; the definition is often presumed to be Plato's meaning of justice. Moreover, it implies how to produce the *just* situation by furnishing characteristics of it: those named previously. So the three methods of definition can all be used at the same time. Therefore, let us not quibble about which definition is best, but use whichever we can to enable us to think better.

USE OF DEFINITIONS

All definitions are general statements, and unless the audience is in the unique position of wanting to hear a definition, these kinds of general statements, however brilliant, will be dull and perhaps somewhat unclear. Definitions must be introduced by, and followed by, supporting material. The most useful kinds of supporting material are examples, both real and hypothetical. Often a negative example, one that illustrates the opposite of the quality being defined, may clarify a definition and make it more interesting. But the use of supporting material is of such great importance that without vivid and clear support, definitions may not have the intended effect.

When a student first discovers the methods of definitions, he tends to think that every term needs a definition. But sentences, paragraphs, and whole speeches can be composed without needing a single definition. On the other hand, for values—particularly when we are trying to give the value a new or more precise meaning—definitions are essential.

As important as definitions are, one must never look upon them as creeds to be enforced. By enforcing his definition of *psychology,* Titchner lessened the significance of his own field. A more productive attitude would have been to recognize that a definition is never right nor wrong, that it can only state what a person means by a term. Some meanings are, indeed, more useful than others, but since there is no way to "prove" a verbal definition right or wrong, it should not be looked upon as a law to which one must conform. But though definitions cannot be either right or wrong, they can be stimulating or stultifying, clear or opaque, narrow or broad, popular or unpopular, insightful or obvious, and therefore useful or useless.

Persuading an Audience to Accept a Value

Often the values on which we base our view of problems, causes, and solutions are implicit in our speech, but occasionally, we must make explicit the values from which we view the world and then persuade the audience to accept them. The means of persuading an audience to accept a value are not difficult to find.

No rhetorician seems to have noted that each school of thought on the matter of ethics and values is itself not only a presentation of a doctrine of ethics or values but also entails advice about how to persuade others to accept that same ethical doctrine. For example, Emmanuel Kant suggested that to be valid, any decision or action must be submitted to the test of being "universalized," of being recommended for all people. What if everyone did the same? If the results would be disastrous, then the decision is unethical; if the results would be generally good, the decision is ethically sound. One way of persuading people that a value is good is to show that if everyone did it, the world would be a better place; one way of persuading people that a value is not good is to show that if everyone followed it, the world would be in worse condition. Hence, the idea of Kant entails means of persuasion.

Furthermore, commentaries and attempts to point out the limitations of theories of ethics are also recommendations for reforming the persuasive power implicit in the theory, or a statement of the limitations of its persuasive power. For example, Aristippus insisted that pleasure was the only good, and that since the keenest pleasures brought the greatest good, one should live life searching for these pleasures. The idea of Aristippus is appealing, especially to the young and to those who know nothing else about ethics. But the idea has a serious limitation: the greatest pleasures often bring with them the greatest "hangovers," and the pain of the "hangover" may exceed the joy given by the pleasure. Hence, Epicurus said that one should not live searching for pleasure, but should instead try to find whatever pleasures brought the least pain. One should "cultivate his garden," Epicurus recommended, searching for mild pleasures that bring little pain. Well, perhaps.

But the point is that theories of ethics and criticisms of theories of ethics extend, limit, and change, and otherwise suggest persuasive possibilities of using the theory. If an audience is ignorant of the criticisms of a theory of ethics, that theory may seem persuasive to them; but ignorance always makes possible a mistake, whether in ethics, in values, or in problems. Nevertheless, a knowledge of theories of ethics and the commentaries and criticisms of these theories provides ideas about persuading people.

He who would persuade audiences about values must have a thorough knowledge about ethics. Regrettably, we cannot supply the student with a complete knowledge of these ethical theories anymore than we could supply him with a complete knowledge of all the problems of the world. But if the student realizes that the study of ethics is desirable not only to help him understand ethics and values but also to provide him with persuasive devices, this discussion will have served its function. It would be even more satisfying if the student began the study of ethics, either in college courses or on his own.

Despite the enormous amount of data and ideas contained in studies of ethics, a very brief and introductory outline of ethical theories may be presented, if only to reinforce the idea that each of these theories is itself a direction for persuading people to accept or reject certain values or certain kinds of acts. The list, however, is not at all complete, nor could it be, within the confines of a single chapter. Omitted are many theories of ethics and values that at some time or other may prove to be persuasive to some audience.

Ethical-Persuasive Theories

Hedonism. Hedonism holds that the highest good is pleasure. The mere fact that we want something may persuade us to try to obtain it, but a significant limitation should be noted. Pleasure may not be the greatest good, at least not alone. Perhaps something more sophisticated, such as happiness, may be what we should seek. But even then, we will do things that will make us unhappy, and probably we should. For example, perhaps we will read a newspaper today or listen to the news on television. Such information as we find in the news will most likely not make us happy; news is so structured that it consists, largely, of bad news. Yet we would rather be informed and somewhat unhappy than to remain blissfully ignorant. Moreover, not all we desire will be to our benefit. We may desire (to be elementary) candy, sweet drinks, and prepared foods that are laced with sugar, but sugar is bad for us and for our teeth. There are many limitations to the idea that pleasure is the supreme good. Once an audience knows of these limitations, it cannot be persuaded by simple hedonism. The study of philosophy, even if it does not provide the perfect answer to what is most important in life, still furnishes one with intelligent commentaries on the limitations and dangers of popularly held notions about the good life. The study of ethics makes one more sophisticated about values.

But the study of ethics may do more, for often a theory of ethics, even if it is not quite the perfect theory for all men and for all times, may contain a kernel of permanent truth—as in hedonism. For if an idea in ethics does not, somehow—in the long or short run—contribute to a satisfying life, if that idea results always in a more miserable life, then that idea cannot be one worth following. An ethical theory must, in some way, contribute to human satisfaction. Hedonism has at least a core of truth.

Authoritarianism. If you wish to know what to believe, go to the person who knows the most about the matter in question; his authority may help you become wiser. Of course, we do not mean that you should go to the most powerful person, or to the most arrogant, or to he who most proclaims his authority. Rather, *authoritarianism* suggests that we consult *genuine* authorities instead of merely relying on our own, possibly half-baked, ideas. We have all been irritated, if not led astray, by those who thought they were authorities. (We have discussed some of the limitations of authorities on pages 68–70.)

Even on the matter of ethics and values, we would be wise to consult a professor of philosophy, or read Bertrand Russell, or study the writings of those whose minds have been recognized as the best informed and brightest.

Yet, when we discover the conclusions of well-informed and bright persons, we must constantly ask: "What reasons can be given for the conclusion?" The *reasons* for the conclusion are most important, for these contain the strength of a conclusion, or show its weakness. Authoritarianism, like hedonism, leaves a permanent core of truth: those who are best informed are in the best position to enrich our own thinking.

Instrumentalism.   Instrumentalism insists that whether or not an act or belief represents a significant value depends on the consequences of that act or belief. One may have fine intentions, noble values, and still cause great harm; however great the values one holds, if they result in tragedy, they are not sound. George Bernard Shaw, in *The Man of Destiny,* says: "There is nothing so bad or good that you will not find the Englishmen doing it; but you will never find an Englishman in the wrong. He does everything on principle. He fights you on patriotic principles; he robs you on business principles; he enslaves you on imperial principles." Englishmen are hardly alone in this matter. At any rate, by the consequences of an act or value, we must judge its merit.

Like all ethical theories, this one has limitations. By no means the least significant is that we can never know all the consequences of a particular act. Just as every cause has a cause, and that cause also has a cause, and so on to infinity, so does every act often (but not always) have consequences that run to infinity. What are the effects of World War II? No one can calculate them, for so many were killed whose genius or skills we shall never know, or whose venality we shall never experience, that we cannot know what the world would have been like with them. The costs incurred, the fears aroused, the ideals crushed, and the events produced were so numerous that no one ever will know them all. The same is true of lesser events. Presumably the learning you receive in one course, or the stultification you experience from one bad professor, may have enormous effects on you and others around you. Probably not every event has such an infinity of consequences. The fact that I have chosen to call my cat *Wu-wei,* which is Chinese for *passive inaction,* may not have many consequences on her, on me, on you, or on anyone or anything. But there is one great difficulty in instrumentalism: often the consequences go to infinity and cannot be calculated. Nevertheless, instrumentalism reminds us that we must try to verify our values by judging their possible consequences.

Utilitarianism.   Utilitarianism affirms that we should seek the greatest good for the greatest number of people. Perhaps it is obvious that what produces a greater good is better than that which produces a lesser good, but don't be too certain. Utilitarianism is more subtle and more sensible than so obvious a tautology. Its contribution is that it reminds us that the good of all is to be preferred to the good of a few;

the good of the people themselves is to be preferred to the good of the aristocrats, or the oil companies, or the food industry. Too often, our own government fails to follow sound utilitarian policies and becomes the tool of the special interests. A strong commitment to utilitarianism would improve the quality of our attempts at democracy.

But utilitarianism is not without difficulties. How, for example, can one judge whether a great amount of good spread among a few people is better than a little good spread among many people? Because that which is better may depend on the case, or may be impossible to judge, even this theory has its limitations. Nor does utilitarianism tell us how to decide when we have a conflict among values. Whenever more than one value is accepted, at some time or other these values will be in conflict. We may wish to enjoy ourselves on a Sunday night, and surely enjoyment is not an evil thing, or at least, some forms of enjoyment are not. But if we go to a party on Sunday night we may do poorly in class on Monday. How do we judge whether going to the party or being in shape for class is the greatest good? Utilitarianism does not always help us decide. And yet it, like other ethical theories, leaves a goal devoutly to be sought: let us try to increase the good that most people receive.

Ethics and values are more complicated than has been suggested here. But we can begin to see that each theory of ethics is persuasive, or at least provides guidelines for persuasion, even though it was not so intended. We can also see that critiques of theories of ethics limit, extend, or otherwise change the persuasive possibilities of the theory. Finally, we can see that studying theories of ethics makes us more intelligent about ethics and values. We can begin to see that each theory of ethics may leave a permanent core of intelligence that can be useful to us. Wisdom decrees that we study theories of ethics and of values.[15]

Questions for Understanding, Discussion, and Research:

1. What conflicts have arisen between your private values and your public values? Between those of the nation as a whole?
2. Study the values of any one of the tribes in South and Central America, Oceana, and Australia that have not yet had much contact with Western culture, and compare their problems, as they see them, with our own, as we see them. Then do the same for the values they hold.

[15] The book I like best to recommend to students interested in ethical theories is John Hospers, *Human Conduct: An Introduction to the Problems of Ethics* (New York: Harcourt Brace Jovanovich, 1961). The book is clearly written, well illustrated, and maintains a certain depth.

3. This chapter discusses values themselves and the values behind such matters as art, customs, and the like. Is the distinction between *values themselves* and *values behind* something an important one? Why? Illustrate.

4. What kind of values do you think might lead to man's survival? Explain. Is there room for differences in opinion among men? How can you say so?

5. What limitations are there to the statement, "Our private values determine the problems we see and the solutions we accept?"

6. What was the value behind fifth-century B.C. Athenian sculpture? Behind fourth-century B.C. Greek sculpture? How do you account for the contrast? How do you account for the contrast between Michelangelo's Sistine Chapel ceiling and his "Last Judgment?"

Speech Assignment: see pp. 225–232.

7

Motivation by Ethos: Individual Determinism[1]

Persuasion by Ethos

Imagine that you are standing in front of a firing squad that has orders to kill you. At that confrontation between you and the soldiers, what alternatives are open to you? Not many: probably only some "last requests," provided these entail nothing more dangerous than a last cigarette. Rack your brain and see if you can think of any paragraph— or any single sentence—that would cause the soldiers to throw down their rifles and accept you as their leader.

One man, faced with the same conditions, spoke one short sentence, and converted the soldiers into followers. The man was Napoleon; the occasion was his escape from Elba and his return to Europe. The

---

[1] Parts of this chapter have been published in Otis M. Walter, "Toward an Analysis of Ethos," *Pennsylvania Speech Annual, 21* (September 1964), 37–45, and *Speaking to Inform and Persuade* (New York: Macmillan Publishing Co., Inc., 1966), Chap. 8: "The Ethos of the Speaker." These materials have been revised and extended for this book.

sentence would not have worked for you, for there is not the slightest "magic" in it, but it worked for Napoleon: It was "Where is the man who would slay his Emperor?" Had Louis XVI used the same sentence while standing at the guillotine, or Julius Caesar, standing near the statue of Pompey in the Roman Senate, or Czar Nicholas II in the cellar in Ekaterinburg, the sentence would have changed nothing. But the sentence did change Napoleon's fate, and that of France, and that of England.

Why did the sentence work for Napoleon? More than a partial explanation is that for members of the firing squad, Napoleon had unique personal prestige, leadership, authority—in a word, ethos. Ethos is that quality that renders the same argument—even the same words—effective when used by some people and utterly ineffective when used by others. Ethos is the audience's idea of what the speaker is. Ethos is the image of the speaker. A strong, favorable ethos can encourage problem solving, whereas a weak one cannot.[2]

---

[2] For a discussion of the history of the concept of ethos, see William M. Sattler, "Conceptions of Ethos in Ancient Rhetoric," *Speech Monographs, 14* (1947) , 55–65. An attack upon the validity of Aristotle's concept of ethos was made by Teddy John McLaughlin, "Modern Psychology and the Aristotelian Concept of *Ethos,*" unpublished Ph.D. dissertation (Madison, Wis., 1952) . For the extent to which ethos is discussed in contemporary rhetoric, see Dennis Gene Day, "The Treatment of *Ethos* in Twentieth-Century College Textbooks on Public Speaking," unpublished M.A. thesis (Urbana, Ill., 1960) . In addition, one should not overlook the relation of ethos to related terms in psychology, anthropology, and sociology. There is an extensive bibliography in these disciplines under such terms as *charisma, credibility, leadership, personality, popularity, prestige, status,* and *halo effect.* The amount of material, together with the poor analysis with which most of this work was done and the dull and unclear style in which it was written (with some exceptions) , make such reading formidable. Yet, regrettably, most rhetoricians have neglected study of such allied fields, and have incorporated into rhetoric only such banal notions as the most simplistic forms of behavioristic theory. Nevertheless, rhetoric would probably profit from a thorough study of cognates of ethos in other social sciences. An attempt to synthesize the work done on ethos has been made by Kenneth Anderson and Theodore Clevenger, Jr., "A Summary of Experimental Research in Ethos," *Speech Monographs, 30* (June 1963) , 59–78, and by Wayne N. Thompson, *Quantitative Research in Public Addresses and Communication* (New York: Random House, Inc., 1967) , but each is limited to those studies published in speech journals; most of the work on cognates of ethos have been done outside the discipline of speech. Moreover, these two works are limited to experimental studies; such studies are not particularly valid because our measures of ethos are gross and fail to analyze and measure the dimensions of ethos. (For a discussion of these dimensions, see Otis M. Walter, *The Measurement of Ethos* (Evanston, Ill.) , unpublished Ph.D. dissertation, [Northwestern University, 1948], 18–21, or the adaptation from part of the dissertation: Otis M. Walter, "The Improvement of Attitude Research," *Journal of Social Psychology, 33* (1951) , 143–46; in this article, for the word *attitude* the reader may substitute the word *ethos,* because what is true of the dimensions of attitude applies to ethos as well.

A worthwhile philosophical treatment of ethos (without using that term) is that of Maurice Natanson, "The Claims of Immediacy," in *Philosophy, Rhetoric and*

ON THE STRENGTH OF ETHOS

Certain men in history with outstanding ethos were followed because of what they were, or at least what their followers thought they were. Sometimes these men attracted attention to the wrong problems and solutions and sometimes to the right ones, but they were not ignored. One can marvel at Alexander leading an army of twenty thousand Greeks against the largest empire in history up to that time, and successfully—and often nearly bloodlessly—creating an even larger empire. One is astounded by the prestige of great religious leaders whose mere touch was enough to achieve medical—or psychiatric—marvels. Gandhi set free the subcontinent of India. Pope John XXIII began a revolution in the oldest organization in the Western world. Nor is the present without men whose ethos achieved the otherwise impossible. Senator Eugene McCarthy attracted an army of college students and made the Vietnam War at last a topic for discussion. Rachel Carson made poisoning of the environment a great issue. Martin Luther King, Jr., began a peaceful revolution to change customs and habits that have burdened and shamed this country since 1619. Even when presidential candidates have a relatively dull ethos, they are often presented to the country by an advertising agency in a way that makes them seem to have an interesting, vibrant, and energetic image.[3]

DEMONSTRATIONS OF ETHOS

Of course, one can change the course of history without ethos. You have probably not heard of one Monsieur Derout, who pulled his cart in front of a fleeing coach, and forced it to stop, making possible the capture and, ultimately, the beheading of both Louis XVI and Marie Antoinette. His effect on history may have been considerable, but only because of his cart, not because of his ethos. The persons who invented the wheel or discovered fire influenced history—because of their inventions, not their ethos. Darwin influenced intellectual history, but not so much because of his ethos as because his ideas helped to explain the origin of species and the extinction of species, and because his support for his ideas was strong enough to convince able intellects. "Nothing is

Argumentation, ed. by Maurice Natanson and Henry W. Johnstone, Jr. (University Park, Pa.: The Pennsylvania State University Press, 1965) , 10–19.

A theoretical analysis of ethos worth studying, both for its own merits and because it differs from my own, is that of Paul I. Rosenthal, "The Concept of Ethos and the Structure of Persuasion," *Speech Monographs, 33* (June 1966) , 114–26.

A summary of the traditional point of view using experimental findings is found in Kenneth E. Anderson, *Persuasion Theory and Practice* (Boston: Allyn Bacon, Inc., 1971) , Chaps, 12, 13.

[3] Theodore Otto Windt, Jr., "The Presidency and Speeches on International Crises: Repeating the Rhetorical Past," *Speaker and Gavel* (November 1973) , 6–14.

so strong as an idea whose time has come": the ethos of Marx and Freud was not, at first, a factor in their influence. Perhaps Rachel Carson's effect —at least early in her career—was the result of the beauty of her style and the soundness of her argument. How can one be sure that there is such a factor as ethos, as distinguished from (but not separated from) other factors such as argument, style, or circumstances?

Some experiments demonstrate that perception of the source of persuasion is a factor in belief. Of course, these experiments are severely limited by the lack of one or more persons who had the ethos of a Joan of Arc, a Mohammed, or a Martin Luther King, Jr. The persons used as subjects possessed no comparable power of ethos. Nevertheless, one can still see, in a number of these experiments that, as Emerson said, "What you *are* thunders so loud, I cannot hear what you *say.*"

In one experiment, three identical copies of a recorded speech in favor of socialized medicine was played for three similar audiences. The first audience was told that the speaker was the surgeon general of the United States; the second, that he was the secretary general of the Communist party in the United States; the third, that he was a university undergraduate. The first audience, believing it had heard the surgeon general, was persuaded to be more favorable toward socialized medicine; the other two were not significantly influenced.[4] If a passage is believed to have been written by a poet of stature, it tends to be rated higher than a passage believed to have been written by an unknown poet; a painting "attributed" to a great artist receives a better rating than the same painting "attributed" to an unknown person.[5] We believe or disbelieve materials found in *The New York Times, The Chicago Tribune, The Christian Science Monitor,* and the *Dallas Morning News* according to our image of these newspapers. So we tend to reject a paragraph if we think it was written by Hitler, whereas the same paragraph might influence us if we thought it was written by Thomas Jefferson or Abraham Lincoln. The perception of the agent performing an act influences our evaluation of the act. The ethos of the speaker changes our perception of his speech.

This powerfully persuasive quality, ethos, is not, however, a mysterious quality totally beyond our ability to analyze and comprehend. On the contrary, one of the best studies of ethos was written over two thousand years ago.

---

[4] Franklyn S. Haiman, "An Experimental Study of the Effects of Ethos in Public Speaking," *Speech Monographs, 16* (September 1949) , 190–202.
[5] See Muzafer Sherif, "An Experimental Study of Stereotypes," *Journal of Abnormal and Social Psychology, 7* (1935) , 386–402; M. Sardi and P. R. Farnsworth, "The Degrees of Acceptance of Dogmatic Statements and Their Supposed Makers," *Journal of Abnormal and Social Psychology, 29* (1934) , 143–50.

ARISTOTLE'S DOCTRINE OF ETHOS [6]

Aristotle believed that one's ethos "may almost be called the most effective means of persuasion" (1356a), and we have every reason to agree with him. His analysis of ethos, moreover, was the most complete to be found in the history of rhetoric, and the most worthy of our attention. Aristotle believes that three qualities are found in those who have a desirable ethos: intelligence, moral character, and goodwill toward the audience. Let us examine each of these.

INTELLIGENCE

We are not persuaded by one who seems stupid. Consider some of your own teachers. If you listed the two or three best teachers you have had, probably no one of them seems to you to be unintelligent. Consider the most effective speakers in the past—philosophical speakers such as Socrates; religious speakers such as Moses, Jesus, and Gandhi; political speakers such as Pericles, Lincoln, and Churchill. No speaker considered "great" by an audience was considered by them to be stupid, at least not insofar as his great speeches are concerned. Indeed, Churchill's wartime speeches were considered great and intelligent, even though his postwar speeches, particularly those on economics, are thought of as being, to put it mildly, uninformed; his wartime ethos held Britain together, whereas his postwar ethos tossed him out of office. Insofar as a person has ethos, he has it only, according to Aristotle, when he is perceived to be intelligent or wise.

CHARACTER

The second quality that constituted ethos, according to Aristotle, was moral character. Moral character, to Aristotle, did not mean what it meant to the Victorians, but was a concept altogether more positive: a man possessed moral character when he did things useful to the audience and did these things for the audience's own sake, rather than for his own. Just as we are not persuaded by a speaker who appears stupid, neither are we persuaded by one who appears to be dishonest or dedicated to preventing us from securing our own welfare. If we perceive a person as being intelligent but crafty, he will not have as much ethos for us. The changes in Nixon's ethos are most instructive. Thus the speaker can achieve high ethos only if he possesses not only intelligence but also moral character in the Aristotelian sense of being of use to others.

[6] *The Rhetoric and Poetics of Aristotle*, trans. by W. Rhys Roberts (New York: Modern Library, Inc., 1954). See esp. p. 25 (Book I, Chap. 2, 1356a); pp. 56–63 (Book I, Chap. 9, 1366a–68a); pp. 90–91 (Book II, Chap. 1, 1377a–78a); pp. 100–103 (Book II, Chap. 4, 1380a–82a).

GOODWILL

Finally, Aristotle insisted, a man cannot develop strong ethos unless he also has goodwill toward his audience. A man, however bright, however devoted to the good of his audience, but thought to lack goodwill toward them will not be accorded high ethos.[7] If the reader examines again those teachers he regarded as most effective, he will find among them none who bore him ill will. Nor will he find any speaker persuasive, regardless of his arguments, who is perceived as having ill will toward the listener.

Intelligence, character, and goodwill—these are the qualities that constitute ethos, according to Aristotle. And surely, those leaders we have already named were perceived by their followers to exemplify these qualities, although often in very different ways. The intelligence of Alexander, for example, was very different from that of Socrates or Pope John XXIII, or Bertrand Russell. Variations exist not only in kinds of intelligence but also in kinds of moral character and in kinds of goodwill. Aristotle did not take note of these variations, nor has anyone else, but we are on safe ground if we accept the idea that some kind of intelligence, some kind of moral character, and some kind of goodwill do, indeed, contribute to ethos.

Aristotle supports his analysis by a kind of reversal in which he answers the question "Why do people give bad advice?" His answer argues that bad advice is given when intelligence, character, and goodwill are lacking:

> False statements and bad advice are due to one or more of the following three causes: men either form a false opinion through want of good sense [intelligence] or, they form a true opinion, but because of their moral badness do not say what they really think; or, finally they are both sensible and upright, but not well disposed to their hearers, and may fail in consequence to recommend what they know to be the best course. These are the only possible causes.[8]

---

[7] To have moral character in Aristotle's sense usually entails having goodwill toward people; few would seek the best interests of people and yet hate them. Perhaps Aristotle had in mind, however, some such situation as a parent who, in an arrogant way, degrades a child by saying, "Eat your spinach or you will have no dessert." The parent is undoubtedly devoted to the "audience," to his health, growth, and happiness; but he enforces the achievement of these ends in a way that reflects a lack of goodwill toward the small spinach-hater. Perhaps the differences between character and goodwill entail some such situation, but the important thing is that *the devices Aristotle lists as achieving goodwill* (in his discussion of Friendship and Mildness in Book II of the *Rhetoric*) *do contribute to ethos,* and whether they overlap with the concept of moral character or not is not, at this point, particularly important. Character makes one *do* the right thing, but goodwill makes one *feel* the right thing.

[8] Aristotle, *Rhetoric*, 1378a, lines 9–16. Other causes of bad advice exist, as we shall see, but the analysis is still helpful.

EVALUATION OF ARISTOTLE'S DOCTRINE OF ETHOS

We have already seen some of the merits of Aristotle's analysis because the lack of these qualities renders one unpersuasive; we are not led to solve problems by speakers we believe to be foolish, to have bad moral character in Aristotle's sense, or to have ill will toward us.

The Aristotelian analysis gains strength because there is something curiously logical about this psychological concept that lack of intelligence, lack of moral character, and lack of goodwill are responsible for much bad advice. The analysis is educationally sound in that we should learn to trust those who have these qualities, and to distrust those who do not. Education should, in part, devote itself to helping us judge whether or not a person is intelligent, devoted to our interests and those of others, and motivated by goodwill toward us. If he has these three qualities, we should acknowledge him as a potentially good source; if he lacks them, we should be wary of him.

Most important, Aristotle's analysis suggests that speech courses should attempt not merely to develop effective speaking but also to explore and teach ways in which students may develop the thoroughly ethical and often compelling persuasive qualities he describes.

That a speech course might aid the development of one's intelligence may not seem possible, yet if intelligence is ability in problem solving (the definition that was one of the starting points of this book), such intelligence can be a legitimate concern of speech courses. Speech courses oriented toward problems and toward solving them may increase a student's intelligence by helping him to locate significant problems, to analyze their causes, and to discover, evaluate, and present solutions to them.

Speech courses can also help him to see and understand the values that underlie his and other's analyses of problems, causes, and solutions. Speech courses, therefore, can increase one's intelligence (provided they eschew superficial subjects and the mechanistic trivia involved in some traditional courses). Moreover, certain kinds of speech experiences can increase one's dedication to others and his goodwill for others. So long as education can help develop the intelligence, character, and goodwill of the speaker and the listener, Aristotelian analysis should find a place in speech courses.

Nevertheless, Aristotle's analysis of ethos, based on intelligence, character, and goodwill is limited because it cannot account for the ethos of some people. Whoever the current film or television personalities, stars, or idols are, their popularity can hardly ever be explained by their intellectual ability. Nor is the fainting of spectators, or their delighted screaming, to be explained by their idol's transcendental moral character or by his goodwill. Aristotle's trinity usually cannot explain the "celebrities," whose styles of hairdo, styles of costume, and styles of life are cherished and imitated. Aristotle's analysis may be a good description of those whom we ought to believe, but it does not account for many in whom we *do* believe. We ought to believe those who are intelligent enough to know the truth and who have the character and goodwill to tell us the truth; yet all of us, at times, have deserted the intelligent, moral, and goodwilled person for someone who lacked one or more of these characteristics. Although often we may follow men of intelligence, character, and goodwill, there are notable exceptions, and these exceptions suggest the necessity for a more comprehensive theory.

Modern works on rhetoric do not offer a more satisfactory understanding of ethos. Modern rhetoric has expanded its list of qualities, adding some Victorian virtues, such as sincerity, and miscellaneous and quasi-Freudian qualities such as pleasing appearance, vitality, virility, and sex appeal. Yet these longer lists give no directions as to how these qualities are to be used. Moreover, the lists do not clarify which qualities are most important in various situations. Mere lists of qualities do not account for the people's worship of stars, of powerful political figures, or of great religious leaders.

PATTERNS OF ETHOS

Both ancient and modern descriptions of ethos seem based on the assumption that we can understand a phenomenon when we determine the elements of which it is composed. Similar assumptions are of value in some disciplines, such as chemistry, and may one day be of value in rhetoric. But as field theory in physics and Gestalt psychology demonstrate, knowledge of elements does not always produce understanding of the phenomenon. Sometimes atomistic assumptions block our thinking.[9] Moreover, there is no assurance that the elements listed are indivisible, i.e. that they *are* elements.

In searching for alternatives to an atomistic explanation of ethos, our understanding of engines furnishes a useful paradigm. Even though

[9] Because psychologists interested in concepts similar to ethos have found atomistic approaches generally unrewarding, the atomistic or "trait" approach to leadership has been largely abandoned. See Alvin Gouldner, *Studies in Leadership* (New York: Harper & Row, Publishers, Inc., 1950), pp. 23–49; see also Dorwin Cartwright and Alvin Zander, *Group Dynamics, Research and Theory*, 3rd ed. (New York: Harper & Row, Publishers, Inc., 1968), Part V, esp. Chap. 24. See also McLaughlin, op. cit., pp. 48–55. A notable exception to those who have given up the "atomistic" approach is Raymond B. Cattell, *Personality: A Systematic, Theoretical and Factual Study* (New York: McGraw-Hill Book Company, 1950), whose ingenious and prodigious application of statistical methods has evolved an approach to traits that reveals "source traits." Source traits are underlying variables in the person and are linked, although in a different way from my analysis, to motivational structures. Because of the magnitude and complexity of his work, rhetoricians (as well as many psychologists) have bypassed his suggestive research.

we know all the elements of which an engine is made—iron, carbon, copper, aluminum, or molybdenum—such knowledge does not tell us how engines work. Strikingly different engines are made of the same elements: a water pump is different from a lawn mower, and yet each can be created out of exactly the *same* chemical elements. On the other hand, identical engines may be made from *different* chemical elements: an excellent automobile engine may be cast from either iron or aluminum. If the same chemical elements can produce different engines, and different elements can produce nearly identical engines, then an understanding of the elements of which an engine is made will not give us much understanding of engines.[10]

The idea that one can know or understand a thing when he knows its parts was a new idea of European science in the seventeenth century, and the idea worked well in chemistry, where soon Priestley discovered oxygen and Cavendish and Lavoisier shortly after came to understand that oxygen was only one of the components of air, and to identify some of the others. For over two hundred years, atomism reigned, but in the twentieth century, relativity theory and quantum theory have laid to rest the idea that always, to understand anything, one must identify the elements of which it is made. Let us try an approach different from atomism and, temporarily at least, abandon the search for elements.

If we do not look for elements, presumably we might look for patterns. The difference among engines made of the same elements lies in their patterns: the lawn mower and the water pump may be made of the same elements, but they are cast in different patterns, and these patterns account for their differences. If engines made from different elements (at least iron or aluminum) are cast in the same pattern, they will be similar in function and power. Patterns may help us understand ethos as well.

PATTERNS AND THE NEEDS OF THE AUDIENCE

But how can one locate a pattern of ethos, and what is it? We may locate patterns of ethos by discovering the needs of the members of the audience. The ethos of Adolf Hitler is instructive: no one can understand the ethos of Hitler without understanding the needs felt by Germans at the time. When men are faced with desperation and defeat, they are vulnerable to anyone who poses as a savior who will lead his people to glory. But Hitler's ethos in the 1930s was perceived quite differently by most Americans (whose needs were different), who regarded

---

[10] One could argue that iron, aluminum, copper, or molybdenum were not the functional elements of engines, and that the carburetor, pistons, and crankshaft were. But then, if determining the elements is as ambiguous as this situation suggests, of what use are they?

him as a lunatic. Today, many Germans (because *their* needs have changed) seem both incredulous and embarrassed by the adulation accorded Hitler decades ago. Hitler's way was paved by the desperation that led men to welcome one who in better times they would have ignored or ridiculed. Thus Hitler's ethos was perceived differently by people with different needs. Needs furnish the organizing principle through which we "construct" the image of the speaker.

Patterns based on need help us also to understand the ethos of the celebrity. Members of a fan club are probably caught in a special social situation that creates certain needs. In the drab existence of the grocery clerk and the mechanic's assistant, identification with the image of the rich, successful, popular, good-looking, and adventurous star offers vicarious fulfillment of a series of needs. This image, which Karen Horney called *the idealized image,* is a perpetual source of frustration. William James suggests that the motivating power of an idealized image can be expressed as follows:

$$\text{The Strength of a Person's Idealized Self-Image} = \frac{\text{Aspirations}}{\text{Achievements.}} \text{ [11]}$$

Thus, one's self-image becomes most painful when aspirations and achievements are most widely divergent. This image is always beyond us, and relief from the tensions it produces can come only vicariously through identification with one who has achieved something like the self we wish to be.

So far, two possible mechanisms for the origin of ethos have been noted: the desire for a savior or father-figure, and the frustrations generated by one's idealized image. The source of ethos is a need, a want, a goal, a frustration, a weakness, a deficiency. Whatever the mechanisms by which ethos is actualized, its starting point is need. *Therefore, ethos is not a separate mode of persuasion, as Aristotle suggested, coordinate with logic and emotion; it is, rather, an aspect of motivation.* The power of ethos derives not from a mysterious "third force" but from the strength of the listener's motives, which are responsible for patterning the image of a person. To an audience with one set of needs, a speaker will have a certain kind of ethos, but to audiences having other needs, he may have a different kind of ethos. With this theoretical construct in mind, we may now set out some hypotheses about the conditions that give rise to ethos.

[11] *Psychology* I (New York: Holt, Rinehart and Winston, Inc., 1890), p. 310. Karen Horney did most interesting work on the frustrations resulting from an idealized image, adapting the concept to an understanding of the neurotic personality in *Our Inner Conflicts* (New York: W. W. Norton & Co., Inc., 1945), Chap. VI.

Although ethos springs from motives and needs, not every need or wish can enhance the ethos of a person who happens to gratify it. When a waiter in a restaurant brings us a glass of water, his ethos is not much enchanced. In the desert, we would feel differently toward the person who gave us a lifesaving drink. The person having ethos for us must fulfill a strong need.

But *strong* has at least three senses. A strong need may be one that is intense: one whom we love can fulfill an intense desire and such a person often has such exceptionally high ethos that we imbue that person with all sorts of good qualities—many of which are not even there. Besides being intense, a strong need may be one that is relatively autonomous: the desire of some to lead a reasonable, intelligent life and to eschew the "unexamined" life may not always be predominant but it may condition more decisions than some momentarily stronger desires. Finally, a strong need may be one that springs from desires that are widespread: a soldier hospitalized far from home and friends has needs not only for survival but for security, for attention, for affection, and for understanding; when his nurse can gratify these, she acquires that unique kind of ethos that begets love. Thus the person to whom we accord ethos must seem to be able to gratify strong—intense or autonomous or widespread—needs.

The needs that result in ethos must be strong, but must also be needs that cannot be gratified by oneself. Even though we were intensely thirsty, we would not accord ethos to someone bringing us a drink that we could as easily get by turning on the tap ourselves. Nor do we feel ethos for one whose effort we take for granted. Moreover, *the person to whom we accord ethos not only must be one who can gratify a strong need but one who has some exclusive ability to gratify the motive or to gratify it better than others can.* We do not feel much ethos for the pharmacist who sells us a prescription that will lead us back to health, for any other pharmacist would do the same.

We also do not accord ethos unless the need or motive is one that we perceive as moral or worthy. As Charles de Gaulle put it: "It is essential that the plan on which the leader has concentrated all his faculties shall bear the mark of grandeur." [12]

---

[12] Charles de Gaulle, *The Edge of the Sword*, trans. by Gerard Hopkins (New York: Criterion Books, 1960), pp. 63–4. The late Charles de Gaulle has written a most insightful analysis of prestige. He describes, however, his own ethos (perhaps unconsciously) rather than any universal characteristics of leaders. De Gaulle, for example, also surrounded his image with a certain mystery, and advocated silence: "Great deeds have never been accomplished by garrulity." Yet these qualities do not describe Castro, Hitler, Theodore Roosevelt, Cicero, or several others with strong ethos. Although the qualities of the successful leader, according to de Gaulle, turn out to be very similar to those of de Gaulle himself, he has one of the best written accounts of leadership.

The addict may be in desperate need of drugs, yet it is doubtful that he perceives his supplier as having high ethos, because selling dope is not an act of moral grandeur. No mere agent of gratification, no matter how strong the drive being gratified or the inability of anyone else to gratify it, can create ethos unless the goal or motive is seen as having moral merit. One must "respond to the cravings felt by men who, imperfect in themselves, seek perfection in the end they choose to serve." [13]

But what of the celebrity? Are such people exceptions to the idea that the need or wish must be tinged with moral grandeur? Hardly. If Elvis Presley and Richard Burton did not achieve admiration because of high moral character, the need they gratified in those who admired them was perceived to be a worthy one: to enjoy the good things of life, to seek and find adventure, to possess vigor and good looks, and to excite admiration. Some of us may have found better things to hope for, yet there is a fulfilling nature in even such "superficial" things as good looks, daring, skill, wit, wealth, and strength. (Who among us would choose to have less of these?) Even the celebrity wins approval because he can, albeit only vicariously, fulfill needs that enrich the lives of some, and these needs are not immoral.

THE RISE OF ETHOS

Ethos is the image of the speaker, a force in problem solving and in historical change. It influences our evaluation of a speech and changes its impact. The best analysis of ethos was Aristotle's, who believed that ethos resulted from the audience's perception of the speaker's intelligence, moral character, and goodwill. Aristotle's analysis is excellent in that if any speaker shows himself to be stupid or dishonest toward his audiences, or if he displays ill will toward them, he will not be persuasive. Moreover, these qualities—intelligence, character, and goodwill —do describe the kinds of people we ought to follow, and lack of these qualities explains why some speakers give unreliable advice. But Aristotle was attempting to analyze the elements of ethos, as have later rhetoricians. We have no guarantee that the qualities that supposedly build ethos are indivisible elements. Aristotle, moreover, considered ethos to be one of three separate kinds of persuasive devices coordinated with logic and emotion. Since ethos seems to be constructed because of a need on the part of the listener, therefore it is an aspect of motivation.

Ethos, therefore, is based on audience needs. But needs that result in ethos must be strong needs that the listener feels another can gratify somewhat exclusively, and these needs must be perceived as being worthy

[13] Ibid., p. 64.

or moral. We are now ready to inquire about the kinds of needs most suited to intelligent—and successful—problem solving.

TRANSFORMING ETHOS

Men and women of great ethos—great teachers, great political and religious leaders—can help or hinder problem solving. The man of ethos becomes the rallying point for others who sense the *need* for transformation and the *possibility* of transformation; he is guide, advisor, and spur. Above all, he converts some or many of his followers into developing their own ethos. The Chinese philosopher Mencius said, "A sage is the instructor of a hundred ages. When . . . [his] manners . . . are heard of, the stupid becomes intelligent and the wavering, determined." Socrates gives rise to two thousand years of brilliant and varied philosophy, for all Western philosophies trace their origin to this one man. After Buddha, annually thousands of new Buddhas arise, and after Galileo, a hundred thousand scientists. Once only Newton and Leibniz could use the calculus; now high school students can. In "The Uses of Great Men," Emerson said: "True genius"—and we could say, likewise, true ethos—"will not impoverish, but will liberate, and add new senses. If a wise man should appear in our village, he would create, in those who converse with him, a new consciousness of wealth, by opening their eyes. . . ." After Thoreau and Gandhi came wave after wave of non-violent protesters who set India free, and who in our own country tried to free blacks and end our involvement in the Vietnam War. The rhetorician known as Longinus said, "But the truly great idea"—and we can add, great ethos—"when introduced at a seasonable moment has often carried all before it with the rapidity of lightning." Thus does the man of transforming ethos, by a reconstruction of personality, ensure that mankind rises. Although transforming ethos is rare, it is one of the great forces of problem solving. Above all, the man of transforming ethos recognizes that the greatest need of man is the need for transformation—of himself and of the society in which he lives.

THE DEVELOPMENT OF ETHOS

The need to solve problems and the need for transformation are the greatest needs of our time or any other. The speaker must try to develop an ethos that suggests that he understands and can help lead the audience toward the solution of these problems. Moreover, if he is to help our culture to survive and to become more rewarding, he is ethically bound to try to develop those characteristics that will enable him to see through confusion, hopelessness, and terror. Our times furnish us with the most desperate needs of humanity, and, consequently, with the most central core for the development of one's own nature. Both logically and psychologically, ethically and pragmatically, a speaker should try to develop ethos that suggests that he can recognize and solve important problems.

In developing ethos that is based on problem solving, we can make use of Aristotle's analysis, making only changes to adapt it to present needs. The image a speaker should try to develop and reflect can be described as problem-solving ethos.

PROBLEM-SOLVING ETHOS
A. *The speaker is a man of intelligence and practical wisdom.*
   1. He has a thorough knowledge of the problem gained from special experience, careful study, and wide information about related matters.
   2. He is alert, sharp-witted, and free from unwarranted doubts and hesitations.
   3. He is uncertain about those matters in which uncertainty is warranted.
   4. He is thoroughly prepared to discuss his subject before this audience.
   5. He understands the causes and solutions of the problems he discusses, and the values behind them.
   6. He perceives the significance of the problems and the goals; his vision shows him what man and society need to be and might become.
B. *The speaker is a man of moral character.*
   1. He is sincere in his recommendations and viewpoints.
   2. He has faith in himself as an agent of good.
   3. He holds his points of view because they are good or correct, rather than because they bring personal gain.
   4. His ideas would bring out the best in the audience.
   5. He is not characterized or motivated by personality problems such as insecurity or overconfidence.
   6. He is worthy of the respect of the audience.
   7. He exemplifies the audience's conception of good moral character: self-reliance, desire for justice, optimism, kindness.
   8. He is dedicated to the audience.
   9. He has the courage to stand by his views.
   10. He can release the powers of members of the audience and give them significance they do not otherwise have.
C. *The speaker is a man of goodwill.*
   1. He knows the distinctive nature of the audience and is sensitive to its needs.

2. He is willing to submit himself to the judgment of the audience.
3. He excels in ways the audience wishes to emulate.
4. He identifies himself with the audience.
5. He admires the good qualities, acts, goals, and attitudes of the audience and, for good reasons, he excuses its weaknesses, mistakes, and shortcomings.
6. He enjoys speaking to and being with the audience.
7. He can unite those of differing abilities, interests, and viewpoints while preserving their differences.
8. He recognizes the better qualities of the audience and can help to maintain and develop these qualities.

Revealing Ethos

REPUTATION

Aristotle pointed out that ethos comes, in part, from the reputation of the speaker. As your speech course has developed, some students in your class already have a reputation for speaking well; this reputation influences your perception of their work, although probably only mildly. Of course, if those with a good reputation for speaking do an abysmally poor job of speaking, their reputations will probably decline, since the audience will be disappointed. In general, however, reputation affects perception.

So great a factor is reputation that very well-known men—presidents of the United States, for example—need not bother with many of the techniques of holding attention prescribed for lesser-known speakers. But even student speakers should be concerned with reputation, and should try to build the kind of reputation that will increase their persuasiveness.

OVERT CHOICES

Aristotle observes that the impression a speaker gives comes, in part, from the choices he makes. The fact that Lincoln, in his Second Inaugural Address, chose to call for a peace "with malice toward none, with charity for all" suggests he was a humanitarian, that he identified with the whole of his people, that he had a high moral purpose, that he had a plan that might have re-established the Union. These choices of Lincoln's gave him an ethos that is cherished long after his death, although his opponents' names are nearly forgotten.

What a man chooses to tell us and the way he tells it suggests something about his attitude toward us, about his intelligence, about his moral purpose, and about the kind of man he is. The student speaker who has chosen not to work very hard on his speech has told us something about himself. The man who has chosen a superficial subject has told us something about the quality of his mind. The pompous orator reveals something of his opinion of himself, and of his opinion of his audience. Even the speaker's choice of words reveals much about his background, his intelligence, his human sympathy and his wit, or lack of it.

The supporting materials the speaker uses may suggest something about his understanding of people, his special experience with the problem, or his concern for the welfare of others. The organization of his ideas may suggest a clear and able mind or a fuzzy one. His sources will reveal much about his background, his knowledge of his subject, his education, and his analytic ability. His choice of words and his grammar may convey to the audience his level of intelligence and education. His ability to speak without notes and to reflect a communicative attitude, his gestures or lack of them, all may say something (rightly or wrongly) about his nature. The number of small matters that reflect his ethos may well run into the hundreds. The speaker builds his ethos through his choice of subject, choice of ideas, by his preparation, his supporting material, as well as his organization, delivery, and attitudes.

MINIMAL CUES

Some of the choices a speaker makes are easily noticed by the audience. If a speaker becomes angry at a hostile question, for example, his anger is noted at once and the audience may infer that he is either pompous or insecure. Many choices, however, have a more subtle effect on an audience: they may hardly be noticed by an audience and yet exert a profound effect.[14] Consider the following case:

X was a woman of thirty-three. Her husband noticed that she had a habit of talking in her sleep. It occurred to him to turn the tendency into account. While she was talking in her sleep, he would say to her in a very low tone, without waking her, "Tell me what you have been doing, today, dearest." She would promptly comply. Soon she came to realize that her husband knew all her activities, even those she would rather have kept to herself and she came to the hospital to see if I could safeguard her against these involuntary indiscretions.[15]

---

[14] Lew Sarett and William Trufaunt Foster, *Basic Principles of Speech*, rev. ed. (Boston: Houghton Mifflin Company, 1946), p. 25. The significance of minimal cues was first suggested to the writer by his major professor of many years ago, the late Lew Sarett, to whom the writer is indebted both for the idea, and for many inspiring hours of superior teaching.

[15] Pierre Janet, *Psychological Healing* (New York: Macmillan Publishing Co., Inc., 1925), pp. 212–13.

This woman's husband may not have known it, but he was using one of the oldest techniques of persuasion: he had circumvented her critical processes. Circumventing her critical processes was possible not so much because she was asleep, but because *she was relatively unaware of the stimulus*. The husband succeeded in getting a response from his wife by establishing an idea without her being aware that it was being established. This stimulus was a minimal cue.

A minimal cue is any stimulus that is only dimly perceived by the audience. One psychologist explains such cues in this way:

> The response called *perceptual* depends, as we have seen, upon the presence of certain stimuli. . . . It is important for us to bear in mind that frequently—if not as a rule—those *cues* or signs are *difficult* to identify. The perceiving person himself is notoriously unable to tell in most cases just what . . . makes him recognize or estimate a situation as he does. . . .[16]

Frequently, it is necessary to establish certain ideas without the audience's awareness that they are being established. This is particularly true for the establishment of a speaker's ethos. Most speakers should not assert directly that they are intelligent. If one announced that he was a man of good character, the audience would either be suspicious of him (recall Nixon's statement, "I am not a crook.") or dismiss him as self-centered and conceited. Nor can a person explain directly that he has goodwill toward his audience. We are suspicious of those who try to win our affection by direct means. If intelligence, character, and goodwill are established, they usually must be established indirectly by the use of minimal cues.

Ordinarily we think that the more aware we are of a stimulus, the more compelling it becomes. Advertising slogans are repeated over and over in order to dominate our attention. That of which we are aware is important, but stimuli of which we are not aware also profoundly influence us.

In one experiment, a group of psychologists at Cornell University were asked to look at a screen and imagine an orange. A picture of an orange was periodically flashed on the screen, but with a light of such low intensity that no one could tell it was there. When the image was not on the screen the psychologists found it difficult to imagine the orange, yet they imagined a rather clear image of an orange whenever the "invisible" image was present.

---

[16] John Frederick Dashiell, *Fundamentals of General Psychology* (Boston: Houghton Mifflin Company, 1937), p. 458. Unfortunately, the study of minimal cues, although once a popular study, reflects the irrational styles of thought and research in psychology. Like the concept of attention, it was once popular, and is now almost never studied. Yet, like attention, the concept of minimal cues is useful for rhetoric and communications. If psychologists abandon these ideas, we need not.

In another experiment, Donald Laird asked a large number of women to choose among four pairs of silk stockings; the stockings were identical except for one irrelevant stimulus: their odor. One pair had the usual odor characteristic of silk stockings—8 per cent believed that pair was the best in quality; 18 per cent preferred the pair with the sachet odor; 24 per cent, the pair with the fruity odor; and 50 per cent, the pair with the narcissus odor. Yet these odors were not noticed, or at least never reported by the women and were true minimal cues that influenced behavior.[17]

A few years ago, minimal cues were used to increase sales in the refreshment booth of a film theater. During the picture, *Time Magazine* reported, in the upper corner of the screen, the words *Drink Coke* were flashed, but so quickly that no one in the audience reported seeing these words. Coca-Cola sales increased that night by 18 per cent; on the same night, *Eat Popcorn* was flashed in a similar fashion, and popcorn sales increased 57 per cent.

Minimal cues are probably responsible for the extent to which we like or dislike a person at first sight. If we dislike him, it may be simply that he has the same feature or mannerism that evokes an unconscious memory of someone whom we once had good grounds to dislike. We should be wary of such first impressions, for although they are sometimes accurate, perhaps just as often they come from an irrelevant minimal cue that is leading us astray.

Sensitivity to minimal cues is often the source of success for interviewers, teachers, and salesmen:

The intelligent salesman perceives that it is time to close his interview. Something about the movements of the auditor's eyes, or . . . his way of sitting . . . or his glancing at his papers . . . something, though, he cannot say just what it is, tells the salesman that it is time for him to go. Most of the so-called "sizing-up" of one man by another is a complex reaction to many obscure stimuli, which are not all catalogued or weighed but simply enter into the total mass of stimulation and help to determine the general impression. It is the operation of such minimal cues that often leads to the intuition or what is colloquially called the "hunch" and gives some basis to the claim that even a guess has a certain value.[18]

Minimal cues have much to do with medical practice. Believe it or not, the color of pills is important in medicine: if patients have responded successfully to a certain type of pill and the doctor changes the color (but not the composition) of the pill from the original bright color

---

[17] Donald Laird, *What Makes People Buy* (New York: McGraw-Hill Book Company, 1935) , p. 29.
[18] Dashiell, op. cit., p. 460.

(such as red or yellow) to blue, often the patient will report, "Those blue pills you gave me just didn't work." For some reason, blue pills provoke more negative response than pills of any other color, whereas reds and yellows provoke positive responses. Certainly minimal cues also enter into the "beside manner." The bearing of the doctor, his calm behavior, his usually conservative dress, his "little black bag," his medicine, and his Latin prescriptions are all devices that establish his prestige as a doctor. He might make as competent a diagnosis dressed in long underwear and unshaven, but it would not so easily be accepted by the patient. Small, irrelevant stimuli establish the idea that the doctor is a competent person in whom trust may safely be placed, or the opposite.

To conceal minimal cues is virtually impossible because one is constantly exuding these small, fleeting stimuli. Probably through such stimuli a horse decides whether its rider is experienced or a novice; the rider's way of mounting and holding the reins, his muscular coordination, and many other tiny stimuli reveal to the horse whether or not it may calmly trot back to the barn. All of us radiate cues, and no great intelligence is needed to interpret them. Children are notorious for being able to size up a substitute teacher in a few minutes, and to estimate the teacher's self-confidence and ability to command them.

So it is with speakers. By the time a stranger has spoken for one minute, you already know much more about him than he has told you. You have already formed an opinion of the kind of person he is, the attitude he has toward life, and his emotional state as he stands before the audience. You know more already about members of your speech class—and the instructor—than anyone has told you, for a speaker conveys his ethos by minimal cues as well as by his reputation and his overt choices.

FAÇADE AND SUBSTANCE IN ETHOS

Can a speaker gain prestige by feigning another character? Can a swindler appear honest? Can a childish person appear mature? Can a shallow man seem profound? Possibly the number of times the Brooklyn Bridge is sold each year would suggest that the answer is affirmative. Yet the best way to *appear* to have good ethos is to *be* the kind of person who is experienced, who is moral, and who genuinely respects and likes people. Virtually everything about you—every muscular contraction, every variation in tone of voice, every word, and every idea—may suggest something about your nature. If you believe you can control all of these factors, you are either more skillful than most people or sadly misinformed. If you pose as a kind of person you are not, there will be a word, an accent, an idea, a facial expression, a certain tension in your voice that may escape and arouse in your audience the suspicion that something about you does not quite ring true. One does not have to be a genius to spot a phony; even horses can. The cues that give us away are too numerous for most of us to disguise or control.

SUGGESTIONS FOR DEVELOPING ETHOS

The wrong way to develop ethos is to ask, "How may I make the audience think that I have intelligence, character, and goodwill?" A better question is, "How may I let the audience know about my intelligence, my character, and my goodwill?" A speaker should demonstrate his intelligence by choosing a subject, a basic theme, and main ideas that demonstrate his intelligence and understanding. He should be willing to work to find materials on which his intelligence can operate. He should put them together so that they are clear, and should find supporting material that demonstrates the rightness of his cause. He should prepare the speech so that he will be at ease and avoid a blundering delivery. He can quote authorities and writers and refer to experiences of his own that suggest his breadth of understanding. He can use statistics to demonstrate his case, and choose language that is clear and vigorous. If he does all these things, the audience will not doubt his intelligence but will perceive him as one who can recognize a problem and bring his intelligence to bear upon it.

How can one suggest that he has moral character and seeks the goodwill of the audience? Again, the same kinds of things that convey a speaker's intelligence can convey his character. His devotion to others is suggested by his theme, by his ideas, by his support, and in subtle ways, by his style and delivery. The same is true of his goodwill. The sarcastic, defensive, critical man will make slips that will reveal him for what he is, whereas another speaker's facial expression, his zest for speaking, and his responses to questions can suggest something of his goodwill toward his audience.

The development of ethos is a program suitable for an entire lifetime, and one can begin that development at once. College provides an excellent place to begin. Some courses can increase one's understanding of social, political, economic, and environmental problems. Good lecturers can increase one's competence in understanding these problems. Every college has a library in which one may discover current and ancient responses to problems. Every curriculum offers courses in literature, as well as in sociology, economics, political science, psychology, and philosophy. Although most curricula are not devoted to problem solving, but merely to conveying information, a bright student can see through the fog of detail to the central core of these subjects. And if he does, he has increased his functional intelligence, his ability to solve problems. Moreover, colleges offer the opportunity to work for causes that develop dedication and human sympathy or, in other words, moral character and goodwill. They offer opportunity for the student to engage in such work while he learns. Character can be learned, too, from a study of literature, from the great epics of the past, from the powerful tragedies that have come to us from Greece and England, and from poetry, whether ancient or contemporary.

Nor need one be in college to develop moral character and goodwill. Perhaps a tour of duty in the Peace Corps or Vista, or a year of travel may arouse one's sensibilities and free him from naïveté and provincialism. From life itself, from the records of the past, from present scenes of strife and terror, from the current literature and magazines that are problem-oriented, from all these come opportunities to develop one's intelligence, character, and goodwill. The important thing is that one decide to explore these opportunities. Many have found that their study of speech begins to stretch their horizons, to develop their potential moral fiber, and to help them discern the fundamental worth of human beings. The difficulty for most persons is not that they cannot develop such qualities but that too few ever try.

The Dangers of Ethos

We must understand not only how ethos may arise but also how we may defend ourselves against the ethos of such men as Hitler or Stalin. If ethos arises in seemingly hopeless situations when the needs of human beings are desperate, one defense is to reduce human desperation and hopelessness. In a word, we must prevent the uniform frustration of a whole people. When needs are too strong, people may turn to the father-figure, or the strong man. When needs are relatively well satisfied, there is more protection against the social pathology of ethos.

A society may also develop resistance to pathological ethos by developing sophistication about which needs are worth developing and which are superficial or neurotic. If the human being can refine his own needs, criticize them, suppress some, and develop others, he can existentially create himself and help determine the kinds of people he will admire and those who will admire him. One great objective of education should be to develop people who will not be subject to neurotic needs and who have a conscious and sophisticated sense of values.

Societies must also produce many men who can meet the legitimate needs of people. Ethos does not become strong unless the agent possessing it seems to have some sort of exclusive power to gratify needs. When only one person seems to have the sharpness to see a people's needs, and the strength to gratify them, the situation is dangerous. Education must help to produce many men who are sensitive to human needs and who search for ways of meeting them. A heavy burden must fall on speakers:

we must need speakers who are sensitive to human needs, who struggle to reformulate those needs, and who become adept at finding ways to alleviate them.

Speech courses often have held the narrow view of using a human need to achieve the speaker's aims: if the audience needs sex or status, use sex or status to sell an idea or product. Instead, we must produce speakers who make the needs of the audience their own. Sophistic rhetoric uses the needs of people as a tool for persuasion; ethical rhetoric— the kind that will prevent men from giving their allegiance to a criminal who poses as a savior—takes the needs of people as the primary end. Thus, another defense against the dangers of ethos is to produce many speakers whose major aim is the satisfaction of the needs of humanity.

If we can create a profound sensitivity to human need, we will produce speakers who have a deservedly powerful ethos. The strongest ethos belongs to him who best serves mankind, provided only that he has the ability to show mankind that he can serve best.

But to serve man best suggests that we must do careful and intense thinking about which needs ought to be ultimate goals of persuasion. What needs are fit to be ends? The need for wealth? For status? Arriving at an answer poses problems of rhetoric, psychology, and philosophy. The problems are subject to constant change because needs may be gratified, whetted, and perhaps created. The needs of man can be sensed from a search through the social sciences, literature, art, and history, and through careful scrutiny of the times. The needs of the affluent may well be those of shattering old barriers, transcending old limits, and reconstructing the human personality. The discovery of which needs are most fulfilling remains perhaps the greatest problem facing education. Whatever these needs are, a speech course that does not focus on the problem of the great needs of man is both sophistic and impractical.

The strongest ethos will be developed by those who can satisfy the strongest and most worthy needs. To an ethical speaker, the needs of man are not means of persuasion but are ends of persuasion. To use human needs as only a tool or means is sophistic; to use human needs as the end is not. Yet the satisfaction of these needs is, itself, an ethical act. Hence the man who is the most ethical is the most apt to have the strongest ethos. Ethics and persuasion unite.

Questions for Understanding, Discussion, and Research

1. Select a person from the past, or from the present, who has high ethos. How, using the concept that ethos is based on need, do you account for his ethos? Does this person have the Aristotelian qualities of intelligence, character, and goodwill?

2. Among people you have known personally, who has the strongest ethos? Why?

3. You have probably been in love, and perhaps more than once. Do feelings of love improve the accuracy of one's assessment of another? Do they sometimes do the opposite? Explain and account for the results.

4. Name some famous and some infamous father-figures from both past and present. How could their rise to power have been prevented? How could their strong ethos have been weakened?

5. Who, in contemporary public life, comes closest to having transforming ethos? Name some people in the last twenty years who have had it. Do you find it significant that many of these people were assassinated or died prematurely? Explain.

6. Set out a five-year program for the development of your ethos. Describe courses you might take, subjects you should explore, and experiences you should seek. Justify your choices.

Speech Assignment: see pp. 232–236.

8

Motivation by Group Behavior: Group Determinism

Groups have much more power than individuals. To solve problems, sometimes an individual must join a group, or organize one himself. Let us examine the power of groups ranging in size from whole cultures to small action groups, and see how groups influence problem solving.

The Importance of Groups

When a Japanese gentleman enters the home of a friend, good breeding requires that he remove his shoes. In our country, the removal of shoes on entering the home of another person may show "bad" breeding; instead, the American gentleman removes his hat (if he wears one) but his wife keeps her on. Muslim women venturing outside the home must be completely covered except for eyes and forehead, but the American or European woman, at the beach, is quite acceptable to others clad in a bikini made of less material than would make a veil for her Eastern sister. What we may or must do depends partly on the group into which we are born and in which we live. When we become members of a group, we begin to reflect its desires and customs. We become, in short, partly group determined, acquiring values, customs, and feelings that shape our lives.

The human being can be shaped by culture into an astounding variety of forms. The problems we locate and the solutions we use depend on the group we are in. In Samoan life, the entire family occupies one room, and by adolescence, children have witnessed all aspects of family life, so that sex and childbirth hold little mystery for them. In Samoa, sexual experimentation is approved and premarital relationships are sanctioned by parents and family. Extramarital relationships are not encouraged, but if a wife is unfaithful, the outraged husband may be placated by the presentation of a mat.[1]

Note how the problems one recognizes and how one solves them are group determined, and why social change and persuasion require the formation of a group. The middle-class American boy grows up in a group that rewards achievement. He grows up hoping to be a "success," to be "outstanding," and if it should be his lot to become richer than others, or more popular, or more intelligent, so much the better. The American may work hard to achieve and, if he wins, will find that Americans admire winners. But for the Zuñi the ideal is different. To the Zuñi, the ideal man is one who is never noticed and certainly never talked about. Hence, a Zuñi avoids office, unless it is thrust upon him, and cooperates with others, gladly lending to others his few personal belongings, always avoiding any show of competitiveness, arrogance, or combativeness. Ruth Benedict epitomizes the mildness of the Zuñi:

> One of the young husbands . . . had been carrying on an extramarital affair . . . The family ignored the matter completely. "So," his wife said, "I didn't wash his clothes. Then he knew that I knew that everybody knew, and he stopped going with that girl." It was effective, but not a word has passed. There were no recriminations, not even an open recognition of the crisis.[2]

Culture produces different varieties of human nature:

> Within one culture, an anthropologist . . . discovers an identifiable and recurrent combination of competitive striving, ambition, violence. The members of a second tribe present, in contrast, a uniformly bland, cooperative, complacent exterior to the investigator. . . . Another society is moralistic, stern, harsh in its discipline of children, hurrying them along the developmental path toward adulthood. Its neighbor has few taboos, lets its children grow up with the pigs and chickens at the edge of the forest. It punishes precocity and over-

[1] Margaret Mead, *Coming of Age in Samoa* (New York: William Morrow & Co., Inc., 1961) , Chap. 7.
[2] Ruth Benedict, *Patterns of Culture* (New York: Mentor Books, 1946) , pp. 98–99.

looks stupidity; and it is as unconcerned about the sexual lives of the youths and maidens as it is about the matings of the pigs and chickens.[8]

Culture can sometimes dramatically influence even seemingly constant physiological patterns. People have been found who "withstood freezing temperatures in rags and plucked potatoes out of boiling water without discomfort." Among the Dobu, magic is believed in so strongly that should a powerful sorcerer suddenly face his enemy with the proper incantation, the enemy would fall writhing to the ground, lose consciousness and die.[4]

The destiny of a group is irrevocably tied to its beliefs and attitudes. John Collier, for example, describes attitudes toward war among the Aztec Indians:

All men were trained for war, and were available as warriors, but the sometimes rather frequent wars lasted . . . only for days or weeks. Battles were events of gorgeous pageantry, waged with a minimum of bloodshed since the object was to capture the foe, not kill him. Indeed, no honor was paid for killing men in battle, while their capture was a prerequisite to the civic advancement of a warrior. Capture was for sacrifice, and to be sacrificed was a public service.[5]

Cortes, with only four hundred soldiers, could not have conquered two million Aztecs had they viewed war as the Spaniards did.

The culture, the civilization, the group, the family, whose ways we have imitated and absorbed—or rejected—partly determine what we are, what we believe, what we can do, what we value, and even what happens to us. The belief that groups of which the individual is a member partly determine his characteristics is called *the theory of social determinism.*

THE NATURE OF SOCIAL DETERMINISM

Social determinism is based on the idea that the whole determines the parts. In the familiar but ambiguous illustration on the next page, the same boundaries seem at one moment to outline two faces and, at another, to outline a vase. Whether the part indicated by the arrow is perceived as a nose or as an indentation in the vase depends upon the whole to which the part is seen to belong. *The nature of the part is determined by the nature of the whole to which the part belongs.*

The practical significance of social determinism is sketched by a well-known social psychologist:

[3] Lawrence Cole, *Human Behavior: Psychology as a Bio-social Science* (Yonkers-on-Hudson, N.Y.: World Book Co., 1953), pp. 49–50.

[4] Ibid., pp. 11, 140.

[5] *Indians of the Americas* (New York: Mentor Books, 1948), p. 47.

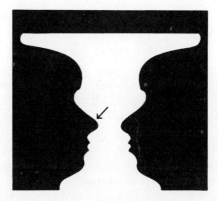

Social scientists . . . have found that an infant's chance to live a year or more is affected by the social class to which his parents belong, that different social classes have distinctive child-raising practices, that attitudes toward education vary with one's social class as does the amount of education youths receive. The courting, marital, and family patterns; how liquor is consumed (to say nothing of what kind!) ; what type of organizations the individual has membership in; how active he is in these; his sexual behavior; which newspapers, magazines, books and radio programs he prefers; even the manner in which breakfast is eaten—all these are influenced by the social class in which individuals are born or belong.[6]

In one experiment social determinism was even noted in marked degree in children's groups.[7] Children were allowed to meet a number of times in a group situation in which they were furnished with toys. During these times, certain group "traditions" were established: seating order, permanent division of objects, "ownership" of objects, and the sequence in which certain games were performed. Once these traditions were set, a "leader" was introduced into the group. The leader was selected because in other groups of children he (or she) had exhibited the following characteristics: he more often gave than followed orders, was more often imitated than found imitating, and was more often the attacker than the attacked. Would such a leader, injected into a group whose leadership, structure, and traditions were already set be able to change the traditions of that group? Would he become the leader of the new group? In the experiment cited, in ten groups, the ten new young "leaders" were generally unable to change the group pattern. With but one exception, they were forced to accept the tradition of the group or

[6] Alvin W. Gouldner, ed., *Studies in Leadership* (New York: Harper & Row, Publishers, Inc., 1950) , pp. 132–33.
[7] Ferenc Merei, "Group Leadership and Institutionalization," trans. by Mrs. David Rappaport, *Human Relations 2* (1949) , 23–29.

be ignored. Thus, the traditions of the group were stronger than the new "leader." We must try to understand how groups become so powerful an influence on those within them.[8]

EFFECT OF GROUPS ON THE INDIVIDUAL

We have all become socialized individuals. In our childhood, doubtless, we at first fought the unnatural idea of wearing shoes; now we have accepted the custom of our society, and not to wear shoes would probably make us both physically and psychologically uncomfortable. The ways, or at least some of the ways, of our culture seem right, as do the ways of every culture and subculture to most of its members. The individual is unaware of any compulsion that has brought about his socialization:

[I]t is not a pleasant experience for him to have his ties upset or severed. He feels uneasy, disturbed, and confused. . . . Conversely, the stability and continuity of the group ties is pleasant—a state to be desired, maintained, and improved.[9]

Others have so much influence over us for many reasons.

THE ORIGIN OF MIND AND SELF

Common sense has it that the nature, variety, and complexity of human society can be explained by the human mind; that is, man's mind makes possible the complex structures and varieties of human societies. George Mead, however, reversed this idea of social causation. He points out, first, that society is already present, ready to make demands, to cajole, approve, or punish, when the child is born into it. Moreover, the human mind develops as a result of living in a society. One's mind, Mead holds, is the result of taking the attitude of others we have known toward ourselves. Mead points out that even the self is socially determined. One experiences himself only by taking the attitude of others he has known toward himself. So the child may take the attitude of his mother toward himself, and later look at himself from the standpoints of others he has known. But, Mead insists, one cannot know himself directly, "for he enters his own experience not directly or immediately . . . but only insofar as he first becomes an object to himself just as other individuals are objects to him . . . and he becomes an object to himself only by taking the attitudes of other individuals toward

---

[8] Groups have limits in shaping individuals, and as we shall see, we cannot always be sure what these limits are. But for now, it is enough to realize that we are shaped by groups in ways that are often beyond our consciousness.

[9] Muzafer Sherif and Carolyn Sherif, *Social Psychology* (New York: Harper & Row, Publishers, Inc., 1969) , p. 145.

himself." [10] The only "others" whose attitudes the child can take are those whom the child has known. The human child takes on the characteristics of those around him, developing himself by looking at himself from their standpoint. "Other men are lenses through which we read our own minds," said Emerson. Thus we become like others because we look at ourselves through the eyes of those we know.

Because we need other people to generate both our minds and our concepts of self, if Mead is correct, children raised apart from other people should lack certain characteristically human qualities. There have been such children—children raised in an attic room apart from adults or other children, or the "wolf-boys" discovered in eighteenth-century Europe when parents sometimes abandoned children in forests. These children, reared without the social setting necessary for them to take the attitudes of other persons, are unable to learn language. Those reared with animals seem to have taken the attitude of animals toward themselves and imitated the animal's posture, snarls, and gestures.

When Emerson said, "I am a part of every man I know," he had grasped one of the central patterns out of which mind and self are built. Samoans will become Samoans, and Americans, Americans, largely through this process of viewing themselves from what they infer to be the attitude of others. If George Mead is correct, when the number and variety of others is lessened and there are fewer standpoints from which the individual may view himself and his ideas, then the individual has been deprived. Perhaps the richest environment in which a child may be raised is one in which he can be exposed to the attitudes of the greatest variety of people. At any rate, our minds and selves develop by taking what we think is the attitude of others toward ourselves. We constantly "monitor" ourselves so that we grow up acting and sounding much like people who were closest to us in our childhood and who in turn, perhaps unknowingly, created us partly in their own image.

FRAMES OF REFERENCE

In an unstructured situation, we tend to decide what to believe or do on the basis of what others around us believe and do. In one experiment, subjects were put into a totally dark room where, because nothing could be seen, there was no frame of reference, and no way of judging distance. A tiny light, about the size of the tip of a matchead, was introduced; it could be seen clearly, but was not bright enough to illuminate any object in the room. Such a light, in an otherwise dark room, displays an "autokinetic effect;" that is, the natural but involuntary and

[10] George H. Mead, *Mind, Self and Society*, ed. by Charles W. Morris (Chicago: The University of Chicago Press, 1934), p. 138.

jerky movements of one's eye muscles make the light seem to move even when subjects *know* it is not moving. The subjects were asked how far the light seemed to move. Now, if the subjects do not know how far away the light is, or how large it is, their judgment of how far the light seems to move can be enormously influenced by those around them.[11]

In this situation . . . there is no "right" or "wrong" judgment. One subject demonstrated this spontaneously during the experiment by suggesting. . . . "If you tell me once how much I am mistaken, all my judgments will be better. . . ." In *the group situation,* the members of the group tend to structure the situation by converging toward a common norm in their judgments. If in the beginning of the experimental session they start with widely different judgments, in the course of the experiment, they come together, the divergent one feeling uncertain and insecure in the solitude given by his judgments. . . .

Yet the subjects were not aware of being influenced by others: "In fact, the majority of the subjects reported not only that their judgments were made before the others spoke, but that they were not influenced by the others in the group." [12] The experimental situation is, however, an artificial one.

It must be said that in our experimental settings the subjects were not moved by a common interest drive such as is found in a group that faces a common danger, such as starvation or the cruel authority of a tyrant. In these vital situations there is a certain gap that has to be filled, some urgent deprivation to be satisfied. Until the need is satisfied, to some degree at least, the instability of the situation continues. If the norms and slogans that arise under the stress of a tense and uncertain situation do not meet the situation adequately, the instability is not removed, and new norms and new slogans are likely to arise until the tension is relieved. For example, in a mass of hungry people searching for food, a leader of a small party may standardize certain norms or slogans as guides to outlook and action. But if these norms do not lead to the satisfaction of hunger, other leaders or interested parties may and do spring up and standardize other norms or slogans. This dynamic process moves on and on until norms or slogans are reached appropriate to the situation.[13]

The degree to which others set—often without our awareness—our standards of achievement is surprising. In Europe, where everyone in college learns several languages, the learning of languages is easy. "What man has done, man can do," is the proverbial expression of the idea. But in our country, the learning of languages is perceived as so

---

[11] By far the most detailed account of the autokinetic effect was in Muzafer Sherif's earlier book, *An Outline of Social Psychology* (New York: Harper & Row, Publishers, Inc., 1948), pp. 175, 202. All citations are from this earlier edition.

[12] Ibid., p. 175.

[13] Ibid., p. 176.

difficult that many universities have eliminated the language requirement for graduation. At any rate, in situations where what to believe or what to do is unstructured, we tend to take our norms—our frames of reference, our guides—from those about us, and we tend to accept these norms more or less unconsciously.

NEED FULFILLMENT

The power of groups over the individual develops, in part, because groups can filfill his direct and indirect needs. *Direct* needs are those that are met by the recognized purpose of the group. Thus, among physicians, the American Medical Association serves as an accrediting agency for hospitals, medical schools, and, to an extent, for physicians; the United Mine Workers' Union, the welfare of coal miners; the John Birch Society serves as a forum for those who consider themselves far right of the political center. Hence, some groups have power because they meet the clear and stated needs of the members.

In addition to these direct needs, each group likewise serves certain *indirect* needs that have little to do with the stated or "official" purpose of the group. Groups may meet the need for status by providing a public office for one to hold, by giving one a cause with which to identify and giving one something to work for that is of greater moment than himself. Some organizations give a feeling of prestige to nearly anyone admitted to them, thus raising the esteem of the member in his own eyes and often in the eyes of others. Other organizations provide recreation, or enable the newly arrived stranger to make new friends easily and quickly, or otherwise provide benefits all the way from low-cost transportation to Europe to special hospitalization and insurance policies. Moreover, from earliest childhood we are dependent on others for our feeding, safety, and comfort. When we contravened the norms they set for us, they showed their disapproval and possibly withheld gratification of one of our needs. Though we cannot remember the process now, we came to develop a certain relationship with others in which we accepted their norms and they fulfilled our needs. To rebel against these norms, even when we think we are right, causes us a certain anxiety that sometimes expresses itself in overreaction. We need others, and to be deliberately ignored or overlooked by the groups we like most can drive some to despondency, and solitary confinement is among the worst of punishments. *Groups can influence us because they contribute to our needs. To go contrary to the influence of a group is to risk leaving ungratified one or more of our direct or indirect needs.*

CREATION AND ENFORCEMENT OF EXPECTATIONS

Groups expect certain kinds of attitudes and behavior of their members and the individual often fulfills these expectations. We behave in one way at the meeting of a religious organization, in another at the reunion of old friends, and in still another in an academic, business, or trade setting. By applause, titles, salary, invitations to the "right' places, access to "inside" information, and by ridicule, ostracism, criticism, and rejection organizations enforce their expectations on us. When individuals in an organization fail to live up to the expectations of the organization, the group can often apply enormous pressure. One might think that the following paragraph was written by a businessman; but it was written about pressures in a military organization:

A member of an organization who cannot do what is expected of him is subject to self-criticism and to criticism, implied or explicit, from his supervisor and from his co-workers. His self-confidence will diminish, and feelings of inferiority emerge; he is likely to become hypersensitive and defensive in his social relations, and [to] blame others for his own shortcomings. . . . Thus, as soon as the strength of one component—in this case that of a specific ability— drops below a certain minimum, other components are similarly affected. . . . Contrariwise, a man whose talents are exactly suited to the job assigned to him and who, therefore, attains or surpasses the level of social expectation for him, will continually be encouraged by signs of approval and of respect from associates, and under these conditions, his energy and initiative, motivation and effective intelligence, emotional stability, and social relations are likely to reach their maximum.[14]

Organizations enforce what they think they have a right to expect, from admission to membership to selection for the highest office the organization offers, and by acts that range from slightly raised eyebrows to murder.

STRUCTURE FORMATION

Groups form, within themselves, a structure—a hierarchy—that specializes the functions of members, fixes the responsibility for certain acts, and helps to perpetuate the group. Thus, officers are elected and committees are appointed to recommend policy changes, to plan programs, to get new members, or to raise money. This structure helps to clarify lines of authority and responsibility for certain functions.[15] Elected officers preside over meetings, take notes, and handle money. The structure serves to guarantee that the functions necessary to the life of the group will be performed, and orderly procedures are devised for choos-

---

[14] U.S. Strategic Services, Offices of the Assessment Staff, *The Assessment of Men* (New York: Holt, Rinehart and Winston, Inc., 1948), p. 456.
[15] On the reasons groups tend to create specialization, and the value of specialization, see Franklyn S. Haiman, "The Specialization of Roles and Functions in a Group," *Quarterly Journal of Speech, 43* (April 1957), 165–74, including the commentaries by Gale E. Jensen and William Utterback together with the reply of Professor Haiman.

ing other members to fill the same functions so that the organization has some assurance of continuity. The structure usually ensures that those in high office have greatest access to the members and exercise maximum influence and control over them. On the other hand, the members have the greatest control over those who want high office, and members can enforce their demands on those who seek office by withholding election, or by withdrawing support from officeholders. At any rate, part of the power of a group develops because the group arranges for roles, for specialization, for hierarchy, and for orderly succession of those who perform the functions of the group.

DOUBLE CHOICE

Groups have influence over us, much of which we perceive, because to participate in a group, we must choose the group, and the group must choose us. Without this act of reciprocal choice, we are not members of a group, but only members of a class. For example, you may be a member of the class *university* or *college student,* but you may not be a *member* of any university or college group—social, academic, or athletic— unless you choose to be and the group chooses you as a member. If you are a college student, you cannot avoid being a member of the class *college student,* but you can avoid being a member of almost any campus group by simply refusing to make the choices necessary to become a member. By the same token, various groups can make the choice to exclude you, making it virtually impossible for you to participate in the group. In this way, groups differ from classes. We do not choose the classes we are in, and classes cannot choose their members: no person with brown eyes can help being in the class of brown-eyed people. But to be in a group, we must usually choose, and be chosen.

One or more of the explanations offered helps account for the power of groups to influence individuals in and out of the group.[16]

Social determinism comes about because we become like members of the groups to which we belong, adopting the attitudes of others we have known toward ourselves, becoming like them and looking to others to set our frames of reference or our levels of aspiration in unstructured situations. Groups have power over us because they can fulfill both direct and indirect needs, and can reward and punish us. When we are in a group, we behave as the group expects us to, or suffer loss of identifi-

---

[16] These explanations are generally in the same tradition as recent theoretical formulations, whether in psychology or in rhetoric. See, for example, the introductions to each of seven parts of Dorwin Cartwright and Alvin Zander, *Group Dynamics, Research and Theory* (New York: Harper & Row, Publishers, Inc., 1968). See also Herbert W. Simons, "Requirements, Problems, and Strategies: A Theory of Persuasion for Social Movements," *Quarterly Journal of Speech,* 56 (February 1970), 1–11.

cation with it. Group structures fix the right and responsibility to perform certain acts. Through reciprocal choice, we choose to be in the group, and the group chooses to accept us.

For these reasons, we do not deviate much or often from the norms of groups of which we are members. We have peace of mind when we accept the ways of the group, and pangs of guilt when we do not. The power groups have over us, both in its conscious and unconscious aspects, perform the same function that instinct does among social insects, keeping us together, giving us roles to fulfill, creating hierarchies, and perpetuating the group.[17]

LIMITATIONS ON GROUP DETERMINISM

In all cultures, some persons ignore, or deviate, or innovate, or revolt from group pressures. Some of these are saints, and others, sinners, but all limit the power of groups. Both individual determinism and social determinism have merits and limitations; neither philosophers nor psychologists are able to state the extent to which either theory is correct, nor to predict accurately where one theory will apply and the other will not.[18] But the theory of social determinism provides insights useful for the study of rhetoric.

RHETORIC AND SOCIAL DETERMINISM

Because groups are powerful determinants of what individuals do, we need to know the rhetorical ways of creating groups. In our society, power is wielded by groups. Small but well-organized groups have made the Federal Communications Commission, which is supposed to be responsive to the public, responsive to the broadcasters instead. On the other hand, newly organized citizens' groups have made the Food and Drug Administration more responsive to the needs of consumers. In

---

[17] See Henri Bergson, *Two Sources of Morality and Religion,* trans. by R. Ashley and C. Breraton (Garden City, N.Y.: Doubleday & Company, Inc., 1954), who believes that habits and customs are the counterpart of instinct among the social insects. These habits and customs are, for the most part, influenced and inculcated by, and derived from the groups of which we are members.

[18] The argument about which theory is preferable began early. One can trace elements of social determinism back to Plato, as does Gardner Murphy, in *Historical Introduction to Modern Psychology* (New York: Harcourt Brace Jovanovich, Inc., 1949), p. 284, whereas individual determinism and atomism go back to Democritus. Most rhetoricians were atomists and individual determinists. Yet the influence of Gestalt psychology and wholeism are not absent. See W. M. Parrish, "Implications of Gestalt Psychology," *Quarterly Journal of Speech Education, 14* (February 1928), 7–29. The theory of individual determinism was defended as early as three years after Parrish's article by Milton Dickens, "The Group Fallacy and Public Speaking," *Quarterly Journal of Speech, 17* (February 1931), 40–49. Regrettably, however, social determinism, Gestalt, and wholeism have not been adapted sufficiently to rhetorical theory.

political campaigns, small groups do much of the campaigning that results in the election of candidates. The group ties determine, in part, the extent to which members are willing to work for the group, and the extent to which the group is effective. Therefore, *one may often need to know how to create a group, and how to help strengthen a group. Since persuasive devices are used in creating and strengthening groups, we must understand the devices that bring groups into being and that make groups function effectively.*

Traditional rhetoric has not concerned itself with the matter. Yet if some of our problems are to be solved, we must form groups to solve them. By what rhetorical means may groups be strengthened or weakened, created or destroyed? How may we change an audience into a group?

THE CREATION OF GROUPS

If a speaker wishes to create or to strengthen a group, he must: (1) create a feeling of cohesiveness among members of the group; (2) create a feeling of striving for common goals; (3) create confidence that the group can achieve the goals; (4) create mechanisms to ensure the continuity of the group.

The Feeling of Cohesiveness. For a group to function smoothly and override obstacles, members must have a feeling of belonging. Sometimes, this feeling is the overiding explanation of the effectiveness of a group. Bill Mauldin, the famous cartoonist, describes this feeling among men in combat in World War II, noting that their cohesiveness stemmed not so much from the cause for which they fought, nor from any great certainty that the cause could be achieved, but rather from the way they seemed to "belong" to the unit into which they were arbitrarily cast:

> Combat people are an exclusive set, and if they want to be that way, it is their privilege. They certainly earned it. New men in outfits have to work their way in slowly, but they are eventually accepted. . . . Once . . . [the new man] has arrived, he is pretty proud of his clique, and he in turn is chilly toward outsiders. That's why, during some of the worst periods . . . many guys who had a chance to hang around town for a few days after being discharged from a hospital where they had recovered from wounds, with nobody the wiser, didn't take advantage of it. They weren't eager to get back to the war by any means, and many of them did hang around for a few days. But those who did hang around didn't feel exactly right about it.[19]

The reader can think of organizations that lacked a feeling of belonging, in which there were serious splits in the group, or in which morale

[19] *Up Front* (New York: Holt, Rinehart and Winston, Inc., 1944), p. 58.

had deteriorated. Perhaps he could think of ways in which cohesiveness could have been imparted or restored.

The feeling of cohesiveness seems to result from three factors: [20]

1. The characteristics of the members of the group:
    a. The group differs from other similar groups: its members are more interesting, generous, hard-working, witty, dedicated, honest, clear-sighted, powerful, or brave, than those of other groups.
    b. Members are relatively equal, and the group lacks subgroups of racial, economic, social, hierarchical nature.
    c. Differences among members do not add conflict but color, life, and charm to the group.
    d. Leaders have more merit, common sense, daring, knowledge, fortitude, power, or liking for the membership than leaders in similar groups.
    e. Members like, respect, and enjoy one another.
    f. Members have the same needs, problems, aspirations, make the same mistakes, possess the same attitudes, and beliefs.
2. The prestige of the group:
    a. The group has a highly regarded or unique function, membership, history, aim, or tradition.
    b. Members acquire, increase, or maintain their significance, status, or prestige by belonging to the group, or the group has raised their significance, or is raising it.
    c. The group may conflict with other groups, but is not ignored.
3. The activities of the group:
    a. The group is bound by mutual experiences, by a tradition of being together in the face of opposition, and by the need to confront shared problems and to stand together in the future.
    b. Superior forces that threaten the group are immoral, unintelligent, selfish, or greedy.
    c. The group has its own characteristic symbols, techniques, cus-

---

[20] My deepest gratitude in the development of these ideas, as classical scholars will note, is to the spirit—if not the word—of Aristotle. Any resemblance between the methods of holding a group together, driving it apart, increasing or lessening its influence, and the intellectual style of *The Rhetoric* of Aristotle, Book II, Chaps. 2–11, is not merely a coincidence. Nor is this part of his work unworthy of respect, as some have said. Here, he draws hundreds of highly probable generalizations about human needs, feelings, behavior and human nature. Those turned off by this sort of highly intellectual activity may prefer generalizations that are a hundred per cent certain, but then, not much can be said about human life. This different style of intellectual activity, so necessary to rhetoric and communication, should be given credit as an alternative intellectual style. Aristotle was among the first to use it, and because of him, we may use it even better.

toms, roles, and procedures, which are more natural to the group, better in themselves, more efficient, and more outstanding than those of other groups.

d. Barriers to a feeling of belonging have been removed, or are in the process of being removed.

The Feeling of Striving for Common Goals. This feeling can be achieved by acceptance of some of the following:

a. The goals of the group are attractive, interesting, necessary, and will benefit the group and others.
b. The goal is deserved by the group, or is more deserved than by those who will achieve it if the group does not.
c. The goal has been fought for in the past by those who were the most intelligent, the bravest, the most admirable, or those who produced the most for humanity.
d. Seeking the goal is a tradition and the rightful function of the group, and is necessary for the group's survival.
e. The undesirable aspects of the goal have been removed, are being removed, or can be minimized.
f. The goal is more important and more valuable than before.
g. Similar groups aim at the goal, but inferior groups lack the courage, intelligence, foresight, and so forth, to do so.
h. The activities of the group are pleasant, easy to participate in, rewarding, and so forth.
i. The goals are selected by the group, can be changed when the group wishes, and are subject to the group's collective will rather than forced upon them.
j. The group must remain together and drop minor differences if it is to survive—if its aims are to be achieved, or achieved with minimum ease and efficiency.

Confidence That the Goals Can Be Achieved. Confidence is always important in achieving goals. We know that persons under hypnosis are capable of performing feats of strength that would be impossible if the hypnotist did not verbally assure them of success. The same is true of groups. The Continental Army nearly fell apart during the Revolutionary War, when it seemed that victory was impossible. Not a few of Washington's strategies—notably Washington's crossing of the Delaware to capture the Hessians at Trenton—were calculated to instill confidence that the enemy could be defeated.

In 1970, the force of the anti-Vietnam War movement began to seriously decline, even though six months before it had brought together more people to demonstrate than any other movement in American history. When the policies of the Nixon administration made it seem clear that such demonstrations were not achieving their effect, the movement began to ebb: many of its leaders resigned and its attractivensss was, for many, diminished—even though, according to most public-opinion polls, more people than ever before were in sympathy with American disengagement in Vietnam.

Let us examine some of the ideas that can give a group confidence that its goals can be achieved:

    a. This group, or groups similar to it, succeeded in the past under similar circumstances.

    b. This group is likely to succeed because it is stronger, more efficient, wiser, more dedicated than those who have failed or who oppose it.

    c. Material help and moral support are on the way, or will come, provided the group remains intact.

    d. New plans and new ideas for achieving the goal are likely to be effective where old ones have been ineffective.

    e. Similar groups, with less chance of winning than this group, have defeated similar forces.

    f. Similar groups have been defeated in the past, but the conditions contributing to their defeat have been removed or their force seriously weakened.

Mechanisms to Found a Group.   When one is trying to organize a group for the first time, some mechanism must be used to arrange for its formation. When all or part of the audience is ready to form a group, certain simple but crucial steps must be taken to ensure that whatever enthusiasm has been generated does not evaporate. Select the following:

    a. A temporary chairman to conduct the organization meeting.

    b. A time and place for the formation of the organization.

    c. Persons to play temporary roles: to arrange for transportation, collect admission fees, secure members outside the immediate audience, enlist the cooperation of similar interested groups, and so forth.

COMPARATIVE GROUPS

So far, we have been talking about what social psychologists call *normative groups,* that is, groups that influence their members. However, other kinds of groups, known as *comparative groups,* exist whose influence goes beyond their members. The comparative group is used as a reference point by which those outside the group may set standards. Harvard University, for example, is a normative group to the students, faculty, and alumni of that institution, but for many other universities in the country, it is a comparative group; other schools often incorporate programs that originated at Harvard, and, at least, feel "safe" if Harvard has the same sort of curriculum. Thus, a comparative group is one that is imitated. Organizations from the National Association of Manufacturers to the Americans for Democratic Action hope to influence not only their members, whom they can hold in line rather easily, but also a wide range of public opinion outside the group. To understand more about motivating group action, we must understand something of the psychology of comparative groups.

More and more frequently, organizations are dedicating themselves to creating goodwill for themselves among those not interested in joining the group itself. Much contemporary advertising is devoted to creating a "good image" for business organizations. The influence a group has beyond its own membership comes, in part, from the extent to which it can engender goodwill in the minds of the public.

The means by which goodwill is created are worth careful examination. These include the following:

a. The organization performs services to humanity; these services are indispensable, or contribute to the welfare of the community, or offer opportunities to many people.
b. The services are performed *as services,* without expectation of direct gain.
c. The organization is a symbol of a great cause, idea, or movement.
d. The services are sometimes performed at considerable risk or loss to the organization's security or to its personnel.
e. The organization fits the popular conception of success: it arose from small beginnings, struggled to get started, faced great problems, and grew (by ethical means) into a position of considerable size, significance, and influence.
f. The organization is affected by the same forces that affect the members of the audience and is hurt or helped by them.
g. The organization contributes to the fundamental values to which the audience is dedicated.
h. The organization has interesting, unusual, and varied techniques, products, objectives, personnel, significance, services, history, physical facilities, relations with the community, and so forth.
i. The organization is fighting individuals, groups, or forces that are unscrupulous, merciless, unjust, and unintelligent.

In general, a speaker will not build goodwill for an organization if he displays bitterness, intolerance, or undue pride in his own organization. An important exception must be noted. When the organization to which one is opposed is recognized as unprincipled, immoral, or cruel, then a less tolerant attitude is more consistent with the situation; righteous indignation has its place.

Since all of us have been in organizations, we have all seen many of the methods of achieving a group used both to strengthen and to weaken groups. Wherever possible, recall examples of both strong and weak groups and try to explain their strength or weakness. What might have been done to have reversed the situation?

DIMINISHING INFLUENCE

Most often, one desires to create a new group, strengthen an already existing group, or secure more goodwill or influence for a comparative group, but there are times when the opposite is desirable: we may want to weaken a group, to reduce its influence, and even to destroy it. The techniques for achieving these ends are, roughly, the opposite of the techniques used for enhancing the power of a group. These include showing that;

a. The group seems to provide services, but its only motive is profit, and the profits far outweigh the services; in fact, the organization pollutes the air, the water or the land; it overcharges for its products, which are often shoddy and badly designed.

b. Profit-making is the only motive of some of the group—the stockholders or officers—who operate the organization for gain while overworking and underpaying the employees and cheating the consumer.

c. The services are performed at the risk of the employees' health but never at the risk to the stockholders or officers of the organization.

d. Because of its unethical and corrupt practices, the organization has grown into the insensitive industrial giant it is today.

e. The organization thrives on conditions that are harmful to the citizen: it manipulates the market in order to raise prices, eliminates competition, pays lower taxes than are equitable, and spends far less money on research in crucial areas than an organization of its size and wealth should.

f. The organization is opposed to the fundamental values of free citizens in a republic: it is authoritarian, dishonest in its advertising, and profits from wars and calamities.

g. The organization uses outmoded techniques, has officers of unsavory character, luxurious physical facilities that drain profits, possesses great wealth and power, has had a sordid history, and has brought the community pain and hardship, and yet expects to be respected and admired.

One can spot, sometimes without much study, the unscrupulous use of the techniques for building goodwill in government and corporation advertising and propaganda. It is good to know the techniques being used, to be able to identify them.

Diminishing the Influence of a Normative Group. Sometimes, it is possible to demoralize a normative group, to weaken it, to encourage much of its membership to resign, to prevent others from joining, and thereby to cause the group to disintegrate. Again, as with comparative groups, the techniques for accomplishing the weakening of an organization are exactly the opposite of those used to strengthen it.

Let us take a sampling of some of these opposites; the reader can then easily see how some of the ideas suggested to build up a normative group can be reversed:

1. Reduce the cohesiveness of the group members by showing that:
   a. Members are no different from similar groups: they are lazy, uninteresting, selfish, dishonest, muddle-headed, cowardly, and domineering.
   b. Leaders of the group lack common sense, a sense of adventure or opportunity, knowledge, fortitude, a liking for humanity, and even a liking for their own people.
2. Reduce the feeling of striving for common goals by showing that:
   a. The goals of the group are repulsive, uninteresting, unnecessary, and harmful to others, and, perhaps, even to members of the group.
   b. The goal is deserved not by the group, but by others.
3. Undermine the confidence that the goals can be achieved by showing that:
   a. The group is unlikely to succeed because it is weaker, less efficient, less intelligent, less dedicated than those who, in the past, have reached the goal.
   b. Any past successes of this group were the result of luck and, in any event, conditions now are so different that success cannot be gained by the obsolete techniques the organization is using.

USING TECHNIQUES OF MOTIVATING GROUPS

The first advice to a critic or analyst of communication, or to a speaker using the techniques of motivating groups, is that one must know the personnel or group about which or to which he is talking. If he is attacking the goodwill that a large company has, he must know the company, its policies, something about its personnel, its products, its techniques, its organization. He must know its research—or lack of research —its production techniques, its policies toward pollution, and its pricing, for only through such knowledge can he select the best strategy and find support for the strategy he chooses.

Such ideas about strengthening or weakening the power of groups as presented here are suggestions, and may help channel one's investigation. But such ideas are no substitute for research, study, content, or documentation. The aim in stating these ideas is to suggest lines of argument to the analyst, to the critic, and to the speaker. But these lines of argument are not comprehensive, nor are they selected, adapted, and supported to fit the particular group, the analyst, critic, or speaker. These functions must be performed by the analysts, the critics, and the speakers themselves.

One can develop his own lines of argument pertinent to particular groups, if he takes the trouble. One need only sharpen his observation of groups, note what seems to make some groups work effectively, and others ineffectively, what increases the prestige of one group and diminishes that of another, what creates one group and destroys another. By his own acute observation, the reader can sharpen his wits about the kinds of things that create, enhance, and destroy the power of groups over the problems and the solutions of mankind.

GROUP DETERMINISM VERSUS INDIVIDUAL DETERMINISM

Now we are in a position to see the merit of both individual and group determinism. We are sensible enough not to ask, "Which is true?" or even, "Which is more nearly true?" A better question is, "How does each work with the other?" The best current answer has been given in a speech by John Kenneth Galbraith. The speech is of merit not only because it touches on the reconciliation between individual determinism and group determinism but also because it serves as an excellent summary of the ways in which we have incorrectly perceived problems and solutions in international affairs since World War II. As you read the speech, keep in mind the following questions:

1. How does Galbraith reconcile individual determinism and group determinism?
2. What false problems did the United States respond to in foreign policy?
3. How did the recognition of these problems as problems entail solutions that we now find repugnant?
4. How might we prevent the recognition of false problems in the future?

JOHN KENNETH GALBRAITH: *The Policy Specifies the Man* [21]

In the following paper, prepared for the Center [for the Study of Democratic Action's], Pacem in Terris III Convocation, Harvard economist John Kenneth Galbraith says that the policy specifies the man and suggests that the new policy of détente may attract better men to government.

The professional discussion of foreign policy is unique among the great social disciplines in that good tailoring combined with a certain assurance of manner is extensively a substitute for thought. For this reason, even on an occasion that so unites erudition with solemnity as this, one can, with a sense of novelty, still make a commonplace point. It is this: while, as commonly imagined, men do have a certain influence on the foreign policy—on those dealings in and with other countries that affect national and general well-being—policy has had an even more profound effect in selecting the people who guide it. This circumstance, I shall argue, does much to specify the kind of policy that we can pursue. There are policies which require a class of talent which we cannot wisely risk or afford. These are matters which even a brief glance at recent history affirms.

The years of World War II and those immediately following were a remarkably compassionate and creative time in the history of American foreign policy. This policy, in turn, attracted the talents and energy of a remarkable group of men and women—George C. Marshall, the earlier and better Dean Acheson, Herbert H. Lehman, W. Averell Harriman, Paul Hoffman, Eleanor Roosevelt, Adlai Stevenson, many others. Nearly all owed their eminence not alone to their perception of the issues but also to their influence with the Congress and the public at large. The policy of the time was accessible to the Congress and the public. Both had to be persuaded. Hard-nosed diplomatic, military, and espionage talent was not especially useful for this work. It was, we may also recall, a golden age in American influence and esteem.

In the second Truman Administration, the policy changed. The ability of the American conservative establishment to make disreputable what does not serve its interests or beliefs was something that Harry Truman, like many since, did not fully perceive. But for ending the earlier policy—and on this there is now a measure of Soviet agreement—there was no small cooperation from Stalin.

That policy was nailed in its coffin by the Korean War. With others, I think that was misinterpreted—that the common assumption at the time, that it was a signal of Soviet imperial intentions, was wrong. It was, like much since in that part of the world, a matter of local inspiration. It remains that the North Koreans went to Pusan and no one could easily imagine they were our clients. Those who argued for working things out with the Soviets were silenced—or committed to saving their skins from Joe McCarthy.

[21] *Center Report,* 7 (April 1974), pp. 3–4. Reprinted with permission from the April, 1974, issue of the *Center Report,* a publication of the Center for the Study of Democratic Institutions, Santa Barbara, California.

From this point on, the foreign policy of the United States became comprehensively anti-Communist. And this anti-Communism caused it, in turn, to be increasingly theological, military, bureaucratic, and secretive. The theology, of course, was that Communism was wicked and, like the devil, relentless. In contrast free enterprise and democracy—terms liturgically preferable to capitalism—were good but, as with virtue over the ages, beset. With the arrival of John Foster Dulles in 1952, the religious overtones of the policy were formally affirmed. Dulles spoke regularly not of Communism but of *atheistic* Communism.

World Communism, as the Korean War was thought to show, relied ultimately on military means; it was, accordingly, something to be resisted primarily by armed power. Thus the military character of the defense. Liberals, retreating from McCarthy or concerned for their security clearances, could still aver that Communism was the consequence of economic deprivation and that the remedy was social amelioration and economic development. But this, through the Fifties and early Sixties, was the soft position. The tougher, more practical view was that resistance depended on troops, fire power, nuclear weapons, and the associated submarines and missiles. Those who so averred got the good notice from Joseph Alsop.

Since the Communist threat was comprehensive—since it discovered and probed points of weakness anywhere in the world, as the Korean experience seemed to show—it had to be comprehensively watched and countered. This required a massive organization. Thus the bureaucratic nature of the policy. The Communists operated by conspiracy and stealth. They had to be so countered. This, and the military character of their threat, necessitated the secrecy.

The policy, and its attributes as just adumbrated, largely determined the kind of men who were put in charge as well as the way policy was conducted. The theological character of the policy required men who were capable of simple, forthright belief—men of dogmatic faith for whom a distinction between good and evil was sufficient. It has been argued in the case of both Dulles and Rusk, the two Secretaries of State who dominated the two decades of the new policy, that the stern Protestantism of their early origins was reflected in their approach to foreign policy. Perhaps there is something to the point. Be this as it may, both were capable of avowing, without seeming doubt, a sternly canonical view of the unrelieved wickedness of Communism, the inherent and even absolute virtue of almost *any* alternative.

The military character of the policy required men who accepted the use of force, who were untroubled by the vast uncertainties as to outcome whenever there is resort to arms, who were impervious to the moral problems associated with bombing and body counts. The bureaucratic as well as the military character of the policy required men who accepted discipline, operated contentedly within a prescribed formula, understood that you get along by going along, protected their "effectiveness" by controlling carefully their dissent, accepted that, ultimately, the goals of the organization must prevail.

The imperatives of secrecy made winning of support unnecessary. It takes very little persuasive talent to say of an action that it is justified by urgent considerations of national security which cannot be revealed. Secrecy was also essential as a shield for the deeper tendencies of a military and bureaucratic policy. For it is known that these encourage the individual who, however accomplished in bureaucratic survival, is otherwise congenitally incompetent. Secrecy, and the frequently repellent character of the clandestine activities so protected, had a further effect on personnel procurement. It attracted those who, escaping from the confining virtue of civilized existence, rejoiced in what seemed to be a professional license for indecency. Nothing growing out of the Watergate episode has been more salutary than its advertisement of the banality, ineptitude, and general unattractiveness of the people who, released from foreign employment, had sought to bring the darker arts, nurtured by our recent foreign policy, to domestic purposes. The demonstration was an accident but it would have been worth arranging.

The old policy propelled us into the Vietnam War, and that was its grave. That this should have happened, given the men that the policy attracted, is not surprising. Those who resolve matters by dogma do not readily reconsider their course. Those whose faith is based on arms do not readily inquire whether soldiers can contend with historical process and revolutionary dynamic. Men skilled in bureaucratic survival do not readily question, or seek to alter, even disastrous bureaucratic purpose. Men accustomed to the protection of secrecy do not have—or else they lose—the capacity to persuade or defend. All who opposed the Vietnam War will agree that nothing was ever so inept as the defense.

The executive and military power did not, nevertheless, readily surrender its commitment to the Indochina involvement. But in what historians will surely concede to be a truly prodigious display of public power, it was eventually forced to do so. We should be proud. Not before has public opinion so asserted itself to halt a war. And with the end of the Indochina involvement has come a drastically reduced view of what we *can* do and what we *need* to do to affect the economic and political development of countries economically, culturally, and geographically apart from our own. Complementing the withdrawal from Indochina has come also a revised view of the intentions of the Soviet and Chinese Communists. This is a matter on which fairness, however uncomfortable in these matters, requires one to ascribe a strongly affirmative role to the leadership to President Richard Nixon and Secretary of State Henry Kissinger.

The new policy, if it persists, will attract a better and safer class of men. A policy of détente and accommodation with the Communist powers requires men of essentially secular view—men for whom intelligent compromise does not mean surrender to the devil. Additionally, if we recognize that we cannot and that we need not affect the economic and political structure of the countries of the Third World, it follows that unilateral military effort in these countries is unnecessary or irrelevant. So military influence on policy is excluded—including the influence not alone of generals but of the civilian Bonapartes whose influence in the last two decades has, if anything, been even more malign. And if we are not reacting to Communism in Chad, Angola, or Paraguay, we no longer need a vast organization to watch and counter Communist machinations, real or imagined. If we are not seeking to counter some hidden enemy, we do not need to hide our own work. What we do in the Third World can be open and visible and the Congress and the public can rightly ask that it be defended. And our actions will be infinitely safer if they are in the hands of men who must defend what they do.

I've been speaking of the Third World—not of Europe, Japan, or the older British Commonwealth. But it was in the Third World, let us remind ourselves, that our policy brought us the disasters in these last years. That is because policy in Europe and Japan, where we deal through strong, sophisticated governments, has not lent itself to simple theological decision. In these parts of the world military influence, if present, has not been dominant and the role of bureaucracy—intelligence, clandestine activities, propaganda, military operations—has been far less comprehensive than in the Third World. Northern Laos has been a natural theater for the CIA but not northern Alberta or even northern Sweden. Our policy in these parts of the world has not required or attracted the wrong kind of men. It has not, accordingly, reflected their genius for disaster.

A policy that attracts the wrong men has another consequence, including the effect on the way the United States is regarded in the world. The men who were brought into positions of prominence by the creative and compassionate policies of the period of World War II and following kept us out of trouble. (Marshall kept us out of China; the faith that motivated Dulles or Rusk would surely have plunged us in.) Such men, by their caution, imagination, and tolerance of differing views caused us also to be well regarded in the world. Men of dogmatic tendency—generals, military or civilian—those who have surrendered to bureaucratic discipline, spies and perpetrators of dirty tricks do not enlist esteem. A policy that nurtures the wrong kind of people also nurtures national disesteem.

Although in foreign policy, as in economics and love, there are few absolutes, the lesson seems plain: men make the policy. But, even more importantly, the policy makes or specifies the men. Henceforth we must be exceedingly suspicious of those policies that get us the wrong kind of men. If there is a hint of simple, dogmatic formula; if there is heavy reliance on military means; if a large organization is required; if secrecy is an imperative; if there can be no defense to the Congress and the public—then our suspicions must be immediately and deeply aroused. Given such policy, the wrong men are inevitable. And whatever the ends to be served, the words of Wellington on seeing his new battalions must be deeply on our minds. The men required by such policy may not frighten the enemy, but, by God, they should frighten us.

Questions for Understanding, Discussion, and Research

1. Select and study another culture that might have qualities, attitudes, customs, and behavior that would be good for our culture to adopt. Explain (a) why we should adopt these devices of another culture, and (b) how we might be persuaded to do so.

2. Merei (see pp. 177–178) describes leaders as (a) those who are imitated rather than who are imitating, and as (b) those who attack more than they are attacked. What do you think of this operational definition of *leader?* Do we need to develop more such "leaders?"

3. Can you find traits, characteristics, attitudes, and views of others that you have adopted? Account for this adoption, using, if possible, the ideas of George H. Mead (see pp. 178–179).

4. In every culture, dissenters exist and often these dissenters are not recorded by anthropologists and sociologists who may be trying to state the general character of the culture. Name some important dissenters in history. Have they changed the culture? Explain how they could, despite the theory of group determinism.

5. Select a group with which you are familiar: a friendship group, a family group, or a religious, political, business, or social organization. What factors add to its strength? To its weakness? Explain.

6. Describe a currently strong group. How could this group be weakened?

7. What kinds of groups does our own culture most need today? Explain how they might be formed.

8. Now that you have studied both individual determinism and social determinism, and see that each has merit, try to formulate some statement of each. Under what conditions will one apply over the other or limit the other, or reinforce the other?

Speech Assignment: see pp. 234–237.

9

Problem Solving and the Varieties of Rhetorical Criticism[1]

On the Power of Communication

Communication, so commonplace in every culture, now and then becomes a powerful force affecting individuals—and whole civilizations, leading at times to greatness and at times to catastrophe. The speaking of Socrates, made famous by Plato's *Dialogues,* resulted in nothing less than a philosophic revolution; hardly a school of philosophy exists in the Western world that does not find some of its roots in Socratic speaking. The speaking of Jesus launched a new religion, and the speaking of the Apostle Paul altered that religion in ways probably unintended by the founder. Speaking lulled the Romans to disregard the poverty—intellectual as well as economic—of the Roman world until impoverishment pro-

---

[1] Some of the materials in this chapter are adapted from Otis M. Walter, "On the Varieties of Rhetorical Criticism," in *Essays on Rhetorical Criticism,* ed. by Thomas R. Nilsen (New York: Random House, Inc., 1968) , pp. 158–172, and are used here by permission.

duced the sleep that led almost imperceptibly to death; only the final result, the barbarian invasion, was cataclysmic. Speaking intensified the senseless ardor of the Crusades, and later helped to split into a hundred pieces the oldest institution in the Western world. In more recent times, the speaking and writing of Lenin helped create the Russian revolution and led the Russians into Communism. The speaking of Hitler was indispensable in building the Third Reich, and was an indirect cause of history's most devastating war. Franklin D. Roosevelt, in his first inaugural address, restored, by a single speech, the confidence of Americans in their economic future; throughout the country, almost universal despair gave way to hope as he announced, "The only thing we have to fear is fear itself." Winston Churchill, despite the disaster of Dunkirk, steeled the British Empire to the seemingly impossible task of achieving victory. Wherever social, political, economic, religious, and philosophic revolutions have arisen, communication has played an important role—sometimes desirable and sometimes disastrous. Today, the power of communication is even greater than in the past, for now a speech can be heard and the speaker seen around the world as his words are spoken.

All of the ideas that affect us, however, do not come to us through speeches: the written word in its many forms is probably our greatest source of ideas. But the spoken word, active and vibrant, has impact that written passages rarely, if ever, can match. Many influences shape our behavior: our biological heritage, physical and social environment, the political and economic system we live in, our training, the whole pattern of needs we experience, intellectual and emotional as well as physical. The communication we hear is not separate from other life experiences. But it heightens (or obscures) political and economic issues, social and religious questions, indeed the whole range of human problems. Clearly we are shaped in a peculiarly significant way by what we hear, say, or read.

The Need for Criticizing Communication

Because communication is a powerful force, man needs profound and searching insight into communications—into their truth or falsity, their wisdom or stupidity, their profundity or emptiness, into their subtle greatness or disguised and hidden meanness. Since man needs such insights, he needs critics of rhetoric and communications.

In a democratic society, rhetorical criticism is especially important, for in a democracy, each man must understand and judge what he hears and reads. Therefore, each man must be, at times, his own rhetorical critic. Unless citizens can judge wisely what they hear and read, a free society is virtually impossible. Since each citizen must distinguish those ideas that should shape society from those that should not, democracy requires good rhetorical critics.

To say that democracy requires good rhetorical critics is to say that rhetorical criticism is a liberal art, an art appropriate to men who are free. (*Liberal,* remember, comes from the Latin, *liberare,* "to free.") Free men must be able to accept or reject the speeches they hear, to modify or qualify these speeches, to question them, to doubt them, or to accept them. Rhetorical criticism, although it has never held a place among the great liberal arts, deserves one, for it is appropriate to free men, and, for the fullest exercise of freedom, ever necessary.

Kinds of Rhetorical Criticism

Despite the need for it, we have little good rhetorical criticism; of such as we have had, three sources are worth noting. Most rhetorical criticism comes as a by-product of, or as incidental to, political, legal, or social opposition: the party out of power needles the administration in power, the defense attorney exposes the weaknesses in the prosecutor's case; the candidates for office clash—or exhibit their dullness—on television; the leftist lampoons the rightist, and so on.

In addition to criticism from opponents, the reaction of the audience (or what psychologists call "feedback") provides a second source of criticism: the audience cheers or "boos" the speaker, or greets him with icy irresponsiveness; the congregation nods in somnolence during the Sunday sermon; the constituents vote their candidate in or out of office or don't bother to vote. *Criticism from opponents and feedback from audiences constitute the main sources of communication criticism today.*

Neither of these forms of criticism, nor both of them together, ensure that we will have the best, or even adequate, criticism, for both are too often tainted. The reactions of opponents and of audiences may spring largely from prejudice; the listeners may be insensitive and ignorant and their reactions inarticulate or haphazard. We need better criticism than that afforded by the unsystematic and uncritical offerings of opponents and audiences.

The trained rhetorical critic or critic of communication constitutes a third source of criticism. One would think, if criticism were important, that interest in the work of the trained rhetorical critic would be great. But there is no such interest. The world at large takes no note of the work of the professional rhetorical critic. The educated part of the world often seeks the work of the dramatic critic, the literary critic, or the art critic, but it ignores the rhetorical critic. The much smaller scholarly part of the world likewise passes by his work. The few who read the works of the rhetorical critic are, themselves, rhetoricians; even they are dissatisfied with much that passes for rhetorical criticism, and more than one is bored by it.

If rhetorical criticism is necessary, why are professional rhetorical critics ignored? Many reasons account for the inability of current rhetorical criticism to capture interest, and most of these reasons are beyond our control. One reason, however, is totally within our power to eliminate; this reason, moreover, is a decisive one. Let us look at it.

The Weakness of Traditional Rhetorical Criticism

Most rhetorical critics use a system derived from Aristotle's *Rhetoric*, a book deservedly listed among the great books because it furnishes insights into people, into the processes of argument, into the means of persuasion, and into the mechanisms of human judgment; it furnishes more of such insights than any similar work. But the *Rhetoric* was not intended as a recipe book for critics; not one line in the *Rhetoric* suggests it was so intended. The uses of this otherwise great work as the basis for speech criticism have been, with some exceptions, largely sterile. But how can so great a book as this be so sterile when adapted to the criticism of speeches? The reason is that the *Rhetoric* is used—or rather, misused—to provide only one aim for criticism, and that aim is not always the most appropriate nor does it provide the most insight. One of Aristotle's stated aims was to ask "What are the means of persuasion?" Adapting this question to criticism, rhetorical critics have asked "To what extent did this speaker use the available means of persuasion?" At one time (in the 1920s) this question appeared to be a good one, for it gave the rhetorical critic a sphere of inquiry that seemed exclusively his, one that no literary critic nor dramatic critic had exploited. The exclusiveness of the "Aristotelian" question blinded many to the fact that the question itself was not always worth asking.

Of course, this Aristotelian question often is worthwhile in the classroom where the teacher attempts to impart principles of effective communication. But even in the classroom, the instructor may wisely abandon an analysis of persuasive devices to point out more important matters. If a student, for example, were to use the best available means of persuasion to convince an audience that there were 10,572 beans in a jar he held, few instructors would feel moved to congratulate him. Criticism of such a speech requires no erudite analysis of the persuasive devices used but, rather, a convincing message from the instructor or the listeners that the subject was a waste of the audience's time and a perversion of the speaker's intellect. Aristotle, very likely, would have said as little.

If an analysis of the means of persuasion is not always the best standpoint from which to look at a classroom speech, it is even less satisfactory as a standpoint from which to view historically significant speeches.[2] Concern only with the means of persuasion often misses important matters. For example, intelligent men still read Pericles' "Funeral Oration." But the intelligent man—even the intelligent rhetorician—does not ask "How and to what extent did Pericles persuade the fifth-century Greeks who heard him?" We don't know who heard him, and couldn't answer the question if we wanted to. Discerning and sensible men have been asking better questions of this speech for 2,500 years, such as, according to Pericles—or was it according to the famous lady, Aspasia, who may have "ghosted" the speech—"What are the characteristics of a free society?" or "How does Pericles' treatment of the free society compare with Milton's in his *Areopagitica* or with John Stuart Mill's in his *On Liberty?*" or "Was ancient Athens the kind of society Pericles describes?" These questions have little to do with the available means of persuasion and yet are better questions than those about the use of neglect of persuasive devices.

Is it, after all, of much importance whether or not the Sermon on the Mount used the available means of persuading the audience of shepherds and fishermen? Suppose we found that the Speaker missed using some means of persuading the Galileans He addressed? Would not one be tempted to say "So what?" To find that the Speaker's means of persuasion were thoroughly consistent—or inconsistent—with His ethical doctrines might be fascinating, yet the most fundamental question would surely be different from the Aristotelian question. More likely it would be "What is the ethical doctrine expressed in the Sermon on the Mount?" or "What changes in Old Testament morality did the Speaker present?" or "Are there inconsistencies in thought and style? If so, where?" Again, neither the most intelligent nor the most fundamental issues are always revealed by asking about the means of persuasion.

Moreover, total reliance on questions about the means of persuasion often results not merely in unimportant answers but sometimes in absurdities. What is the best way—the most intelligent way—to view Hitler's anti-Semitic diatribes? Is it to ask, "Did Hitler use all the available means of persuading Germans to hate Jews?" And who would assign to Hitler a lesser degree of significance if we discovered that these diatribes failed to use some way of making men hate, or much admire him

2 Even here, however, it is sometimes worthwhile. The aim of Lincoln's "First Inaugural Address" was to prevent the Civil War. It is intriguing to ask "Did Lincoln use all the available means of preventing a civil war?" as did Professor Marie Hochmuth [Nichols] in *American Speeches* (New York: Longmans, Green and Co., 1954), pp. 21–71.

if we found he used all of them? Indeed, we ought to note the techniques that the demagogue uses, but however well or ill adapted to the audience these techniques are is somewhat beside the point. One could better ask "What conditions produce such a speaker and such audiences?" and "How can such conditions be prevented?" Indeed, the devices that Hitler used illuminate Hitler and Hitlerism, but the effectiveness or ineffectiveness of the devices is not always the most critical concern. The same is true of the speeches of the late Senator Joseph McCarthy and Richard Nixon.

The analysis of the Gettysburg Address presents nearly an impossible case for the Aristotelian. He must ask "How well did Lincoln use the available means of persuasion on his audience?" But the question cannot be answered because we do not know Lincoln's audience. According to Alexander Woolcott, Lincoln did not address the speech to those who stood before him; Lincoln did not wait for the crowd to be quiet when he gave the speech, and never spoke loudly enough to be heard by more than a small percentage of those present. The speech was addressed, rather, to posterity. How well adapted was this speech to posterity? We cannot answer the question for we do not know the nature of posterity, or even, in these days, whether we will be fortunate enough to be followed by posterity. Since we do not know the nature of posterity, we cannot tell if the speech is adapted to it. It is ridiculous to avow that the only proper way of looking at a speech is the "Aristotelian" way when that way would sometimes leave critics with nothing to say!

Thus, to ask, "Does this speech use the available means of persuasion?" is not always the best question. Critics were attracted to the question because it offered one that rhetoricians could exploit exclusively. "Aristotelian" criticism, however, does not meet even the requirement of exclusiveness. Studies of the means of persuasion are not unique to rhetoric; psychologists and sociologists also inquire into the devices of persuasion. Uniqueness, moreover, is hardly a guarantee of excellence. Too much concern with mere uniqueness will relegate studies in rhetoric and communication to only those questions about which no one else cares. We should be more concerned with our *intelligence* than with our *uniqueness,* for uniqueness is easy to come by; simply do a rhetorical criticism while standing on your head, for example. Intelligence is somewhat more rare, and at the same time more beneficial to humanity.

Regrettably, however, rhetorical critics made from Aristotle a canon, a creed for criticism. We must not forget that a creed, although it sometimes clarifies and illumines, may become a subtle "enforcer," a guide to the stupid, a tool of the arrogant, and a wall in front of one who realizes that what is intelligent in any given case cannot be dogmatically proclaimed by a code. Instead of guaranteeing good criticism of communication, the current use of the *Rhetoric* formalizes a way of looking at a speech that is not always the best way, and is sometimes an absurd or impossible way.

Alternative Suggestions for Criticism

Rhetorical and communication theory can help free rhetorical criticism from the Aristotelian approach. Although Aristotle defined rhetoric as the art of discerning the available means of persuasion, rhetoric, broadly speaking, is *any idea about communication.* Ideas about communication, from the time of the pre-Socrates to the present, are characterized by great variety. Indeed, many writers on rhetoric have not been predominantly interested in persuasion (see pp. 4–6). These other theorists of communication have ideas that can be adapted to criticism of communication, and, thereby, can help provide the sense of variety in approach that rhetorical criticism needs. Let us adapt some of their ideas to criticism.

Protagoras, you may remember, presented a series of fragmentary ideas about rhetoric that contrast markedly with the ideas of those who were simply interested in persuasion. He started with the idea that speech should be as intelligent as possible rather than as persuasive as possible. His idea of intelligence was a unique one, and was the ancestor of Hegel's dialectic: When intelligence pushes to its furthest limits, it reveals "two *logoi* in opposition," or two opposites, each of which is true. Protagoras based his theory of rhetoric on the idea that, metaphysically, the world consisted of irrefutable and irreconcilable contradictions. Speech, to be as intelligent as possible, must reveal these contradictions, for they are present in every subject.

A complete rhetoric following Protagoras' idea was never written. If it had been (and I suspect it wasn't written because the product of intelligence, most likely, is not two contradictions), we would have had a description of how to locate, step by step, each of the "two *logoi* in opposition," and how to present each of them so an audience would recognize that they represent intelligence pushed as far as intelligence can go. Even from this brief analysis, we can see, again, that Protagoras was concerned with kindling the intelligence of the speaker and then of the audience; kindling intelligence is often different from discovering a way of persuading an audience.

The problem now arises: how can we use "the rhetoric of intelligence" in criticism? Well, first of all we can not do so immediately, because it has not been completely formulated. No rhetoric demonstrates how a speaker may push his intellect as far as it can go. Yet one can ask of a speech, "Is this speech the best that intelligence can do on this subject with this audience?" The question is sometimes a better question than "Did this speaker use the available means of persuasion?"

Many other views of rhetoric are available, and most of them are about as undeveloped as that of Protagoras. Yet they contain the unifying *principle* of a possible rhetoric, the *starting point* for further inquiry, the *basis* for a different rhetoric, a *productive assumption* leading to a theory about communication, a *pattern of inquiry* leading to new principles of symbolism, or a different *definition of rhetoric or communication*. That different emphases exist is utterly beyond dispute. Let us examine some of these differences.

A major objective of Isocrates was to produce the ideal citizen, the orator-statesman. His interest was not merely in producing those who could persuade, but rather in producing those who would speak in such a way that they would guide an entire culture wisely. Isocrates wanted to produce articulate world citizens, identified with more than achieving their own immediate needs, dedicated to the good of the culture as a whole. His rhetoric, although sometimes more fully formulated than that of Protagoras, was still incomplete. Cicero's rhetoric has glimmers sometimes of a rhetoric of citizenship, but it seems corrupted by the traditional rhetorical practice of the day so that he is seldom devoted to the question "How may speech be taught so as to produce the best civilization?" Sometimes he slips into expediency that is not entirely compatible with his ideal and most of his best work, *De Oratore,* is a work explaining how to persuade. Nevertheless, these men represent an interest that is distinct from an interest in mere persuasion. The study of their ideal of producing fine citizens and civilization might suggest ways of looking at speeches that might be more appropriate than the way of Protagoras or the overused one of Aristotle.

One can return to Aristotle and find an emphasis different from the one that rhetorical critics have traditionally exploited. One of his more difficult themes is that the rhetorician must have both a deep and a broad competence. Rhetoric, for Aristotle, was concerned with politics, and hence, the speaker must use political themes; he must also know what subjects are being argued and understand the era's problems, possibilities, and dangers. But politics to Aristotle was merely *ethics in the large.* The speaker must be master of *ethics,* for many lines of argument will be derived from ethical principles, and he who knows the most about them will have the greatest assortment of arguments from which to choose. But the rhetorician must also be a psychologist to judge which arguments appeal to persons in various situations. Thus, to judge a speech one must be a master of politics, ethics, and psychology. Few critics have asked "To what extent does this speaker exemplify the breadth and depth required to speak well?" Thus, the present use that critics have made of the *Rhetoric* by no means exploits the whole of the work; other aspects of it might furnish more productive questions than the traditional one.

Finally, insisting that Aristotle was concerned largely with analysing the means is a distortion of Aristotle's intent. He seems more intent with pointing out the kinds of knowledge that a speaker needed, especially outside rhetoric, than in merely listing persuasive devices. Hence, he has emphasized a knowledge of politics, logic, ethics, and psychology, all of which together are given greater space in the *Rhetoric* than is rhetoric itself. As we said on pp. 3–5, the notion that Aristotle's overriding concern was with listing the available means of persuasion is the conventional wisdom of twentieth-century rhetoric.

Rhetorical theory furnishes many other suggestions for rhetorical criticism. We might expound on the possibilities of idealism in Plato's works or in *On the Sublime,* attributed to Longinus. One can find ideas that could be applied to criticism in Quintilian's educational emphasis, in Augustine's insistence that his religion demanded a characteristic rhetoric, in Bacon's approach to rhetorical logic and to faculty psychology, in the esthetic concerns of Blair, in Campbell's many-sided *Philosophy of Rhetoric,* in Whately's logical emphasis, in Winans' adaptation of the psychology of William James to rhetoric, in I. A. Richards' definition of rhetoric as "a study of misunderstandings and its remedies," and in other ideas of rhetoric and communication as well.

The study of theory, therefore, can help inject variety in view and freshness in approach into the practice of criticism. Once the "cake of custom" is broken, rhetorical theory, provided it is viewed in its diversity, may stimulate the development of ways of looking at communication that do not yet receive treatment in rhetorical theory. For example, there is no "rhetoric of sanity," but one might ask "What kinds of communication help lead to serious maladjustment, and what kinds to mental health?" That there are such kinds of communication is suggested by the speaking of Hitler, which seemed to convert a whole nation to insanity. Although we need a "rhetoric of sanity," it has not been written, and although we also need to know the ways in which a people may be *led away from* sanity by communication, we have little understanding of what these ways might be. In addition, communication is one of the links in the chain of causes that leads whole civilizations to develop and grow; there are kinds of communication that are more civilizing than others and we need to know what these kinds are. (See pp. 11–21) . We need to understand, likewise, the kinds of rhetoric that may weaken or destroy the civilizing propensities that are present in a culture.

Indeed, the points of view from which rhetorics might be written seem unlimited. What kinds of communication lead us toward (or away from) the open society? What kinds of communication lead to creativity and to the lack of it? What kinds of communication lead to violence and what kinds to problem solving? What kinds lead to understanding, to high morale, to learning, to dedication, and to their opposites? We need to look at communication from all these points of view. More worthwhile "undiscovered" rhetorics exist than developed ones, and, therefore, there are more ways of looking at a speech critically than even the diverse history of rhetoric suggests.

So far, we have talked about *explicit* rhetorics: consciously formulated theories of communication. Only a few societies have produced such rhetorics, the most notable being the Greco-Roman civilization and Western civilization. Nevertheless, every culture and every subculture has an *implicit* theory of rhetoric—a theory of how communication ought to proceed, and of what is appropriate, dangerous, unusual, or sane. Unexpressed and implicit theories of rhetoric exist in all cultures and subcultures: in aboriginal tribes, in schools, in prisons, in slum cultures in our large cities, and in "in-groups" and in "out-groups." These implicit modes of communication are the distinctive marks that stamp one as a taciturn New Hampshire farmer, as a child of the slums, as a product of a university education, or as an introvert or as a hippie. Yet we have not uncovered these implicit assumptions about communication, perhaps because we have been too dominated by the study of "the available means of persuasion." Nevertheless, we could uncover implicit rhetorics by studies of the communication of almost any group. Such studies would help reveal the ways in which such groups communicate and help us criticize the communication they hear. Moreover, such studies would provide additional points of view from which a critic might look at a speech.

Formulas and Criticism

To assume that rhetorical and communication theory can furnish a formula complete with a step-by-step procedure to be followed by the otherwise thoughtless critic is in error. Formulas may work well in elementary physics, but in the humanities, formulas somehow result in mindless mechanicalness, giving evidence sometimes of hard work but less often of brilliance. Brilliance and hard work are not the same thing; but criticism that is brilliant is always criticism that could *not be easily prescribed, that is somewhat unexpected, that fits the unique speech for which it is designed* and perhaps no other speech, that is the most appropriate thing to say at this time about that speech.

To say that criticism cannot be formulated in advance is only another way of saying that rhetoric and communication belong to the liberal arts (or humanities) and not to the natural sciences. Although the humanities at their best do that which is unpredictably and even surprisingly appropriate, the way to such achievement, at least partly, can be prepared. We must remember, nevertheless, that in the humanities, the perfect idea for criticism springs from the keen intelligence and sensitivity of the critic and not fully grown from a formula out of the past. In a real sense, *fine* criticism cannot be taught by rhetorical theory or by any other device.

On Learning to Be a Critic

To say that *fine* criticism cannot be taught is no more than saying one cannot teach great speaking, or brilliant writing, or indeed, great virtuosity in any field. Nevertheless, schools can impart a sense of what is worthy, competent, and sensible. If medical schools, for example, cannot automatically produce great surgeons, they still can teach students procedures of good surgery, the problems involved, and dangers to avoid. Rhetorical and communication theory can likewise point out varieties of criticism that might free the young critic from the notion that there is only *one true way* of criticism; it can suggest to him that there are several ways, some of which are sometimes more appropriate than others. In short, rhetorical or communication theory can suggest to the student not just one, or four ways of looking at a speech, but many. The study of rhetorical theory can especially impart flexibility, for rhetorical theory itself is varied; rather than treating only persuasion, some rhetorical theories are not even much concerned with persuading, but with a dozen other matters. Hence, the study of rhetorical theory can help provide the student with divergent standpoints from which he may view speeches, and perhaps help develop the flexibility needed by a good critic. Rhetorical theory can, in addition, present some procedures that might help the critic exploit these standpoints, and give him a sense of the difficulties and dangers involved in criticism. Rhetorical theory cannot be expected to furnish the perfect way for the mature scholar, nor will it instruct the unusually brilliant critic, who himself will erect landmarks. Rhetorical theory, like the Emersonian conception of books, should be used "to inspire," although it cannot furnish the one true key to criticism.

Of course, other ways to assist the development of good criticism should be used: one can practice criticism of speeches and criticize his own practice; one can find *examples* of criticism and analyze and perhaps emulate the examples; but one function of rhetorical theory can be to give the student some broad *principles* of good criticism and have him try them out. Some combination of the three is probably best.

Problem Solving and Criticism

A natural series of suggestions comes from the major concern of this book: problem solving. Looking at policy speeches from the standpoint of problem solving may, in fact, be the most useful mode of criticism. Policy speeches, of course, are speeches that recommend changes—solutions—whether the changes are recommended from the legislator's halls, from the pulpit, from a candidate seeking office, from the president of any organization, by a parent, by yourself, or by a friend of yours. Let us look at some questions that might be useful in evaluating a speaker's ability and intent when the speaker is recommending a change in policy.

PROBLEMS AND CRITICISM

1. Is the speaker concerned with the most significant problems? What problems are they? Which problems does he seem to be uninterested in? Does he have a sufficient grasp of the range of problems?

2. How strong is the validity of the arguments the speaker uses to support his concern with those problems? Does he avoid spurious arguments?

3. If one examines the speaker's communication over a long period of his life, how does his selection of problems change? Is the change intelligent or not? If he does not change, is it because he arrived at intelligent formulations long ago, or is he falling behind the needs of the day?

One can use these and similar questions to look at one speech, a lifetime of speaking, a cross-section of speeches from a particular movement, or the state of speaking in a city, country, or in the world at any given moment. But one must not restrict oneself to only these questions, for new questions, particularly pertinent to the task at hand, may occur to you. But to evaluate speakers effectively we must inquire into the extent, depth, and intelligence of their analysis of the problems of people.

Criticism of the grasp of problems is a logical first step in criticizing problem-solving, for if the speaker's grasp of problems is poor, one may terminate further inquiry. But if the grasp is good, or if further inquiry would illuminate the speakers excellence or stupidity, one should proceed to other categories of problem solving.

CAUSES OF PROBLEMS AND CRITICISM

1. Does the speaker seem aware of some of the major causes of the problems of which he speaks? Does he state these causes clearly and intelligently? Has he omitted some important causes? Has

he misstated or misunderstood the causes of the problems? Is his analysis of causes up-to-date or out-of-date?

2. Does the speaker support his analysis of the causes of problems strongly, either by Mill's Cannons and/or by describing the conditions that produce the effect? Or, does he merely list causes without support? How valid is his support for a causal relation?

You will see that most speakers and many writers omit consideration of the causes of problems; few politicians include any mention of the causes of inflation, shortages, or unemployment, and when they do include such mention, it is unsupported, and out of touch with the best thinkers of the day. Politicians will continue such sloppy speaking, until the American public insists on better speaking. Intelligent criticism may help encourage audiences to demand better speeches and, especially, better causal analysis.

SOLUTIONS TO PROBLEMS AND CRITICISM
1. If the speaker selects the most significant problems, does he offer any solutions? Is he aware that many kinds of solutions are available and that many kinds of solutions may be needed?
2. How valid are the solutions he offers? Does the speaker attempt to show that his solutions will work, or that similar solutions have worked in similar situations?
3. What new difficulties might his solutions raise? Might some of these difficulties be prevented? If not, are the new difficulties preferable to the old problem? To what extent does the speaker show that they are?

VALUES AND CRITICISM
1. What values underlie the speakers choice of problems, his selection of causes (if any) , and his solutions (if any) ? What are his opinions of his fellow human beings, of the society in which he lives, and of himself?
2. How can you be sure these values *are* his values? Does he, at any point, try to explain or justify his values? If so, how clear does he make these values and how good is the justification?

Techniques of Communication and Criticism

For the most part, unless you are going to become a teacher of speech, rhetoric, English composition, or communication, you need not focus on the techniques of the speaker, unless, of course, these techniques illumine his analysis of problems. When the techniques are those of the demagogue, the racist, the man who still lives in the nineteenth century, or the schemer, then techniques become important. Or when the man is surpassingly honest, when he is trying to be extremely clear and fair, when he is leading people out of the morass of problems we have imposed on ourself, sometimes a study of the techniques of speaking he uses are important. But the citizen should focus, most of the time, on the problems, causes, solutions, and values the speaker represents or fails to mention.

Summary

To recommend that citizens look at policy speeches from the standpoint of problem solving is a natural consequence of the main interest of this book. But no single way of looking at a speech is best in all circumstances. We must re-emphasize that man needs the best insights possible into speeches. Rhetorical criticism, however, has become calcified by adopting a portion of Aristotle's *Rhetoric;* that portion cannot always provide the insights we need. We need, rather than a single approach to criticism, a great variety of approaches suggested by the explicit rhetorics of the Western world, and that might be suggested by the yet undescribed implicit rhetorics that exist everywhere.

To put it more succinctly, we need a kind of "natural selection" among rhetorical theories. But for natural selection to occur, one must first have variation in the same sense that Darwin recognized in *The Origin of Species.* When variations occur, they may compete with the effect that the best adapted at the time will more likely survive. But the starting point must be variation. When we have a number of standpoints from which to criticize speeches, we will be able to select those that most meet our needs. Of these standpoints, that of asking questions about problem solving in communication is among the most promising and most suitable to a democratic society.

Questions for Understanding, Discussion, and Research

1. Find communications that present one or more intelligently chosen problems and some that present poorly chosen problems. In each case, why do you say the choice was intelligent or poor? Whether the problems were chosen intelligently or not, were the means of presenting them vivid? Were they valid?
2. Do the same for sermons, or essays, or television productions that present problems, causes, solutions, or values.
3. Since you will probably hear more speeches than you will give, formulate some standards by which you can focus your critical

faculties while listening to communication that presents problems. Would these standards differ from the standards you wish to apply to a classroom lecture? Why?

4. If democracy requires intelligent criticism of communication, and there is little such criticism, how do you account for that fact? How would you remedy the situation?

5. Does criticizing a poem, a play, a novel, a movie, or an opera differ in significant ways from criticizing a speech? In what ways? Justify your answer.

6. Criticize any communications where problems in the following are discussed: politics, religion, economics, international affairs, health, education, or values. Make the basis of your criticism clear and support that basis with enough direct materials from the original communication to justify your answers.

7. Find some kinds of communications in which a problem solving approach to criticism would be inappropriate. Explain.

8. Besides a problem solving approach to the criticism of communication, what other approaches have been recommended by people in speech, rhetoric, and speech-communications? Your instructor can give you a bibliography.

9. Compare the approaches to speech criticism to approaches for the criticism of art or literature. To what extent can the techniques appropriate to speech criticism be used in art and literature and *vice versa?*

10. Examine great literary, artistic, and rhetorical criticism and determine the extent to which you can state the principles on which the critique was based. To what extent are common themes and common difficulties found in the theory and practice of artistic, dramatic, musical and rhetorical criticism?

Appendix

SPEECH ASSIGNMENTS [1]

Problems
Causation
Solutions
Definitions
Values
Eulogy
Comparative Groups
Normative Group

OUTLINING

Outline on Outlining
Sample Outline

DELIVERY

---

[1] I have included in this appendix difficult assignments. Instructors should reduce the difficulty whenever necessary to meet the needs of their classes.

Speech
Assignments

Problems

INTRODUCTION

Great speeches are always responses to great problems. Problems seem to be the starting point of much that is best in man. When man reacts intelligently and vigorously to certain kinds of problems, he often rises to his highest level. It may seem strange that problems, which are also sources of human misery, may sometimes bring out the best in man, but since problems are the starting point of all civilizations, and the starting point of thought, of motivation, and of creativity, it is not strange that whatever stimulates intelligence, energy, and invention leads to a higher level of culture. Solutions to problems of certain kinds reduce human misery, substitute new strength for former weakness, unleash new energy, and enable life to begin at a new level.

We must understand our problems not only because such understanding can lead to an improvement in life but also because problems of certain kinds cause human degradation and suffering. Some of these problems, moreover, can weaken us, and may destroy us.

In a free society, problems usually can be recognized, understood, and solved more quickly and surely than in any other society. Especially, the free society can meet those problems that are not so clearly visible, although in solving certain kinds of clearly visible problems a dictatorship sometimes performs more efficiently than a free society.

The speaking done in any culture helps to transmit energy from one part of the culture to other parts, steers the culture, and propels it toward worthwhile ends. The aim of your speech must be to present, vividly and powerfully, a significant problem.

ASSIGNMENT

Give a six- to eight-minute speech in which you select an important problem and lead the audience to perceive it as a problem and to recognize its importance. Your aim is to present a significant problem vividly and powerfully.

Do not include the causes of the problem, because the techniques of presenting causes are different from the techniques of presenting problems. For the same reason, omit the solution, except when the solution is so obvious that it would be inappropriate to omit it; in such a case, you may present a one-sentence solution, but do not develop the solution further. Your time should be spent *presenting* the problem, and your objective is to make that problem clear, vivid, and important to the audience.

If you choose, you may give a speech showing that something ordinarily considered a problem is *not* one, or is less significant than most people realize. Pointing out false or pseudo-problems is often as important as recognizing real ones. The instructions in these assignments apply equally to such a speech, except that you must use the opposite of the strategic techniques listed as follows. That is, you must show that the problem is *not* a source of danger, of suffering, or of degradation to those who experience it.

TECHNIQUE OF PRESENTING PROBLEMS

1. *Strategy* (Main Points). Select a few ways (usually, the fewer the better) of leading an audience to understand the importance of the problem. Select these ways so that they are (1) few in number, (2) briefly, clearly, and vividly stated, (3) appropriate to the audience, and (4) related to each other. When you know a problem thoroughly, you can often select two or three best ways to lead an audi-

ence to feel its importance. These ways then furnish the strategy of the speech. Rhetorical strategies are, roughly, the equivalent of military strategy. Spare no effort in discovering the best possible strategic ideas to lead the audience to grasp the significance of the problem. These ideas will be the main points of the speech. (See *Standards*). The following will suggest ideas for strategy:

  a. The problem is a source of danger, suffering, or degradation to those who experience it.
  b. The problem directly or indirectly injures the audience.
  c. The problem has harmed or destroyed others like us in the past.
  d. The problem prevents the operation of an ideal or growth toward it.
  e. The problem is already great or is growing in importance.
  f. The problem is a fundamental one in that it causes other problems.
  g. The problem is recognized by others: experts, large numbers of people, admirable people, a majority of citizens, and so on.
  h. The problem makes our society or its institutions operate ineffectively.
  i. Use other methods if they are appropriate to you as a *speaker,* to your *audience,* to your *problem* and to the *occasion* on which the speech is given, but be sure to select the *fewest possible and best strategic ideas.*

2. *Tactics* (Supporting Material). After selecting a significant problem and deciding on the best strategic ideas, support those ideas with vivid and logically valid tactics. The kinds of support best suited to making a problem vivid are statistics, real and hypothetical examples, instances, testimony, visual aids, and summaries. *Your speech should consist almost wholly of these kinds of materials. Speeches that consist largely of general statements, however appropriate, will nearly always be dull, unclear, and unconvincing. Your greatest task will probably be to discover and select intensely interesting and logical supporting material.*

SUBJECTS

One function of a course in speech is to help you decide which problems are most important. Your judgment about the importance of various problems improves with study and with listening to discussions and arguments about problems. The problems you consider important, therefore, will change with your information, experience, and maturity. Because in a free society you must make your own decisions about which problems are most important, no list of subjects is presented here. (You can, however, look through books on social problems and find many suitable subjects.) Think about which problems are most important and then improve your analysis throughout your college career and throughout your life.

One of the best aids to the selection of the most important problems is the "competition of ideas." Justice Oliver Wendell Holmes once said that the best test of truth is the ability of an idea to survive in the competition of the marketplace. Try to subject yourself to a free competition of ideas so that you can select more intelligently from among the countless problems that cry for solution.

STANDARDS

1. *Subject:* Was the speech about a problem of significance?
2. *Opening:* Did the opening of the speech fix attention at a high peak at once?
*3. *Strategy:* Did you use the best possible strategy?
    *a) *Limitation:* Did you limit the number of main points to the fewest possible; were these crucial and indispensable? Could some have been omitted?
    *b) *Statement:* Did you state each of the main ideas briefly and vividly? Did you make coordinate points parallel whenever possible?
    *c) *Selection:* Did you select as main points those ideas that were most likely to lead the audience to understand and feel the importance of the problem?
    *d) *Organization:* Did you relate points to one another? Were they parallel wherever possible?
    *e) *Arrangement:* Did you take up these ideas in the best order?
**4. *Tactics:* Did you support your general statements with vivid and valid instances, real and hypothetical examples, statistics, testimony, visual aids, and summaries, so that the speech was interesting, clear, and logical?
5. Did you summarize skillfully and frequently? It is nearly impossible to summarize too frequently. Use, especially, evidential and cumulative summaries.
6. *Delivery:* Did you demonstrate by your delivery that you had practiced to develop a vivid realization of your ideas at the moment of utterance (see pp. 246–247)?
7. *Conclusion:* Did you conclude with a clear, and if possible, vivid restatement of the importance of the problem?
8. *Outline:* Did your outline follow the recommended form?

9. *Time:* Did your speech fall within the time limits?
10. *Questions:* Did you answer questions clearly and intelligently so as to show that you had a broad and deep understanding of the subject? Be sure to "plant" a question, to be sure that at least one will be asked.

* or ** or *** indicates the standard is especially important.

Causation

INTRODUCTION

The test of wisdom, Aristotle observed, is whether or not a man can understand the causes of events. People suffer and civilizations decline because they fail to analyze or make clear the causes of their problems, and thus fail to find solutions that remove these causes. Too frequently, we try to solve a problem by treating its symptoms; but when only the symptoms are treated, the original cause of the problem may still operate, and the problem may intensify. To solve problems, we must learn to find and remove their cause. However, even if we decide (as sometimes we should) to treat the symptoms of a problem, we cannot make even this choice intelligently unless we first know the causes. After knowing them, we can know that we cannot or should not remove them. Clearly, intelligent speaking demands that we discover causes.

ASSIGNMENT

Prepare a six- to eight-minute speech in which you present a phenomenon of significance and demonstrate that a given cause is at least partly responsible for it. If many causes are responsible, select only one cause or very few causes, according to their significance.

If you wish, take the reverse of this assignment, and demonstrate that what we usually think are the causes of something are not: e.g., that speeding does *not* cause automobile accidents, or that price controls do not keep prices low.

TECHNIQUES OF DEMONSTRATING CAUSES

Use any of the following techniques that give the strongest support to your analysis of the cause (s) . Especially recommended are the Canons of Causation, which follow:

1. Demonstrate *that* a cause operates by *showing that the cause and effect are related.* Mill's Canons of Causation perform this function. You may wish to read about these Canons (sometimes called *inductive methods*) in John Stuart Mill's *System of Logic,* or discussions of them in most contemporary logic books. Use the Canons of Agreement, Difference, and Correlation.
2. Explain *why* a cause operates by *describing the conditions that produce the effect.* (In using this category, remember that each alleged cause is a general statement and often will need to be supported by statistics, examples, testimony, and other supporting evidence, both to maintain interest and to supply logical strength.) Use single causes, a chain of causes, multiple causes, or functionally related causes.
3. Use the method of consequences by discovering additional consequences of the cause (s) .
4. Use the testimony of experts.

SUBJECTS

The cause of any phenomenon in agriculture, anthropology, art, current affairs, economics, geology, government, history, language, literature, philosophy, physics, psychology, sociology, theology or other area is acceptable, provided the phenomenon is sufficiently important and the cause sufficiently unknown to merit a speech.

Limit yourself to only one or two causes, whenever possible. These causes should be important in the sense that they might be easily removed, or that they are widespread, often misunderstood, or not generally known. If other causes can produce the problem, perhaps you should acknowledge and mention them, but avoid more than a mention of them.

Present the cause (s) of any of the following: inflation, depression, absenteeism, fluctuations in the stock market, child abuse, forgetting, absent-mindedness, riots, crime, dreams, an historical event or movement, the evolution of any part of the body, the decline of any civilization, water or air pollution, intelligence, prejudice, good grades, safe driving, maladjustment, energy shortages, corrupt government, aging, rapid learning, underdevelopment or poverty in any part of the United States (e.g., Appalachia), monopolies, war, genius, accidents, happiness, psychosis, drug addiction, continental drift, smog, slow reading, or any other subject worth the time of the audience.

Avoid using tautologies ("Heat is caused by an increase in temperature") and causes that are already understood by most of the audience.

STANDARDS

*1. *Subject:* Was the subject of sufficient value to the audience in that it helped them understand the causes of a significant problem?

2. *Opening:* Did you open with a brief but powerful presentation of the problem so that it arrested attention at once and made the audience want to know the cause of the problem?

*3. *Strategy:* Did you limit yourself to one or two important causes so that the speech did not have too many general statements? Did you state these clearly and if possible vividly?

**4. *Tactics:* Did you support the cause (s) you selected by explanations, examples, statistics, testimony, analogies, and, particularly, the Canons of Causation?

5. *Summaries:* Did you make your analysis of the cause (s) clear to the audience by a clear statement of each cause, by repetition, restatement, and frequent summaries? Use some of the following kinds of summaries: forecast, cumulative summary, evidential summary, and final summary.

6. *Delivery:* Did you deliver your speech with a vivid realization of the idea at the moment of utterance (see pp. 246–247) ?

7. *Conclusion:* Did you conclude with a strong restatement of your causal analysis?

8. *Outline:* Did your outline follow the recommended form?

9. *Time:* Did your speech fall within the time limits?

10. *Questions:* Did you answer questions clearly and intelligently, demonstrating a thorough knowledge of your subject? "Plant" a question with a friend in the audience to be sure that one question will be ready for you. After one question is asked, usually others will follow.

Solutions

INTRODUCTION

Once one understands the importance of a problem, and tries to analyze the causes of that problem, he is in a position to find a solution. In the past, many societies were unable to meet their problems with the rigorous research and creativity that the problems demanded. These societies have perished. If our own society is to grow, or even to continue to exist, we must be able to solve certain problems that beset us. Each of these problems represents a sign of weakness in our culture; some problems such as war, poverty, caste, tyranny, and disease have destroyed previous civilizations. Our existence is not assured unless our speakers can diagnose our great problems, grasp the causes of these problems, and devise convincing solutions.

Solutions have a further significance: sometimes few people recognize a problem until others propose solutions to it. Debates and discussions about solutions focus attention on the problem. More important, we often accept as problems only those situations that seem to have some possibility of solution. Those that cannot be solved, we ignore, or even unconsciously repress. Hence, discussion of intelligent solutions may not only help to solve a problem but may make more people aware of the problem, and eventually lead to a better solution.

Above all, let us not forget that Western culture can become the first culture to dedicate itself to the solution of the problems of its people. This goal, unique in human history, may be the one that makes our culture, unlike previous civilizations, capable of surviving forever. More important, should Western culture prove capable of solving the problems that have destroyed men and nations throughout history, it will be the first culture to deserve survival. Surely this generation, which will make decisions that may lead us to survival, has opportunities never offered before in history. Let us, then, turn to the solutions of our problems, for we must, if we are to flourish or even if we are to survive.

ASSIGNMENT

Give a six- to eight-minute speech in which you present a significant problem to which you offer a solution justified by the use of analogies. If you wish, you may take the reverse of this assignment and show that a certain frequently advocated solution will not work. Sometimes the refutation of a proposed solution is a valuable service. In either case, however, you are required to use *at least two analogies* to show that a similar solution has (or has not) worked in similar circumstances.

TECHNIQUE OF PRESENTING SOLUTIONS

In the introduction, spend a few minutes making the audience realize the significance of the problem before you offer your solution. Your introduction, therefore, should be a short but excellent "problem speech." Once you have made the audience realize the importance of the problem, state your solution and use analogies to *show that a similar solution has worked in similar situations*. Two operations are necessary.

Use the best supporting material—examples, comparisons, testimony, and statistics to:

1. Show that a similar solution has worked well elsewhere. Show that the solution removed the problem, or a significant part of it, that its cost in time and effort was not prohibitive, and that it brought with it no new problems that were insurmountable. Avoid generalities and use specific support.
2. Show the audience that the two situations are comparable in that the same cause that made the solution work elsewhere is operating here. Significant parallels can often be found in places far removed in time and distance. At all costs, avoid an analogy in which the two situations are significantly dissimilar.

    Sometimes, however, similar solutions may come from widely diverse circumstances. In such cases you will be supporting the idea that the solution works under nearly all conditions. You will not have to meet this requirement provided you use a barrage of analogies from widely diverse situations.

In addition, use any of the following techniques to support your solution:

1. Use Mill's Canons to demonstrate that the solution worked elsewhere.
2. Show why the solution will work by describing the conditions that solve the problem.
3. Use chains of causes or multiple causes to demonstrate that your solution will be causally effective.
4. Show that experts approve of the solution.
5. Show that the solution will prevent the symptoms of the problem from recurring.
6. Show that the solution will remove the cause of the problem.

Subjects

No list of subjects is given because those that are appropriate should be arrived at after careful study, discussion, and debate. Only through the competition of ideas can we safely discover either the problems to be solved or the solutions that are best.

You may, if you choose, show that a well-known and popular solution will *not* work by demonstrating that the opposite of one or two of the techniques is true; e.g., that the solution has not worked when it was tried or that the situations in which it worked are too different from the present one.

STANDARDS

1. *Subject:* Did you use the most informed and intelligent sources available?
*2. *Opening:* Did your introduction fulfill with distinction the requirements of the "problem speech" so that the audience wanted to hear the solution?
*3. *Strategy:* Did you limit your speech to one solution to avoid having too many general statements?
***4. *Tactics:* Did you demonstrate the value of your solution by intelligent use of analogies?
   **a. Did you use specific supporting material to demonstrate that the solution worked well elsewhere? At least two analogies are required. Often the best speeches will use a barrage of analogies as well as a number of the other methods suggested under *Techniques*.
   **b. Did you show that the other situations in which the solution worked were, in all significant respects, like the one for which the solution is being advocated? (Note the exception discussed under *Techniques*.)
*5. *Summaries:* Did you make use of skillful summaries?
6. *Delivery:* Did you re-create your thought at the moment of utterance (see pp. 246–247)?
7. *Conclusion:* Did you have a strong conclusion?
8. *Outline:* Did your outline follow the recommended form? At the bottom of your outline indicate whether your solution is symptomatic or causal, individual or group, "villain" or social. Some solutions do not fit these categories, or are of mixed types; if yours is one of these, be sure to note that fact.
9. *Time:* Did your speech fall within the time limits?
10. *Questions:* Did you answer questions clearly and intelligently, showing that you understood your subject thoroughly? "Plant" a question with a member of the audience.

VARIATIONS ON THE ASSIGNMENT

1. Present a solution to a problem for which you believe there is no precedent—a contemporary problem of such nature that it has not been faced before. Support your solution by whatever techniques seem sound.
2. Examine a bill currently before the Congress, the Legislature, or the City Council, and evaluate it as a solution, giving both its strengths

and weaknesses. Conclude the speech by taking what you consider to be the most intelligent attitude toward the bill, and support your attitude with the best possible reasons.

Definitions

INTRODUCTION

If one wants to know if he is in love, or if a certain painting is beautiful, he cannot find out unless he knows, in the first case, what love is, or in the second, what beauty is. Thus, careful definition is often a prerequisite to knowledge. The failure to understand what others mean when they use a term may confuse one or make him subject to propaganda. More important, interest in the nature of certain kinds of ideas has been a powerful generating force behind all high civilizations. A high civilization gathers much of its fire from taking the nature of art, of science, of truth, of the good life as problems. The extent to which we understand the problems involved in analyzing the nature of these great generative ideas is, also, a measure of our own personal degree of "civilization." Thus, the definition speech represents a special and extremely important kind of problem solving. Inquire into the nature of some of the great ideas that have made our culture rich, outstanding, and complex.

ASSIGNMENT

Give a six- to eight-minute speech in which you present a definition. Your objectives should be (1) to arouse an interest in any of the concepts listed; (2) to present a carefully phrased and intelligent definition; (3) to make the definition clear and interesting. You will be cross-examined by the class on your definition, to test its merit. To be sure that there is at least one question for you, arrange with a friend to ask you one.

TECHNIQUES OF USING DEFINITIONS

1. *Strategy.* You must decide what kind of definition you will compose.
   a. *Platonistic:* A concept based on Plato's metaphysical notion of the Theory of Ideas, in which one attempts to discover the timeless, transforming meaning of a term. The Platonistic definition is of special use in the definition of values.
   b. *Aristotelian:* A statement in which the concept is classified.

Aristotle's theory of definition is the best known, and until the discovery of Operationalism by Charles Peirce and Percy Bridgman was the most used, because of its clarity and compactness. Aristotelian definitions should have the following parts: a *genus* or class to which the concept belongs; a *species* or way in which the concept differs from other members of the same *genus*. For example, William James' definition of instinct was "A way of acting without previous experience in the matter." *Way of acting* is the general class to which instinct belongs; the phrase *without previous experience in the matter* shows how instinct differs from other ways of acting. More than one species may be required.

c. *Operational.* A statement of the properties or behavior of the matter being defined, or a statement of what produces the thing being defined. This form of definition is based on the metaphysical idea that a thing is only and exactly what it does. It has greatest utility in defining certain processes and concepts that do not seem to be definable in Platonistic or Aristotelian terms, such as subject-matter areas (e.g., psychology), and matters still not fully understood (e.g., electricity). A second form of operationalism is to explain how to produce the thing being defined. Either form of operationalism may be used.

Regardless of the kind of definition you select, your definition should not be unnecessarily verbose. Make the definition as compact as intelligence permits. Your definition should not contain words whose meanings are not clear. Do not use, for example, figurative words, words whose meaning is unknown to the listener, or words that are a form of the word being defined. Finally, your definition should contain all the essential characteristics of the term being defined, but no accidental or unessential characteristics.

2. *Tactics.* Use the most vivid supporting material possible to clarify the concept and to give the audience a lasting interest in it. Of the following forms of support, a, b, and c are especially recommended; the other kinds of support should be used with caution, and only when they clearly contribute to our interest in the concept and our understanding of it.

*a. *Illustration:* Give a number of illustrations of the definition. The illustrations should be as vivid and varied as possible.

*b. *Comparison:* Use comparisons that help the audience understand your concept. Compare the idea with a similar one. Even figurative analyses are of help.

*c. *Contrast:* Tell what the concept is *not;* give negative illustrations of it.

*d. *Repetition and restatement:* Frequent repetition reinforces the understanding of your audience.

e. *Division:* Often, breaking a concept into its parts helps us to understand the concept; division should not be used, however, unless it does clarify the definition or add interest, because division consists of general statements.

f. *Synonym:* Sometimes a synonym will help to clarify the concept. Avoid synonyms, however, unless one would work particularly well.

g. *Etymology:* Sometimes a concept may be clarified by giving the original meaning of the word, or by explaining what it means in another language. Often, however, etymology is a poor guide to current meaning.

SUBJECTS

You are limited to only these words, unless you have permission from your instructor: aesthetics, Americanism, aristocracy, art, beauty, Buddhism, capitalism, Christianity, civilization, classicism, communism, cynicism, cubism, dialectic (Hegelian or classical), economics, Epicureanism, ethics, evil, existentialism, freedom, functional autonomy, functionalism, God, health, Hinduism, intelligence, Islam, idealism, impressionism, jazz, Judaism, justice, literature, logical positivism, materialism, metaphysics, music, mysticism, naturalism, normality, phenomenology, philosophy, poetry, pragmatism, realism, reason, religion, romanticism, scholasticism, science, socialism, stoicism, surrealism, Taoism, theology, transcendentalism, truth, utilitarianism, Zen.

In order to devise an acceptance definition, use the following procedure:

1. First, consult some general works such as the *Encyclopedia Britannica,* the *Oxford English Dictionary* (the largest dictionary in existence, and many times the size of *Webster's Unabridged*), and *The Syntopicon* by Mortimer Adler. The last two sources will be of great use in defining philosophic terms, but poor for definitions of terms from such disciplines as economics, psychology, or sociology. The *Britannica* is almost always worth looking into, even if dull.

2. Consult dictionaries and special encyclopedias in the special field of your definition; nearly all disciplines have several dictionaries available, and some have an encyclopedia. Ask your librarian.

3. Read widely in that field about the word you are defining.

STANDARDS

**1. *Subject:* Did your definition and your support of it show careful thought and study on your part, revealing that you were cognizant of the best sources?

2. *Opening:* Was your speech introduced so as to arrest attention and arouse interest at once? Do not, of course, open with the definition; it is a general statement.

*3. *Strategy:* Was your definition clear, compact, and sound? The definition, which constitutes the point of the speech, should exemplify the qualities listed under *Techniques*.

**4. *Tactics:* Did you support the definition with concrete material that clarified the concept and its definition and created interest in them?

*5. *Summaries:* Did you repeat the definition frequently enough so that the audience understood it? Watch the audience, particularly when you give the definition the first time, to see if they understand it. If you suspect that they have not grasped the definition, you should repeat it carefully, perhaps more than once.

6. *Delivery:* Did you re-create your thoughts as you expressed them (see pp. 246–247)?

7. *Conclusion:* Did you conclude with a clear summary of your speech?

8. *Outline:* Did you turn in an outline that followed the recommended form? Indicate the type of definition you used at the bottom of your outline.

9. *Time:* Did your speech fall within the time limits?

10. *Questions:* Did you answer questions clearly and intelligently so as to show that you understood the subject thoroughly?

Values

INTRODUCTION

A cynic, as Oscar Wilde said, is a person who knows the price of everything and the value of nothing. At any rate, values are important because values help to determine our choices, and to determine whether or not our choices are intelligent. Men require more than to sleep in safety with stomachs filled with food; once we find our physical needs met, we feel uneasy, lost, and discontented until we discover a higher need and work to achieve it. The absence of higher needs, which we call *values,* can make life a bore, but a keen perception of them makes life meaningful, satisfying, and often, by any standard, successful.

The perception of high values puts in motion the giant wheels that carry people in the directions characteristic of great civilizations. For our own satisfaction, but also for the sake of our civilization, we must discover, understand, refine, and remold the values that serve as the basis of the choices made by us and by the rest of the world.

Assignment

Give a six- to eight-minute speech in which you select a single value and persuade the audience to accept it. You may, if you wish, choose to attack a popularly held value that you believe to be a false one. The speech should aim at changing our ways of thinking and feeling: it should, ideally, change our lives. Remember the definitions of "value" given in class or in the text. (Speeches on "the value of baseball" or "the value of higher taxes" are *not* acceptable because neither baseball nor taxes are values.)

Techniques of Presenting Values

1. *Strategy.* The *Value* assignment provides you with an opportunity to use many of the techniques of strategy learned in previous assignments:

   a. Demonstrate that a certain false value (or the lack of a certain value) presents a severe problem or series of problems. Use the techniques of presenting a problem given in the *Problem* assignment.

   b. You may use causal argument to demonstrate the cause of, or effects of, a value. Review the methods of causal argument presented in the *Cause* assignment.

   c. You may use analogies to show that under similar conditions the value has had good (or bad) effects. Review the techniques presented in the *Solution* assignment.

   d. You may wish to use a definition to make the value more clear. If so, review the techniques of definition and plan to use tactics that will create interest in the definition. Review the strategy and tactics presented in the *Definition* assignment.

   e. These techniques do not exhaust the possibilities for persuading the audience to accept a value. Some philosophers believe that appeal to consequences is the most fundamental approach to persuading people to accept a value, and that all other additional methods are reducible to it. But others insist that there are other ways: showing the audience that admirable men and/or authorities approve or adopt the value whereas others do not; showing that the value is a fundamental right;

or, that honor or duty requires us to adopt it. Other techniques can be found in works on ethics. You will find a study
of ethics indispensable. Read books and take courses in philosophy to enlarge your grasp of the problems involved in analyzing values.

    f. The most intelligent speeches on values generally try to de-
scribe the *limits* of the value as well as its merits. All values,
perhaps, have some limits. (Honesty is generally preferred to
dishonesty, but we would not be honest with a madman who
wanted to know where our family was so that he could murder
them.) A short section should be included—when the section
would help understanding—explaining these limits.

2. *Tactics.* As in all previous assignments, the power and validity of
your speech will be closely related to the amount and quality of
supporting material. By this point in the course, you are expected
to use supporting material *with distinction*.

SUBJECTS

1. Persuade us to accept (or reject) a value that is central to another
society. Do not be so naïve as to think that even primitive societies
might not make a contribution to us; some of them have cultures
in which suicide, insanity, and crime are nearly nonexistent. Examine such cultures as the Iroquis, Kwakiutl, Fiji, Zuñi, Dobu,
Arapaho, Manus, Pueblo, Watusi, Trobriander, or any culture on
any continent. Try to find a central or driving value of the culture
and construct a speech to make us accept or reject that value.

2. Persuade us to accept a value that is central to any great period of
history, or important in the genesis of any civilization. Try to discover a central value from any period of the following: Western
culture, Roman culture, the Golden Age of Greece, the Renaissance,
the Reformation, the Age of Reason, Africa, India, China, the Aztecs, the Incas, the Jews, or our contemporary civilization. Demonstrate that the value was important to the achievement of any of
these and that it would be to us, or that we should reject it because
it brought about strife, ignorance, terror, and so on.

3. Choose a value that is central to any of the following: the kibbutz,
Taoism, Judaism, Buddhism, Catholicism, Protestantism, Islam,
Hinduism, agnosticism, atheism, Quakerism, humanism, Unitarian-
ism, Zen, Stoicism, Epicureanism, existentialism, phenomenology,
rationalism, romanticism, utilitarianism, formalism, Confucianism,
conservatism, liberalism, anarchism, skepticism, cynicism, optimism,
pessimism, or the philosophy of any of the following: Plato, Aristotle, Saint Augustine, Saint Thomas, Origen, Occam, Bacon, Des-

cartes, Spinoza, Leibnitz, Locke, Hillel, Berkley, Hume, Bentham, Mill, Wittgenstein, Einstein, Russell, Whitehead, Gandhi.

4. Persuade us to accept a value that was central to the life of men worthy of note: Moses, Socrates, Galileo, Beethoven, Buddha, Newton, Gandhi, Pasteur, Lincoln, Mohammed, John Huss, Pope John XXIII, Radhakrishnan, Norman Thomas, Charles Darwin, or anyone from any time or country, provided you choose one that will demonstrate your ability to use the library to gather ideas and information.

5. Persuade us to reject (or accept) a value represented by the snob, the "success," the middle class, the jingoist, the intellectual, the protester, the bigot, the authoritarian, the apathetic, the hippie, the militarist, the racist.

6. Persuade us to accept the value of the beautiful, or of art or of aesthetics, or explain the central value behind any period of art, music, literature, drama, or any great artist, writer, or thinker.

7. Find a value central to any form of architecture, science, philosophy, literature, law, or period in art, and persuade us to accept or reject it.

8. Persuade us to reject or accept as values the following: love, hate, anger, compassion, worry, knowledge, fear, democracy, emotion, authority, obedience, patriotism, courage, freedom, altruism, hedonism, chauvinism, egoism, naturalism, empiricism, idealism, experimentalism, scientism, psychologism, deism, mysticism.

9. Persuade us to return to the values that some say we seem to be deserting, or persuade us to abandon them with greater speed: loyalty, sincerity, individualism, self-sufficiency, Calvinism, heroism, piety, purity, honesty, chastity, horse sense, practicality, virility, patriotism.

10. Formulate a new value needed, but not followed, by men and persuade us to accept it.

STANDARDS

**1. *Subject:* Did you give evidence of thorough reading, careful analysis and, if possible, inspired thought?

2. *Opening:* Did your opening arrest attention at once?

*3. *Strategy:* Did you analyze the value so carefully that you could distill its essence into a small number of clear general statements that would lead the audience to accept and adopt the value? See *Techniques*.

*4. *Tactics:* Did you support your points with concrete material that was psychologically compelling and logically sound?

5. *Summaries:* Did you use cumulative summaries whenever possible?
6. *Delivery:* Did you apply the principles of good delivery so that your voice and body showed that you had a vivid realization of your ideas at the moment of utterance (see pp. 246–247)?
7. *Conclusion:* Did you have a strong conclusion?
8. *Outline:* Did your outline follow the recommended form?
9. *Time:* Did your speech fall within the time limits?
10. *Questions:* Did you answer questions intelligently and clearly?

Eulogy

INTRODUCTION

A eulogy is a special kind of persuasive speech that appears to the audience to be a speech in praise of a person. Actually, the eulogy is a persuasive speech in which the speaker uses indirect methods to persuade the audience to accept an idea. The attention of the audience is, of course, directed toward the person being eulogized. But the person being eulogized is only a "vehicle" for the idea. *The real purpose of the speaker is to have the audience accept and follow the idea that the man being eulogized concretely exemplifies.* In giving a eulogy on Socrates, for example, one would apparently be discussing the life of this great thinker, but the real aim of the speech might be to persuade the audience to live a life of sacrifice. Such a speech can be extremely compelling because it is indirect and hence disarming, and because it furnishes the audience with a concrete model. A carefully prepared eulogy, therefore, may be among the most powerful of persuasive forms.

ASSIGNMENT

Select an idea you wish the audience to follow; such an idea is usually chosen from ethics and ideals. Find and study a person, living or dead, or a group, who exemplifies this idea. Prepare a ten-minute speech eulogizing this person.

TECHNIQUES OF THE EULOGY

1. Describe the person—how he looked, acted, sounded, dressed, or talked, so that the audience has an image to carry through the speech.

2. Humanize the person or groups. One way of humanizing a person is to relate humorous anecdotes—pointing out minor mistakes he made.

3. *Most of the eulogy should support an idea that this person exemplified.* In no sense should the eulogy be a biography, or, worse, a chronology. Decide upon the idea you wish the audience to accept and then supply vivid descriptions, narrations, and examples from the person's life that exemplify this idea.

4. You must, while talking about the person, establish those ideas about your own intelligence, character, and goodwill that build ethos. For the most part, these ideas must be established indirectly. But use every possible device in choice of ideas, composition, and delivery that will establish your ethos. If you succeed, you will complete the assignment with distinction and be able to establish ideas indirectly about both yourself and others.

ALTERNATIVE ASSIGNMENTS

1. Give a speech on an important subject that will best enable you to reflect your intelligence, character, and goodwill. Use as many devices as possible in the choice of ideas, organization, supporting material, and delivery to establish your ethos.

2. Analyze the ethos of any well-known public figure, living or dead, and explain the nature of his ethos, and the reasons for which he achieved it. Where possible, point to cultural, sociological, and psychological origins of his ethos.

3. Write a paper on any "villain" in history—living or dead—and explain how people might have prevented his ethos from developing, and how they might have avoided his rise to power.

4. Write a paper or give a speech on a person whom you admire but who was something of a failure. Some persons of very high ethos were, at times, quite unsuccessful in appealing to their audiences. Among these men are W. E. B. DuBois, Winston Churchill, Adlai Stevenson, Lyndon Johnson, Malcolm X, Eugene McCarthy, and others. Explain why they failed, at least at one point in their lives, to captivate more people than they did.

Comparative Groups

INTRODUCTION

We often set our aims, our level of production, and our degree of honesty by noting what others do, and doing likewise. No one feels particularly upset when he breaks a traffic law, for example, because other people in our culture do so with impunity. At any rate, we often decide how hard to work or how high to aim by observing those around us, and we decide what to do by looking at comparative groups. Comparative groups influence us particularly in unstructured situations in which we have no established customs, habits, values, or other guides. Thus, we may define a comparative group as one whose achievements or actions are used by nonmembers to help make decisions. Much of the process of using comparative groups is unconscious; if our parents are professionals we will probably decide to enter a profession, too. If none of our peers takes school very seriously, the chances are that we will not—unless we are "monitoring" our behavior by comparing ourselves to a group other than our peer group. At any rate, we use others, particularly in an unstructured situation, to decide what we shall do and what we shall feel.

ASSIGNMENT

Give a six- to eight-minute speech in which you make use of comparative groups to persuade the audience. You have several options in this assignment. Use one or more of the following: (1) persuade the audience to accept an idea or work for a cause because admirable groups believe in it; (2) persuade the audience to accept an idea or work for a cause because a group you can make the audience dislike is against the idea or cause; (3) attack an organization or group by destroying the goodwill they may have, and bringing the audience to be suspicious of, to dislike, or to withdraw from the organization; (4) build goodwill for an organization that merits the goodwill of the audience.

TECHNIQUES OF USING COMPARATIVE GROUPS

1. *Strategy.* Use ideas that increase the influence of the organization. Select ideas that are most appropriate to the organization and to the audience and to the speaker (see pp. 189–191).
2. *Tactics.* Whatever ideas you select must be clearly stated (avoid using the terminology on pp. 189–191 so that your speech does not contain the technical terms of the chapter). Most important, sup-

port each idea with powerful evidence that makes the idea interesting: real examples, testimony, statistics, comparisons, and so on. Keep general statements few and support them well, or your speech will be dull and possibly unclear.

SUBJECTS

Each of the following may be used as either a positive comparative group (one we admire and look to for guidance) or a negative comparative group (one we abhor and revolt against):

1. Any past culture or current subculture that possesses outstanding merit or demerit—the Zuñi, the ancient Greeks, Chinese-Americans, the Japanese, the Incas, immigrants, farmers, teachers, businessmen, labor unions, political parties;

2. Any current business, professional, or service organization—Bell Telephone Company, American Medical Association, National Association of Manufacturers, Chamber of Commerce, American Farm Bureau Federation, National Education Association, American Pharmaceutical Association, the oil lobby, Tobacco Research Council, National Rifle Association, American Civil Liberties Union, Rotary Club, electric and gas companies, moving and storage companies, Nader's Raiders, Red Cross, Salvation Army, Gay Liberation, Women's Liberation, John Birch Society;

3. Any agency of government—the Federal Bureau of Investigation, the Selective Service, the Department of Agriculture, the Interstate Commerce Commission, the Supreme Court, Congress, the Federal Trade Commission, the Forest Service, the House Un-American Activities Committee, the Senate Foreign Relations Committee, the presidency, the local or state police;

4. Any organization dedicated to conveying information to the public —the *Encyclopedia Britannica; The New York Times,* the local newspaper, the Columbia Broadcasting System, the local radio or television station, *Reader's Digest,* the *New Republic, Time,* the current presidential press secretary, the "information" division of any lobby, business, government, educational, or religious organization;

5. Any of the "big" organizations in government, education, religion, business, labor, consumer protection, crime, politics, and so on;

6. Any past group: the Hitler Youth, the Minute Men (1776 version or the more recent group), the Know-Nothings, the Confederacy, Abolitionists, and so on.

STANDARDS

Set your own standards for his speech, keeping in mind that the speech should be on a subject worth taking the time of the audience, and should follow the techniques for the assignment with distinction.

Normative Group

INTRODUCTION

The group of which we are members exerts pressure on us to do things that we, as individuals, might not otherwise do. Our own cultural, national, economic, social, and family groups have all exerted pressures on us to conform to certain patterns, to perform certain acts, and to hold certain beliefs. *To get a program enacted one must sometimes create a group.* When the group has high morale and operates efficiently, it will be doing far more than any single individual or any number of single individuals may do alone. Therefore, occasionally it is necessary to create a new group.

ASSIGNMENT

Give an eight- to ten-minute speech in which you try to turn the class audience into a psychological group to perform a function you believe to be a worthy one.

TECHNIQUES OF CREATING A NORMATIVE GROUP

Strategy. To create a normative group, each of the following clusters of ideas must be established, though not necessarily in this order: (1) a feeling of striving for common goals; (2) a feeling of cohesiveness, of belonging; (3) the confidence that the goals can be achieved; (4) the naming of a temporary chairman, the delegation of certain responsibilities on a temporary basis, the selection of time and place for meetings, and so on (see pp. 185–191).

SUBJECTS

Because all ideas begin with a minority of one, all influential organizations have begun with a small normative group, from the disciples who were instrumental in the formation of Christianity, to the minority that first formed the United States. Select, therefore, any subject of local, college, state, national, or international significance and create from the audience a group to perform a significant service.

STANDARDS

By this time, you will be able to set your own standards of performance. For this speech, however, remember that your ability to form a group from the audience is not a reliable standard. It may be impossible, at the time you give your speech, to form a group and to get it to act. Therefore, do not judge your speech on whether or not you were able to form a group but on whether or not you used the right methods of bringing the audience as close as possible to that objective. Just as a surgeon may use the best possible techniques and yet lose the patient, so may the speaker use the best possible techniques yet fail in his objective. Bear in mind that many of the best speeches in history have been failures from the pragmatic standpoint; nevertheless, even if the Sermon on the Mount has not made better people, and even if Lincoln's First Inaugural Address did not prevent the Civil War, or his Second Inaugural Address prevent the Reconstruction, these speeches were technically superior. The standards you should apply to your speech should be not pragmatic, but methodological.

ALTERNATIVE ASSIGNMENTS

1. Analyze Western civilization as a normative and comparative group, pointing out its distinctive nature, and its inherent advantages in recognizing and solving certain problems, and its limitations in recognizing and solving other kinds of problems.
2. Analyze the group structure of any organization with which you are thoroughly familiar. To what extent do members of the organization have a feeling of belonging, of dedication to mutual goals, and confidence the goals will be realized? Explain specifically the part that speaking (conversation, conference, discussions, speeches) has played in the development or weakening of the group structure.
3. Select an organization of which you are a member and make a list of its traditions: the kinds of leaders it selects, its habitual attitudes toward outside groups, toward certain practices among its members, its ways of doing things, and so on. Point out the effect that these traditions have had upon whatever changes in those traditions have been recommended.
4. Analyze the relation of the following to the groups with which they

dealt: Alexander the Great, Napoleon, Socrates, Jesus, Julius Caesar, Gandhi, Hitler, Galileo, Pope John XXIII, Franklin Roosevelt, Winston Churchill, Dwight Eisenhower, Richard Nixon, Malcolm X, Martin Luther King, Jr.

5. Prepare a six- to eight-minute speech in which you select one or two points and persuade the audience to believe these points for either or both of the following reasons: (1) a normative group of which they are members expects them to accept the points; (2) a comparative group has already accepted the points.

Outlining

An Outline on Outlining

I. The purpose of an outline is to reveal the structure of a speech by showing the following, graphically:
   A. The order of materials in a speech.
   B. The relation between general statements (points, ideas) and the material that supports these statements. All general statements and all supporting materials—including statistics, poems (identified by title and author), examples, and so forth—should appear on the outline.
II. General statements (points, ideas) should be written as complete sentences with the following characteristics:
   A. *Limitation:* Did the speaker limit the number of general statements to the fewest possible? Only indispensable general statements should be used (see pp. 49–51).
      1. General statements are usually dull and often unclear.
      2. General statements are made vivid by graphic supporting material; therefore, enough support must be included to make each general statement vivid.
   B. *Statement:* General statements must be brief, clear, and if possible, vivid (see pp. 51–56).

239

C. *Selection:* Those points must be selected that best fit the subject, the audience, and the speaker (see pp. 52–56).

D. *Organization:* Points must be related to each other, and must be parallel wherever possible. Perhaps the easiest way to emphasize the relation of points to one another is to cast coordinate points in parallel structure.

    1. Parallel points are points of roughly equal importance and are cast in the same grammatical structure.

    2. Coordinate points can often be parallel:

        (a) Parallel structure makes the points of a speech easy for the speaker to remember.

        (b) Parallel structure makes the points of a speech easy for the audience to remember.

E. *Arrangement:* Ideas must be taken up in the best order.

III. Supporting material should be indicated, not by complete sentences, but by key phrases, and should have the following characteristics:

A. All supporting material must be on the outline, subordinated to the appropriate general statement.

    1. Subordination may be either deductive or inductive.[1]

    2. Outlines usually follow a deductive order. That is, they proceed from a general statement to more specific material, as follows:

(gen st.)	I. Many great speeches have been failures.
(inst.)	A. William Pitt's speeches in support of American independence.
(inst.)	B. Lincoln's attempt to restore goodwill in his Second Inaugural Address.

    3. Outlines may follow inductive order whenever a general statement can be introduced more effectively by prefacing it with concrete material as follows:

(inst.)	A. William Pitt's speeches in support of American independence.
(inst.)	B. Lincoln's attempt to restore goodwill in his Second Inaugural Address.
(gen. st.)	I. Many great speeches have been failures.
(inst.)	C. The Lincoln-Douglas debates.

B. Avoid *contentless* entries for supporting material; they indi-

---

[1] The terms *deductive* and *inductive* are not used here in the sense in which they are used in books on logic; they indicate supporting materials that come after or before the general statement, respectively.

cate only the kind of material to be included, not their specific nature. The following are *contentless:*

(stat.)   1. Number of automobile accidents; number preventable.
(test.)   2. Quote from Ralph Nader.

  C. Use only "contentful" entries, such as:

(stat.)   1. Over 55,000 killed in auto accidents; 65% are preventable.

(test.)   2. Ralph Nader: "The gap between designs of automobiles and attainable safety has widened enormously since World War II."

(qual.)   a. Ralph Nader, advisor to a Senate subcommittee investigating auto accidents, conducted an investigation on automobile safety, and published his findings in *Unsafe at Any Speed.*

IV. Use deep indentations to indicate the subordination of ideas and to make the outline easier to remember. Your outline should *not* look like this:

I. Insensitivity seems built into all civilizations, including our own.
  A. Those who suffer have little power to reduce their own suffering.
  B. Those who have power never suffer, and hence never understand the urgency of problems that cause suffering.
  1. Who understands the urgency of hunger best: a rich and powerful person, or one who starves?
  2. Who understands the sufferings of a minority group better than the group itself?

Instead, items should be indented according to their relative importance:

  I. Insensitivity seems built into all civilizations, including our own.
    A. Those who suffer have little power to reduce their own suffering.
    B. Those who have power never suffer, and hence, never understand the urgency of problems that cause suffering.
      1. Who understands the urgency of hunger best: a rich and powerful person, or one who starves?
      2. Who understands the sufferings of a minority group better than the group itself?

V. Use marginal notes to indicate that you understand the kinds of supporting material you are using, and that you understand when you are using general statements. These notes should be entered in the left-hand margin, and abbreviated. The following abbreviations are acceptable:

(gen. st.) .... General statement, point idea
(stat.) .... Statistics
(real ill.) .... Real or historical illustration
(hyp. ill.) .... Hypothetical illustration
(inst.) .... Instance
(test.) .... Testimony of expert
(qual.) .... Qualifications of expert
(fig. comp.) .... Figurative comparison or figurative analogy
(lit. comp.) .... Literal comparison or literal analogy
(s.) .... Summary
(s. com.) .... Cumulative summary
(s. evi.) .... Evidential summary

VI. Sources should be listed as footnotes following each item listed (see Sample Outline, p. 243).

    A. Sources will be judged for both quality and quantity. Locate and use the best sources available for whatever subject you have chosen, and use a sufficient number of them.

    B. Footnotes should indicate the source of material. The following forms should be used for footnotes:

        1. *Periodical:* Name of author, title of article in quotation marks, name of periodical underlined, date of publication and page. See footnote 2 on p. 243.

        2. *Book:* Name of author, title of book underlined, city of publication followed by a colon (:), then publisher's name, date of publication in parenthesis, and page. See footnotes 1, 3, 4, 5 on page 243.

VII. Use any or all devices—symbols, underlines, colors, arrows, and the like—to make the outline easy to learn and easy to use.

    A. Asterisks (****) may separate parts of the outline.

    B. Underlining may point up some parts of the outline.

    C. An arrow (   ) may help you find a place you often forget.

    D. Colors may help you locate materials—for instance, underline various parts of the outline in different colors.

Sample Outline

John Jones

What is a Great Speech?

(real ill.)		A. Demosthenes' speeches to keep Greece free
(real ill.)		B. Sermon on the Mount to change man's motivation
(gen. st.)	I.	Many great speeches have been failures.[1]
(gen. st.)		C. William Pitt's speeches on the American Revolution:
(real ill.)		1. His Parliamentary speeches.
(real ill.)		2. His political speeches.
(inst.)		D. Lincoln's Second Inaugural Address.[2]
(fig. comp.)		E. A good surgeon who fails to save a life.
(stat.)		F. Of 300 great speeches, 156 were failures.[3]
(gen. st.)	II.	Many poor speeches have been successful.
(gen. st.)		A. Political speeches often poor but wildly applauded.[4]
(hyp. ill.)		B. Dismissal of class.
(fig. comp.)		C. Poor surgeon makes mistake but patient lives.
(gen. st.)		D. Successful speeches often appeal to prejudice.
(gen. st.)	III.	The test of a good speech must not be whether it succeeded or failed, but whether or not it used the available means of persuasion.[5]
(gen. st.)		A. Yet this test is not a test of greatness, but only of technical excellence or rhetorical virtuosity.
(gen. st.)		B. Technical virtuosity does not make a great speech.
(gen. st.)	IV.	A great speech is one that is concerned with a great problem.
(inst.)		A. Moses
(inst.)		B. Socrates
(inst.)		C. Pericles
(inst.)		D. Jesus
(inst.)		E. Kennedy
(S.)	V.	To speak greatly is to be greatly concerned with problems.

----

[1] Aristotle, The Rhetoric, trans. Lane Cooper, New York: Appleton-Century-Crofts, 1932, p. 6. 1355b.

[2] John M. Jones, "The Gettysburg Address," Quarterly Journal of Speech, 31 (June 25, 1958), 428.

[3] Meryl T. Rand, Political Parties, New York: Smith & Co., 1959, p. 87.

[4] Rand, p. 241

[5] Aristotle, p. 6. 1355b

Delivery

"[D]elivery is—very properly—not regarded as an elevated subject of inquiry."

—ARISTOTLE [1]

If one reviews writings on delivery over the past century, one must agree that while delivery may not be a subject of elevated inquiry, it surely is a subject of inflated discussion. Sometimes whole books, many of them quite thick, are given over to it. (Until forty years ago, only the most daring speech books allotted to delivery less than half their pages.) Most of these discussions were long, tedious, and pointless, because the authors could not define precisely what distinguished effective from ineffective delivery, nor could they instruct one in developing this skill. But, new insight into the nature of delivery now makes it possible to treat the subject rather briefly but adequately.

NATURE OF GOOD DELIVERY

Good delivery is simply that kind of delivery than intensifies the meaning and spirit the speaker intends to express. When a speech is well delivered, it should influence the members of the audience more power-

---

[1] *The Rhetoric of Aristotle,* trans. by W. Rhys Roberts (New York: Modern Library, Inc., 1954), *1404a.*

fully than if they had read it. The speech, when well delivered, wrings all the meaning and feeling from the words. Good delivery helps to hold an audience's attention and, in addition, is highly individualistic: the speaker is uniquely himself; his delivery helps suggest the kind of person he is. Good delivery, therefore, reinforces the speech, suggests the speaker's ethos, and makes the speech more effective.

But how do we attain the kind of delivery that makes a good speech better? The first step is to develop confidence, for stage fright frustrates the techniques of good delivery.

DEVELOPING CONFIDENCE

With confidence, one can do almost anything better, from making speeches to making love, provided that one does not become overconfident. Within our reach are two important sources of help for developing confidence: competence and commitment.

Competence

One admires the confidence of the surgeon who, making an incision, shows no tremor of hand or bead of sweat upon his brow, but who confidently proceeds with consummate skill. And we admire the football player: the pass flies toward him while his opponents charge, and he, with the eyes of everyone in the stadium on him, jumps to catch the ball, then charges through a weak place he has spotted in the defense. Both men are skilled—they know what to expect, but they also know how to reach to the unexpected. In a word, they are confident because they are competent in their respective fields. Put the football player in the operating room with a scalpel in his hand and the surgeon in the stadium, and almost surely the surgeon would drop the ball, and the football player, unless he dropped the scalpel, would probably faint should he be required to open the patient's abdomen. Neither has the necessary courage, because courage, in large part, comes from knowing what to do.

One of the aims of a speech communication course is to help you to develop competence. You should, when the course is over, feel you are competent in many aspects of speech making. You will, with competence, be able to:

1. Choose a subject of worth.
2. Find material on the subject, both in the library and elsewhere.
3. Present problems vividly and intelligently.
4. Discover and present the causes of problems.
5. Analyze and present solutions to problems.
6. Analyze and present values.

7. Develop ethos that can stimulate audiences to solve problems.
8. Develop the ability to create a group, or to weaken or destroy the power of groups.

Because one by-product of the course will be the confidence that springs from competence, you will develop less fear of speaking—and a greater desire to speak.

Commitment

Another source of confidence is total commitment to an idea. After he had consumed the hemlock, "Socrates alone retained his calmness," Plato reports. He was calm because, even by dying, he was "living" for his commitments, one of which was the idea that "Nothing can ever harm a truly good and just man." Whether this statement is true or not is beside the point; the point is that his intense commitment produced courage. The martyrs of history died because of their commitment, and very few feared dying or cried out even when consumed by flames. Intense commitment can lead to confidence and even to courage.

How does one find that to which one should be committed? How can one decide whether a principle, a cause, or an ideal is worth total commitment? No easy answer is possible, and some have taken as long as a lifetime to decide. But the search for commitment ought to occupy all of us. College is not a bad place to begin, because, in addition to the classroom and the library, there are many arenas where great ideas, ideals, and principles are disseminated, and where you can test your own thoughts and emotions—lectures, seminars, drama and music festivals, and so forth.

And do not believe, as some might, that you are too young to make a decision for commitment, and to act upon it. (Joan of Arc was in her early teens when she led the armies of France, and Alexander began his expansion of Macedonian power in his late teens.) Make a commitment and you will find that the resulting courage and sense of direction are remarkably confidence-producing.

REALIZATION OF CONTENT

Effective delivery usually differs from ineffective delivery in that the former has a full realization of the content of the words as they are uttered.[2] Develop this sense of responding to your own words, your own ideas, in the way you might have when you first thought of them. Good conversation has this quality. Your instructor can demonstrate it for you,

[2] See James Albert Winans, *Public Speaking* (New York: Appleton-Century-Crofts, 1917), p. 31.

or you can demonstrate it for yourself: Have a brief conversation with someone, then see if you can write down the conversation as you remember it. Then, each of you try to read your respective parts. While conversing, you probably had a vivid realization of the idea at the moment you uttered it, but when you read your part of the conversation, you very probably lacked that quality of spontaneity.

If this spontaneity is an important quality in delivery, how can one attain it? *You can develop it simply by working hard to grasp each word, each phrase, and each idea, and to respond to it before or while you say it.* If you respond to each word, you will find that you will be using gestures, facial expressions, and variety in voice and manner, because all these come from responding with immediacy to a significant idea. To practice, speak a single sentence of your speech and then ask, "Did I really respond to those words as I said them?" As you continue through the speech, monitor yourself to see whether or not you are intensely aware of each word, phrase, and idea as you utter it.

THE END OF ELOCUTION

The subject of delivery was not always this simple. Seventeenth-century science evolved the idea that one can understand things if we know their elements. Rhetoricians applied the same technique to the study of speech. The search for elements blocked progress not only in the study of ethos (see pp. 158–162) but also in the study of delivery. Soon the number of elements numbered in the hundreds, and the attempt to control several hundred elements simultaneously proved impossible for most students. One could not learn to speak well by following the directions of the atomistic elocutionists, and some rhetoricians were bright enough, or brave enough, to admit it. Bishop Richard Whately was among the first, for, in 1828, he produced the theory of a *vivid reealization of the idea at the moment of utterance.*[3] In the twentieth century, his principal followers were James Albert Winans and Wayland Maxfield Parrish, from whom I learned the idea. Whately's system did away with any reason to search for the "atoms" of delivery. *Good delivery is that kind of delivery that comes when you are confident and at ease and responding intensely to your own ideas.* You may speak more quietly than others when you so respond, or you may increase your volume; whichever you do will be in your own style. You may speak melodiously or in a monotone—but, again, what you do will be your habitual way of expressing yourself and will be characterized by spontaneity and variety.

Winans wanted to add a second quality: a communicative attitude,

[3] *Elements of Rhetoric,* Section IV.

without which, he insisted, one is merely soliloquizing. Perhaps, and the point is not worth much discussion, but if you truly understand what you say as you say it, that understanding implies that you understand the importance of your ideas, so perhaps adding a communicative attitude is unnecessary.

WATCHING THE AUDIENCE

The final matter for good delivery is that you should watch the audience so that you can tell when they don't understand or don't agree with a point. You can tell if they become fatigued, or if they want and can absorb more information. As you develop more and more confidence, you will not only speak with a full realization of your content but also more responsively to the reactions of the audience.

Three matters, then, are enough to start you on the road to good delivery: develop confidence, learn to speak with intense realization of the content, and learn to receive impressions from the audience. Follow these three, and you will probably need no more help in the matter, and your delivery will be interesting, original, and supportive of the ideas of your speech.

Index

A

Agreement, Canon of, 78–81
"Amazon Valley" structure, 35–36, 41
Analogy, 118–19, 122–24
Anderson, Barry, 103n
Anderson, Kenneth, 152n, 153n
Aristotle, 5, 8, 10, 22, 155–58, 201–204,
    206, 244
Arts, liberal, 6, 22
Associational methods of causation,
    78–87
Authority, 68–70, 127

B

Bakal, Carl, 120
Barzun, Jacques, 2–3
Benedict, Ruth, 175
Bergson, Henri, 14
Binet, Alfred, 8–9

Blankenship, Jane, 143n
Braybrooke, David, 113n
Breasted, James Henry, 76
Brophy, Ira, 121
Brown, Dee, 134
Browning, Robert, 1
Bruner, Jerome, 72
Bryson, Lyman, 2n
Bryson, Reid A., 93, 110

C

Carlson, James, 121-22
Cartwright, Dorwin, 158n, 183n
Caste, 29–30
Cattell, Raymond B., 158n
Causation
    canons of, 78–96
    and speech assignment, 219–21
Causes
    chain of, 92
    discreet, 91

249

Causes—*Continued*
  functionally related, 94
  multiple, 90
  simple, 90
  and values, 140
  (*See also* Chapt. 4)
Characterization, 63–65
"Christmas Card" structure, 34–35
Citizenship, 9–10, 22
Civilization, 7–8, 10–21, 22
Clarity and solutions, 116–17
Clark, Kenneth B., 92
Clevenger, Theodore, 152n
Coherence, 51
Cole, Lawrence, 176
Collier, John, 176
Commitment, 246
Communication, democratic, 6–7, 22
Comparative groups, speech assignment on, 236–38
Competence, 246
Confidence
  and delivery, 245–46
  and solutions, 117–18
Consequences, method of, 95
Connectional methods of causation, 88–96
Correlation, Canon of, 84–86, 121
Creativity
  and criticism, 207–208
  and solutions, 102–103
Criticism, need for, 199–200
  rhetorical (*See also* Chapt. 9)

D

Dashiell, John Frederick, 167, 168
Day, Dennis Gene, 152n
Delivery, 244–48
Definitions
  speech assignment on, 225–28
  of values, 141–43
Democratic communication, 8, 22

Description, 62–64
Dewey, John, 100
Dickens, Milton, 184n
Difference, Canon of, 80–84
Disease, 30
Disorders, civil, 91–92
Dougherty, Richard, 120n
Dubos, René, 31–33
Duhamel, P. Albert, 2n
Durant, Will, 40

E

Ethics and persuasion, 147
Ethos,
  dangers of, 171–72
  developing, 170–71
  patterns of, 158–63
  transforming, 163
  (*See also* Chapt. 7)
Etzioni, Amitai, 105, 106, 107
Eulogy, speech assignment on, 232–37
Examples, 60–68
  hypothetical, 60–61
  real, 61–62

F

Farnsworth, P. R. 154n
Freedom, 136
Freeman, Kathleen, 4n
Frieden, Betty, 96n
Foster, William Trufaunt, 166n

G

Galbraith, John Kenneth, 4n, 94n, 192–96

de Gaulle, Charles, 161
Gibson, James, 2n
Gottshalk, Louis, 77n
Gouldner, Alvin, 158n, 177
"Great Pyramid" structure, 37–39, 41
Griffin, C. W., Jr., 121, 122
Groups
    comparative, 189–92
    creation of, 185–92
    normative, 185–88
    (See also Chapt. 8)
Growth, personal, 136–37

H

Haiman, Franklyn S., 154n, 182n
Harris, Sydney, 69–70
Heard, Gerald, 26
Hedonism, 147
Heisenberg, Werner, 5
Herrenstein, Richard, 9
Hoffman, Paul G., 129
Horney, Karen, 160n
Hospers, John, 149n
Hunt, Everett Lee, 22n
Hyman, Ray, 103n
Hypothetical examples, 60–61

I

Imagery, 62–64
Instances, 65–66
Instrumentalism, 148
Intelligence, 8–9, 21
Isocrates, 5, 8, 22, 205

J

Jacobson, Lenore, 114
James, William, 160

Janet, Pierre, 166
Jensen, Gale, 182
Johannesen, Richard L., 2n, 143n
Johnson, Gerald, 33
Johnstone, Henry W., Jr. 2n, 152–53n
"Johnstown Dam" structure, 24–25, 34

K

"Kallikak, Martin," 82–83
Knowledge, 22
Krutch, Joseph Wood, 142n

L

Laird, Donald, 168
Langer, Susanne K., 15
Lao-tzu, 132–33
Life styles, 131–36
Lindbloom, Charles E., 113n
Lundberg, Ferdinand, 58n
Lyle, David, 58n

M

McCullogh, David, 25n
McLaughlin, Teddy John, 152n
"Magnificent Façade" structure, 36–37, 41
Maslow, A. H., 142n
Materials, finding, 42–45
Mauldin, Bill, 185
Mead, George Herbert, 142n, 178–79
Mead, Margaret, 2n, 112, 175
Merei, Ferenc, 177
Mill, John Stuart, 78–87
Minimal cues, 166–69
Motivation (See Chapts. 7–8)

Muller, Herbert J., 40
Murphy, Gardner, 184n

N

Nadar, Ralph, 68, 104
Narrative, 65–66
Natanson, Maurice, 2n, 152–53n
Newman, Dale, 70
Newman, Robert P., 70
Newspapers, indexed, 44
Nichols, Marie Hochmuth, 202n
Nilsen, Thomas R., 198n
Normative group, 236–38
Novak, Michael, 134–35

O

Oliver, Robert, 2n
Outlining, 239–43

P

Parallelism, 51–52
Parrish, W. M., 184n
Pauling, Linus, and vitamin C, 88–89
Persecution, 18
Philipsen, Gerry, 2n
Piccard, Jacques, 30
Plato, 4, 8, 22
Poetry, finding, 44
Pomerans, Arnold J., 5
Poverty, 28, 127–28
Protagoras, 4, 8, 18, 21, 90–91, 204
Problems
    assignment on, 214–21
    classical, 26–29
Protest, 32
Puzzles vs. problems, 9–10

R

Realization of content, 246–47
Reference works, 43–45
Rhetoric
    classical, 3
    explicit and implicit, 1–2
Rhetorical criticism (See Chap. 9)
Roberts, W. Rhys, 155n
Robinson, Richard, 141n
Rosenthal, Paul I., 153n
Rosenthal, Robert, 114

S

Sardi, M., 154n
Sarett, Lew, 166n
Sattler, William M., 152n
Schwartz, Robert L., 79, 120
Sevareid, Eric, 101
Sherif, Carolyn, 178
Sherif, Muzafer, 154n, 178, 179–80
Sherrill, Robert, 58n
Simons, Herbert W., 183n
Social determination, explanations of,
    176–84
Solutions
    causal, 108–10
    as causes, 119
    false, 103–04
    individual and group, 113
    prevention vs. treatment, 115
    rhetoric of, 116–21
    speech assignment on, 221–24
    symptomatic, 105–09
    and values, 137–39
    "villian" and "social forces," 115–16
    (See also Chap. 5)
Sorokin, Pitirim, 16n
Starr, Roger, 121–22
Statistics, 57–59
Sterling, Claire, 66–67
Strategy, 46–56
    evaluation of 52–53
    and solutions, 116

Summaries, 72–73
Survival
  and solutions, 99
  and values, 131–36

T

Tactics, 56–74
Testimony, 68–70, 77–78
Thompson, Wayne N., 152n
Tompkins, Peter, 38n, 75n
"Torquemada" structure, 39–40
Toynbee, Arnold J., 12n, 102n
Twain, Mark, 2
Tyranny, 29–30

U

Untersteiner, Mario, 4n
Utilitarianism, 148–49
Utterback, William, 182n

V

Values
  speech assignment on, 228–32
  (*See also* Chapts. 6 & 9)
Visual aids, 71

W

War, 28, 126–27
Welch, Holmes, 133
Wieman, Henry N., 143n
Wilhoit, Robert, 143n
Winans, James Albert, 245n
Windt, Theodore Otto, Jr., 153n

Z

Zander, Alvin, 158n, 183n